THIS BOOK COULD CHANGE YOUR LIFE

"Why is it important to read this book? It is my belief that all of us have entered the Earth Plane with a basic "blueprint" of our life plan. However, because of the existence of free will, many of life's major decisions and their consequences are a matter of private choice.... Dreams, intuition, and psychic impressions offer productive opportunities to envision future possibilities." —Joan Ruth Windsor

***

Joan Ruth Windsor is a licensed professional counselor. She has been the director of the Personal Development Institute since 1972, and has taught and lectured throughout the country, making radio and television appearances and writing the "Dreamlife" column for *Body, Mind & Spirit*.

Berkley Books by Joan Ruth Windsor

THE INNER EYE
DREAMS AND HEALING
(coming soon)

THE INNER EYE

A GUIDE TO SELF-AWARENESS THROUGH YOUR DREAMS

JOAN RUTH WINDSOR

BERKLEY BOOKS, NEW YORK

This Berkley book contains the complete text
of the original edition.

THE INNER EYE

A Berkley Book / published by arrangement with
the author

PRINTING HISTORY
Prentice-Hall Press edition published 1985
Berkley edition / November 1991

For information address: The Berkley Publishing Group,
200 Madison Avenue, New York, New York 10016.

ISBN: 0-425-13035-5

A BERKLEY BOOK ® TM 757,375
Berkley Books are published by The Berkley Publishing Group,
200 Madison Avenue, New York, New York 10016.

PRINTED IN THE UNITED STATES OF AMERICA

10 9 8 7 6 5 4 3 2 1

Contents

PART TWO
Expanding Your Own Personal Consciousness

Foreword

Readers seeking self-mastery and spiritual applications of their psychic potential will find a rewarding experience awaiting them in Joan Windsor's *The Inner Eye.* Sharing her own discoveries of the psychic dimension of understanding, Ms. Windsor keeps us at her side as fellow explorers—and shows us how to manifest self-healing and direction in our lives. Her balanced perspective between the spiritual and the practical derives much from her study of 5000 dreams—a remarkable accomplishment in itself.

Drawing on the wisdom of Edgar Cayce—and spicing it with candid examples from her own experience—Ms. Windsor sets out a really useful manual for cultivating dream revelations and psychic exercises to help readers make sense of it all—and achieve a higher sense of knowing about their own destinies.

Although aimed at beginners, the book will also give seasoned explorers of the psychic something new and valuable. Ms. Windsor has a way of getting down to spiritual brass tacks that makes *The Inner Eye* as helpful for aspirants to self-knowledge as Julia Child's books are for novice cooks. Nothing mysterious or threatening here—it's all carefully laid out to entice you to follow her path but with your own special directions.

If Joan Windsor makes the psychic dimension less mysterious, she also makes it more accessible and quite sensible. If you are preparing to climb the mountain of truth, she will remind you to wear the right kind of shoes. You just can't beat that practical down-to-earth approach to a topic so often obscured by the esoteric. She really helps us to make the best of ourselves.

Alan Vaughan

Preface

The Inner Eye is designed to provide you with a new and exciting life orientation gained by psychological and spiritual understanding of your own dreams and psychic exploration of present and future realities.

This book is divided into two parts. The first part relates personal experiences during a three-year period of psychic expansion. The second portion challenges you to develop your own psychic abilities through the phenomenological study of experiential aspects of dream incubation, dream interpretation, psychometry, and psychic readings.

Part I, "Adventures in Transpersonal Consciousness," supplies the impetus for the novice psychic explorer to begin a spiritual journey by removing the aura of mystery that often shrouds synchronistic events and interweaving them into the pattern of ordinary daily living as experienced by me from 1981 to the present.

Part II, "Expanding Your Own Personal Consciousness," takes the do-it-yourself approach to psychic and spiritual development. After examining the nature of consciousness, dream theories, and ESP from a historical perspective, Chapter 7 launches the student into the exploration of inner space. This is accomplished through an explanation of the sources of dreams, the types of dreams that emanate from each source, the purposes for recalling our dreams, and suggestions for enhancement of their recall. Chapter 8 offers the dreamer 15 rules for successful dream interpretation and describes how the dreamer can recognize and work with each. In Chapter 9 the dream researcher is encouraged to master an eight-step program to increase the likelihood of incubating a dream that contains answers to specific questions posed by the dreamer.

A new dream classification system is proposed in Chapter 10 based on my study and personal interpretation of more than 5000 dreams combined with an extensive review of dream literature. Chapter 11 discusses the sources of psychic readings, defines five types of readings, and relates how each can prove helpful to the recipient. In Chapter 12 a practical approach to psychometry and psychic readings is presented by means of the medium of elementary exercises for training the inner eye. Dangers encountered during psychic growth are cited as well as guidelines to promote spiritual attunement for accurate psychic readings.

The final chapter charges you to acquire the proper physical, mental, and spiritual attitudes to be assumed in living each day successfully and prompts you to internalize them into your own personality structure.

One of the most important features of the book is the presentation of a new twelve-category system of dream classification. This novel schematic arrangement furnishes inquiring minds with a unique format within which to begin compartmentalizing dream information before attempting to personalize its nocturnal message.

Why is it important to read this book? It is my belief that all of us have entered the Earth Plane with a basic "blueprint" of our own life plan. However, because of the existence of free will, many of life's major decisions and their consequences are a matter of private choice. Therefore, in the final analysis, it is up to the individual to determine the degree to which you can fulfill the life plan previously chosen.

Dreams, intuition, and psychic impressions offer productive opportunities to envision future possibilities. If, through *both* cognitive and intuitive "intentional focusing" on future realities, we can invoke the Creative Subconscious to self-actualize these blueprints by the selection of the best of all possible worlds, does it not then behoove each and every one of us to channel our energies in this direction? *Subconscious intentions ultimately influence future realities, and we are, in the truest sense, all Co-creators with God.* Will you then join with me as a fellow Co-creator in developing your own Inner Eye?

Acknowledgments

Books are not written in isolation. *The Inner Eye* could not have been brought to fruition without the participation of many of my close associates and mentors. Therefore, I wish to express my gratitude to the following people for their ideas and contributions to this work.

Betty Hall, my secretary and friend, for her patience and good humor while retyping several versions of the manuscript.

Mark Thurston, whose publications and insightful theories of dream incubation and dream interpretation served as an impetus to continuing dream experimentation during the beginning phases of my development.

Harmon Bro, for his invaluable evaluation of my initial manuscript. The scope of the book would have been severely limited without the benefit of his keen intellect and superior wisdom expanding my narrow perceptions.

Alan Vaughan, fellow psychic and parapsychologist, whose recommendations and exercises in *The Edge of Tomorrow* contributed immeasurably to the refinement of my own precognitive skills.

Roger and Nancy Pile, psychic instructors extraordinaire. Without their practical demonstrations and unwavering confidence in my fledgling efforts, I never could have taken more than a few tottering steps down the spiritual path.

My dear friends *John and Elizabeth Hollis,* with whom I have shared so many personal psychic adventures. Thanks for making them fun as well as educational.

Kevin Riley, one of my finest precognitive dream students, for generously sharing his biblical research. His extensive knowledge regarding biblical dreams added immensely to that section of the book.

My thanks to my sister, *Arlene Helmus,* for her creative suggestions that enhanced the book's readability.

Thanks to the members of my parapsychology class, from whom I learned far more than I could have possibly imagined.

A special hug to the library staff of the Association of Research and Enlightenment for furnishing special books and information on the life and works of Edgar Cayce.

Accolades to my Prentice-Hall reviewer, *Cynthia Ryan,* spiritual healer of Hackensack, New Jersey. I will be forever indebted to her for the discerning commentaries and inspirational guidance offered me during the final revisions of *The Inner Eye.* Through her substantive suggestions she made my book reach out beyond the occult reader and embrace all those who dream and who wish to build castles from their dreams in which to live. She truly epitomizes the personification of spiritual creativity.

And finally, my husband, *Jim.* He brings sensitivity, intelligence, encouragement, and unselfish devotion to all our endeavors. I have truly come to realize that I am privileged to be involved in a loving and self-actualizing partnership beyond my wildest dreams.

Introduction

The social sciences have not been able to contribute very much to the resolution of the persistent human conflicts that threaten our very existence because they do not have an agreed-on image of the nature of man. In their haste to be "scientists," the social scientists have tended to reduce humankind to those characteristics that can be examined empirically in the laboratory. This tunnel vision perspective greatly limits our understanding of human behavior. It also cripples our progress by restricting areas of research.

Generally accepted scientific methodology requires that a phenomenon be subject to observation, experimental control, quantification of the data, and statistical analysis. We should meet these requirements when we can, but if we restrict our research to those characteristics that can be studied by this methodology, we will fail to examine many of the attributes that make us uniquely human.

The human person is more complicated than the conditions that can be duplicated in the psychologist's laboratory. Human beings are apparently the only animals that pray, or that know they are going to die. We are concerned with our physical needs for food, shelter, water, and sleep, but we are also interested in God, love, music, literature, dreams, talent, and values. We seek more than material things or knowledge. We seek a raison d'être, a spiritual dimension. These expressions of the human spirit are subjective, difficult to quantify, yet no less important to our understanding of behavior.

Although some parapsychological data can be examined under the most rigorous scientific conditions, much of it cannot. Herein lies the problem for the interested scientist, who must decide to study only that which can come under his methodology; or realize that there are realms of experience that seem to lie outside of time and space limitations that are worthy of investigation. In any event, the scientist must be careful not to be inexcusably nonscientific by dismissing as untrue that which he has not studied.

William James spoke of a "general sense of dramatic probability." He insisted that a thing was not necessarily untrue simply because it conflicted with known principles of science. It is in this spirit that the subject of this book is approached. With respect for scientific methodology—and its limitations—this book ventures into the world beyond the five senses. The story is worth telling not because these experiences are unique, for others have traveled a similar road before, but because the implications are so significant to our understanding of human psychology that they deserve emphasis. It is our hope that the sharing of these experiences will encourage others to explore openly their own "inner space" and the unrealized potential that resides therein.

As a psychologist, I have always had a deep interest in the nature of consciousness and perception. The experiences described in the pages which follow have given me an opportunity to explore these subjects in a unique setting. My wife, Joan, who had astounded me with her precognitive dreams for 26 years, became my regular inductee a few years ago when I was training in hypnosis and needed a subject. We began to discover psychic phenomena of which we still stand in awe. We have concluded, *experientially*, that there is indeed perception beyond the five senses. Our future efforts will be directed toward further validation and replication of these experiences. You are invited to share in this venture.

James C. Windsor

Preface to the Berkley Edition

When I took pen in hand in 1984 to give birth to my first book, *The Inner Eye*, I was totally unaware of the powerful impact its concepts would have on thousands of individuals earnestly engaged in the pursuit of self-growth. I felt assured of the merit of my dreamwork theories based on the unqualified success enjoyed by both our Parapsychology students at Christopher Newport College and the counseling clientele that comprised our private practice. I rather suspected we were "on to something" as time progressed, but not until the late 1980's was I fully cognizant of the intrinsic potency of their transformational and self-healing potential.

Once again I lift the pen, this time to compose a new preface to *The Inner Eye*. We have moved forward seven years in time. From a global point of view, at this moment we stand poised on tiptoe peering beyond the time barrier to capture glimpses of the advancing Age of Aquarius. A new decade is upon us. Humanity balances on the brink of a worldwide spiritual revival with starbursts of spirituality exploding in shimmering cascades of light from every corner of the globe. Each macrocosm of light is composed of infinitesimal numbers of microcosms emblazoned with personal spiritual illuminations. If we examine these spiritual microcosms, we perceive that each illuminate has achieved his or her Spiritual Truth uniquely; yet each has utilized the transcendental tools of meditation and dreams in its journeys in self-discovery. To many spiritual truth seekers the transcendental quality of dreams provided the pivotal point for metamorphic change.

The spiritual transformation I experienced in 1981 has deepened. The boundaries of dream power vanished with each and every successive physical, mental and spiritual healing I was associated with or witnessed as counselor/teacher or research/investigator. *Thus, as the year 1991 unfolds it is no longer a question of "Do the techniques purported in* The Inner Eye *work?" but rather "Just how far are you willing to progress on your chosen path using* The Inner Eye *techniques as a ticket to your spiritual destination?"*

The Inner Eye is divided into two parts. "Part One — Adventures in Transpersonal Consciousness" provides a chronicle of my husband, Jim's and my early investigations in the paranormal realm. The time span ranges from 1981 - 1984. The second book of the set, *Dreams and Healing* continues the narrative through the late eighties.

"Part Two — Expanding Your Own Personal Consciousness" takes a "do it yourself" approach to intuitive and spiritual development. Chapter 6 examines higher awareness, dream theories and ESP from an historical perspective. Chapters 7 and 8 contain "tried and true" formulas for dream recall, dream enhancement and accurate dream interpretation. In nine years of teaching dreamwork I have yet to encounter a student who could not eventually recall and successfully work with his or her dreams employing *The Inner Eye* techniques. Chapter 9 encompasses perhaps some of the most thought-provoking material. The fact that we can incubate dream guidance seems inconceivable to the analytically minded individual. Yet dream students have proven again and again that true seekers of wisdom, once having opened the door, find Revealed Truth waiting on the doorstep.

Chapter 10 contains one of the most important features of the book. The twelve category system of dream classification has withstood the test of time. It continues to furnish novice dreamers with standards and clearly identifiable dream models to use in compartmentalizing and interpreting their own personal dream messages.

For those dream students who desire to expand their level of transpersonal awareness to include intuitive readings, Chapter 11 discusses varied sources, defines five types of readings, and then relates how each will prove beneficial to the recipient. Chapter 12 provides elementary exercises for the pyschometric training of one's inner eye and sets forth guidelines for the promotion of spiritual attunement. The final chapter charges the reader to achieve physical, mental and spiritual balance through the diligent pursuit of divinely inspired ideals integrated into personal daily living patterns. Through activation and energizement of one's chosen ideals one blesses not only one's soul's intimates but humanity as a whole.

Why is it important to read this book? Dreams, visions and intuitive readings are the hallmarks of the Creative Expression of God. They are the harbingers of evolving future possibilities. *Subconscious intentions ultimately influence future realities since we are, in the truest sense, all Cocreators with God.* Creativity takes root in the process of self-growth, but it is seldom the work of an isolated mind. A single thought form, like a luminous spark, cannot endure unless it can attract other enlightened thought forms. Furthermore, the mind of man is clothed in The Oneness, the tapestry of which is continually woven through the giving and receiving of loving thoughts and actions. *Thus, through Creative Expression the nucleus of a new reality is born.*

We are all starbursts of light eternally creating present and future realities through the illuminated vision of our Inner Eye. Cognitive and intuitive "intentional focusing" and singularity of vision let us, as fellow Cocreators, Self-Actualize The Best of All Possible Worlds. *The Blueprints for His Kingdom lie within. Will you not join me in welcoming its joyous advent?*

To my father, Thomas Clifford Laurent, the giver of the gift, who passed from this life into the next on January 26, 1983, and to my husband, James Clayton Windsor, whose loving support and encouragement are responsible for the development of the gift

PART ONE

Adventures in Transpersonal Consciousness

1

The Awakening

There are none so deaf as those who do not want to hear.

Doris Agee, *Edgar Cayce on Dreams*

"What did Dr. Bell say?" my husband, Jim, asked with a note of concern in his voice.

"The same as usual," I responded disheartedly. "I have to have surgery to remove the cyst, which will leave a deep indentation in my chest, or I can endure the discomfort and leave the cyst alone."

I had just returned from a consultation with our family physician, Dr. Baxter Bell, who was a friend of long standing and an excellent physician. His patience, understanding, and expertise in the practice of medicine had seen us safely through many medical crises in the past 20 years. I remembered how as a new mother I was reassured by his gentle manner and confident diagnosis when my children had contracted a mild case of the flu or when they were about to blossom into 1000 tiny chicken pox. I had always been certain before the office visit that some mysterious and dreadful disease had struck them down in the prime of youth with little hope of recovery — a mother's overreaction, to be sure. I was also reminded of the sense of relief and thankfulness that flooded me when his long-awaited phone call brought us the news that my husband had not suffered a heart seizure but instead had been caught in the throes of a hiatal hernia attack that could be treated successfully through diet and exercise.

Although Dr. Bell was a friend and adviser to my entire family, I now seemed to be the patient on whom his attention centered. I had developed cystic fibroid disease of the breasts and had been hospitalized on three separate occasions during the past five years for removal of cysts. With the discovery of each new cyst, the fear of a possible malignancy intensified. These fears were not unfounded because throughout my family history deaths resulting from malignant growths ran rampant. This included my mother, whom death claimed at the early age of 55 through a misdiagnosis of breast cancer. The six-month delay of the operation cost her her life. Although all my surgeries revealed the presence of benign cysts, with a history such as this, the unwelcome news of the possibility of a fourth bout with the surgeon sent new discordant notes of terror reverberating through my soul.

This depressing scenario began unfolding at the end of July 1981. The usual feelings of frustration, defenselessness, and futility that accompanied the tidings of impending surgery now enveloped me. To further complicate the situation, my mother-in-law, Mrs. Mary Windsor, along with my sister-in-law, June Moses, and her husband, Earl, had planned to visit us for a few days at the end of the week. I had always felt close to Mrs. Windsor since the death of my mother in 1960. My mother-in-law's loving generosity, sense of humor, and indomitable spirit had forged a close bond between us, and her periodic sojourns in Williamsburg, Virginia, over the years had tended to heal the wound sustained from the loss of my mother.

My sister-in-law, June, and her husband, Earl, had proven themselves to be amiable and stimulating company during my marriage to Jim, which had lasted almost a quarter of a century, so I had been anticipating a friendly family reunion until the prospect of a fourth surgery had reared its ugly head. How would it be possible for me to exhibit a carefree and tranquil facade while, with each passing moment, I was becoming more and more embroiled in a tempest of conflicting emotions. These seemingly irresolvable frustrations seethed just below the surface, and as yet I had devised no successful method of escape.

I summoned up all the courage and fortitude at my command and with the support of my husband began making preparations for the forthcoming visit. I would "grin and bear it."

Our company arrived on schedule, and I felt myself relaxing somewhat as I temporarily busied myself in the daily business of meal preparations, sightseeing in Williamsburg, and that inevitable but delightsome trek to Williamsburg Pottery. Accompanying all our activities was a ceaseless barrage of family gossip — much of which revolved around health problems of others. This was not surprising because my mother-in-law had for many years served as a nurse's aide in Oak Hill Hospital, Oak Hill, West Virginia, and June had always displayed a keen interest in matters of this nature.

Gradually, the conversation took a personal turn as June described an eye problem that seemed resistant to treatment. She had visited an ophthalmologist in Cleveland several weeks before and been given an appropriate medication, but the affliction persisted. In an effort to seek further treatment she proposed an excursion to the Association for Research and Enlightenment (ARE) headquarters in Virginia Beach. It was there she hoped to research the Edgar Cayce readings housed in the ARE library in the expectation of discovering among his medical readings a successful prescription for healing her ocular ailment.

The Association for Research and Enlightenment was vaguely familiar to me. Some 15 years ago I had read *There Is a River* by Thomas Sugrue, a biography of the life of Edgar Cayce, the "sleeping prophet" of Virginia Beach, Virginia. In his book, Sugrue described how the psychically gifted Cayce, while in a self-hypnotic trance state, was able to diagnose physical illnesses and prescribe effective cures for patients' diseases. His amazing accuracy has been documented in publication after publication, and the general applicability of his occasionally unorthodox but universally healing medical prescriptions has withstood the test of time.

The material received through the unconscious Cayce was entitled *Readings*. Elsie Sechrist describes these readings as follows: "The files containing his Readings are in the custody of the Edgar Cayce Foundation, an affiliate of the Association for

Research and Enlightenment (ARE). The ARE itself is a nonprofit benevolent organization established in 1931 to preserve, study, and present the Edgar Cayce clairvoyant Readings. The Association preserves 14,253 Psychic Readings by Cayce in its national headquarters at Virginia Beach. An approximate breakdown of the Readings according to subject matter indicates there are 8976 on physical or medical subjects; 799 on business; 401 on mental and spiritual; 24 on home and marriage; 2500 on personal life problems; 879 miscellaneous readings and 1009 on dream interpretations."[1]

My initial contact with the ARE had been through my husband, Jim, a professor of psychology at Christopher Newport College in Newport News, Virginia. He had been a frequent guest speaker at the ARE during the late 1960s. At the request of Hugh Lynn Cayce, Edgar Cayce's son, he had presented a paper during a 1968 conference entitled "A Psychologist Looks at ESP." I recalled having attended the lecture. He had also researched the files intensively one summer after having received a grant from Hugh Lynn to study Cayce's theories on the causes of mental illness.

Through Jim's association with the ARE we began to collect a small library of works concerning Cayce. I had digested *There Is a River* along with several others and remembered being absolutely astounded that anyone could perform such amazing feats. This amazement was undoubtedly tempered with a grain of skepticism as that rational voice in my analytical mind frequently whispered, "Impossible! Impossible!"

In 1970 my husband was appointed president of Christopher Newport College and became so absorbed in his duties that the stimulating activities of the ARE years faded into obscurity and the spark of interest that had been ignited in me was extinguished. I myself became more involved in child rearing and also enrolled in the Counseling and Guidance Program at the College of William and Mary, in Williamsburg, Virginia, for my M.Ed. Upon receiving my degree I set up my own counseling practice and began to provide diagnosis and prescriptive evaluations for children with learning disabilities.

"Time to go." My mother-in-law's voice broke through my reverie. Everyone was eager to be on the road. As I closed the door behind me, I paused to wonder exactly what kind of hand the Fates had dealt this deeply Christian organization that so devotedly and diligently continued to carry the Cayce banner.

And so it was on the bright, balmy morning of August 3, 1981, that seven of us set forth for Virginia Beach intent on a visit to the ARE — a visit that would generate a complete reassessment of my orthodox religious philosophy and eventually, revolutionize my own raison d'etre.

Upon arriving at our destination the Moses clan and my mother-in-law eagerly climbed the ARE library stairs to the second floor and settled in for several hours of concentrated research. My daughter, Robin, and her fourteen-year-old companion immediately headed in the direction of the beach to pass the day rebronzing their gradually fading suntans, and Jim and I delighted in the prospect of having several free hours at our disposal — a rare opportunity indeed given the rapid pace our careers often imposed upon our lives.

"Let's browse in the bookstore first," Jim beckoned.

"Great idea!" I replied enthusiastically,chuckling inwardly as we walked in that general direction.

My husband and I are chronic bookstore browsers, and the usual outcome of these browsing expeditions is a rash of newly acquired books destined to join the already towering pile on the nightstand next to our bed. Although we are both voracious readers, the pace of purchase far exceeds the rate of digestion.

As we passed the stairway leading to the second floor, I noticed a sign advertising a castor oil pack demonstration later in the day. I vaguely recollected that this was a favorite Cayce prescription, but that was the extent of my meager knowledge.

The bookstore was alive with activity during this hot summer day. I found a quiet section containing publications dealing with nutrition and health and began to thumb through paperbacks concerned with vitamins, natural foods, and diets of all kinds that purported to cure a variety of the common illnesses that plague humanity.

"Here's a book written with you in mind," my husband exclaimed with a grin as he held up Jean Campbell's *Dreams Beyond Dreaming*. I detected a more serious note beneath his jovial exterior. "There is a section in one chapter that explains precognitive dreams and the circumstances surrounding them. Aren't these the kind you always experience and continually deny exist?" he chided. How true! How true!

I had experienced this phenomenon ever since I was a child and could recall dreaming. However, as I grew older and more sophisticated in the ways of the world, it rapidly became apparent to me that the mere mention of dreams that came true resulted in finger pointing, head shaking, and muffled giggles among my peers. Determined not to be considered "a weirdo" by my fellow students, I began suppressing such dreams and vigorously denied their existence.

Years passed with continuing suppression and more forceful denials, but in spite of my relentless struggle to eliminate such dreams from my life, vividly colorful nighttime productions completed their runs on Saturday morning only to be replayed in actuality on Tuesday afternoon. The characters and settings frequently were exactly as seen on the dream stage. The only variation that stirred feelings of consternation within me was the fact that this dream replication had now intruded upon my waking reality.

I took the book Jim offered me and skimmed the section on precognition. The description of the phenomenological aspects of precognitive dreaming fit my experiences precisely. Amazing! Here in print before me to read and internalize was a narrative that not only granted me permission to indulge myself in this type of dreaming but offered additional instruction on how to derive benefits from such activities. There were more books discussing the subject of dreams that lined one shelf of the ARE bookstore. As I eagerly "eyeballed" the wealth of literature that lay before me, my husband laughed in amusement at my obvious lack of knowledge on a subject that had been an integral part of my being for over 46 years.

"Weren't you aware that Edgar Cayce was an expert on dreams and dream interpretation?" Jim continued. The tone of his voice was obviously encouraging me to begin the reeducation of my corsetted psyche. It was as if the floodgates were opening wider and wider, setting free a torrent of suppressed emotions and irrational fears whose release was long overdue. These negative emotions were replaced by a desire for psychic knowledge that would grow into an almost unquenchable thirst in the years to come. Would I allow myself to let go?

Together we reviewed the variety of books before us and selected *Edgar Cayce on Dreams* by Harmon Bro and *Dreams: Your Magic Mirror* by Elsie Sechrist. After paying our bill at the counter, we ascended the stairs to the library and settled in for an afternoon of pleasant reading.

By four o'clock we had all completed our projects. We returned to the car to begin our journey homeward. Conversation was at a minimum during the trip home. I seized the opportunity to finish reading *Dreams: Your Magic Mirror* and began *Edgar Cayce on Dreams*.

After a congenial supper drew to a close and the dishes were dried and put away, I excused myself and retired to bed leaving Jim and his relatives to engage in family talk. I did not choose the top book from the dusty pile beside my bed as was my usual practice but continued to speed-read Harmon Bro's literary work. Thoughts spun around and around in my head. I had read one section which suggested that answers to one's problems as well as all healing energies reside within the self, and that by the simple act of requesting guidance solutions would be received through dreams. This was too mind-boggling a concept for me to accept just yet, but at least I now felt I had begun to make progress in understanding the nature of precognitive dreaming. I began to entertain thoughts of somehow manipulating the dreams so that they might provide useful information and benefits for myself and others of my acquaintance. My mind kept returning again and again to my own health problem and that of my sister-in-law. Wouldn't it be nice to request and receive a dream that would provide healing solutions to both afflictions! This must have been the last thought I focused on before I drifted off into one of the most peaceful nights of slumber I have ever known.

I began to regain consciousness just after first light and realized in astonishment I had three rather lengthy dream sequences stored in my head. Two of these I was absolutely certain discussed the steps necessary for healing my cyst and eliminating June's eye malady. The dream that dealt with the healing of my cyst was not literal and had to be interpreted through dream symbology. The message, however, was clear: Hot oil pads applied over the afflicted area would provide the necessary treatment for healing. The dream was as follows:

MY CYST

I am in my own house and I see a small fire in the basement. It is an oil burner and has red flames shooting out from it. I panic but realize it is not serious. I think I can put the fire out by applying hot oil to it and regulating the amount.

I remembered the advertisement for the castor oil demonstration and felt that this was the type of oil treatment to which the dream referred. I immediately searched through my husband's Cayce books and located instructions for using a castor oil pack. *Within 10 days of faithfully applying the heated castor oil pack for one and one-half hours daily accompanied by 1000 milligrams of vitamin E to soften the lump internally, my cyst broke open, drained, and disappeared forever.*

My sister-in-law fared equally well. I intuitively knew from seeing the appearance of June's eyes in my second dream that the problem was allergy-related. An appointment with Dr. James Hartwright, an allergist who practices in the same office complex where my husband and I rent space, would provide us with the correct answers. I could not bring myself to confide in my sister-in-law that I knew her eye problem was the result of an allergic reaction because of information received while in the dream state. I did confide in my husband, because he was more a believer in my dreams than I was at this point. He tactfully persuaded June to seek medical assistance from Dr. Hartwright on the pretext that her condition was not unlike that of the allergy-prone children diagnosed as learning-disabled by Learning Development Service.

Her appointment was made for three o'clock that afternoon, and by four we had the verdict. The encrustations on her eyelids were a definite symptom of the existing allergies. Dr. Hartwright prescribed the appropriate medication and suggested she undergo a complete battery of allergy tests upon her return to Cleveland. This advice combined with some of the treatment recommended in the Edgar Cayce readings proved of incalculable value in placing her on the road to recovery.

The first tottering steps had been taken. I now began to realize that it was possible to use my dreams to gain access to higher knowledge and perceptions that lay beyond my scope of knowledge in waking consciousness. I also became more fully cognizant of the significance of an observation made by Edgar Cayce to one of his psychic students concerning dreams. Cayce stated that "the function of dreams . . . was not alone to solve problems. It was also to awaken the dreamer to his full stature as a person."[2]

The acceptance of the idea that it was conceivable that my dreams could portend future events seemed to set my steps on the right path. I began recording my dreams daily. A curious phenomenon seemed to occur simultaneously with the inauguration of my own dream journal. Not only did I begin to dream more prolifically, but, upon awakening, I immediately recalled each and every nightly tale I had witnessed. Even more amazing was the fact that I often knew the meaning of 90 percent of the material channeled through me without laboriously having to consult my books on dream symbology. There would be an occasional stumper, but eventually I mastered all my personal dream symbology associations. I began to rely generally on my own intuition for accurate dream interpretations.

As I grew more comfortable with myself and my nocturnal returns to the theater of the future, I was able to view more objectively some of my most vivid precognitive dream experiences of yesteryear. Three of the most dramatic had always remained with me in spite of repeated attempts at suppression. A precognitive dream in 1958 had involved the purchase and building of our home on the James River near Williamsburg, Virginia.

The dream presented itself in this fashion:

OUR SHELLBANK HOME

Jim and I are seated on a beautiful patio above a river having breakfast. The area is one of the loveliest places I have ever seen. I am impressed with its wooded beauty. A lush green marsh is situated to the left of the patio.

The happiness and serenity I experienced during the dream remained with me weeks afterward.

I was 24 years old at the time. My husband and I resided in Rochester, New York, where he attended Colgate Rochester Divinity School. We both were graduates of the College of William and Mary in Williamsburg, Virginia, and had enjoyed the mild climate of the colonial town. After spending a frigid winter in the frozen north, we decided to return to a warmer climate for the summer. We applied and were hired as lifeguards at the Williamsburg Inn swimming pool.

One day that summer, while driving home from Richmond on Route 5, we saw a For Sale sign that advertised waterfront lots. After spending four years living in Williamsburg as college students, we thought we were aware of all the places that had waterfront development, but this one was new to both of us. As students we had no money, nor did we expect to have any for several years in the future. Out of curiosity we drove down the main road and turned off to the right. The road wound around several curves along the James River, ending on a high bluff that overlooked one of the river's widest points. Jim and I stepped out of the car. It was an incredibly lovely view.

As we walked up the bluff, I turned to look to my left. *There before me, as if reflected in my mind's eye, was the same lush green marsh I had observed in my dream! I knew immediately that here was the place I had seen the dream house with the patio where we had been eating*. I recounted my dream vision to Jim, who suggested we inquire about the price of the lots, perhaps for a future investment for one of our families. The lot was apparently destined to be ours, however, for at an appointment with the real estate agent we learned to our delight that, because of a minor problem with the road, the majority of prospective buyers were unimpressed with the land.

With the help of our attorney in rerouting the old road and a small inheritance left me by my aunt, we cleared away the initial hurdles to acquiring the land and in 1959 became the proud owners of one and one-half acres on the James River. Three short years later, when my husband accepted a position as instructor at Christopher Newport College, we returned to Williamsburg with our new son in tow and proceeded to reconstruct the exact house I had foreseen in my dream. Was it coincidence that brought us to the site of our future home or synchronicity? Today I would opt for the latter.

One of the most enduring, and perhaps among the most visionary dreams I have ever encountered, was given to me in 1954 at the age of 20. My mind still bears witness to the following drama:

THE VEIL OF THE FUTURE

I see an angelic being standing in front of a black curtain. She turns to me and says, "Would you like to see the future?" and begins to draw aside the curtain's folds. I am aware that beyond the curtain lies the future of all mankind in its entirety and, if I wish to observe it, I need only to keep my gaze fixed upon the screen. I close my eyes!

At age 20 I was being given hints of my psychic abilities, but as the dream so vividly portrayed it, *I closed my eyes to all of it for 26 more years!*

I believe the dream epic that finally attracted my attention was a dream I call "The Office Robbery." The events and emotions were so powerful that I could no longer deny the extraordinary content of my dreams. I work in an office complex surrounded by physicians, psychologists, dentists, and other professionals. At the time of the robbery dream, a psychiatrist and several psychologists had rented office space next to mine. The robbery dream went something like this:

THE OFFICE ROBBERY

I open the door to the waiting room and go directly into my office. I notice a large gaping hole in the wall between my office and that of my neighbors. I say, "Bob, we cannot conduct business in private with this hole here."

He replies, "Don't blame me. It was those people who came to visit you recently."

I woke up with a sense of apprehension and disorientation. The dream had been so real I actually felt as if I had been there. What seemed even more strange was an unexplainable sense of alarm that grew in intensity the closer I drew to the Denbigh Professional Park Office Complex. Upon entering the door I noted things were in disorder. *I entered my office to find a huge gaping hole in the ceiling between my office and the adjoining one.* The police told me after a thorough investigation that the robbers were probably after drugs in the psychiatrist's office next door. Cutting a hole in my ceiling provided them with easy access to the neighboring office. The shock of that dramatic episode undoubtedly accomplished more than all the years of ordinary precognitive dreaming had ever done.

Looking back I am now more keenly aware than ever that my psychic development was largely dependent upon the nurturing bestowed upon me by the two male influences in my life: my father, Thomas Clifford Laurent, and my husband, James C. Windsor. I credit my father with my psychic inheritance and my husband with my psychic progress.

My father was a highly intelligent individual and a man of strong religious convictions. He held the position of an elder in the First Presbyterian Church of Rahway, New Jersey, for more than thirty years. He served on the YMCA board for more than a decade and was a staunch supporter of a multitude of fellowship and sports activities connected with the social life of our church. As a child of eight I recall tagging after my father to baseball games and clapping my hands with glee when he hit a home run or caught a fly ball in left field.

As I grew older, he encouraged me to follow in his footsteps and engage in athletics. I loved basketball and became a member of the First Presbyterian Church team during my last two years in high school. Now it was my father's turn to sit on the sidelines and cheer us on to victory as our team won first place in our league for two years in a row.

Scholastically, he was my strongest supporter also. If I had trouble understanding a concept or needed clarification on some minor point in a night's lesson, I would often seek his guidance. Instead of supplying me with the answer, however, he would discuss the issue with me, and, in time, I was often able to perceive the correct solution myself. As a young child he appeared to me to be the source of all knowledge. Therefore, a strong bond existed between us.

My sister was my mother's child — the musical one who was outgoing and always surrounded by a host of friends, as my mother was. I was my father's daughter who excelled academically and athletically but was always a rather shy and inward person. There seemed to be no competition between my sister and myself. Our personalities complemented each other. I can truly say she was in my childhood and to this day still is one of the best friends I have ever had.

In the course of growing up, and in the years of caring for my two young children, there were numerous incidents that should have made me realize how truly psychic my father was. I often would receive an unexpected call from him at college when I was faced with some seemingly insurmountable academic or social problem and had become despondent. He would say, "I had a snow dream about you last night, Joan, and just wanted to call to see if I could help." ("Snow dreams," I was to learn later, was the term he used for precognition. He often told me snow dreams ran in the Laurent family.) Snow dreams would appear to him during my own children's illnesses and on several occasions when I fell into ill health.

There would always be that mysterious phone call coinciding precisely with the peak of the illness. The voice on the other end of the line would inquire anxiously, "How are things in Virginia? Are you ill? I feel your problem stems from mental and physical exhaustion. If you will take [a dietary prescription followed] and walk two or three miles a day, you'll be feeling better in no time." When I followed his advice, the crisis passed and vibrant physical and mental health returned immediately.

It was only toward the last year of his life that we had the father-daughter conversation that should have come 30 years before. Perhaps because he was near death, or because I had been struggling with my precognitive dreams and rapidly developing psychic abilities for more than one year, we had a much-needed talk. My husband and I were visiting my father on his eighty-third birthday. I had finally decided that I should broach the subject of my precognitive dreams. I found him sitting alone in his bedroom on the second floor while the other members of the family were busily engaged in the kitchen making preparations for his birthday dinner, and I hesitantly began to recount the events of the past year. Before I had completed my résumé, he interrupted me excitedly saying, "Accept the gift you have been given, and thank God for the blessing every night. The snow dreams that I always referred to were the same type of precognitive dreams you have been experiencing. It is a family trait. That is how I always knew you were in trouble and needed help."

I gazed at him in astonishment and, for a time, was speechless. "Why didn't you tell me about this years ago?" I finally managed to utter. "It would have saved me so much anxiety and would have been so much easier for me to understand and accept."

He shook his head solemnly. "Things of a psychic nature were taboo in my day," he replied in a quivering voice. "Though I did not discuss my gift, I always availed myself of it whenever possible to provide aid for those relatives and friends who were in need. I believe it is a spiritual gift whose source is the Almighty. I endeavored to pay my debt to Him for it through my activities and participation in the life of our church."

So there it was finally out in the open! I truly was my father's girl. The gift that he had possessed and used all his life was now being passed on to me. I would realize the truth of this statement more and more as the years wore on.

For the last three years of his life my father was afflicted with Parkinson's disease, gradually losing control of his muscles to the point where he was literally starving to death from his inability to control his throat muscles. As the disease progressed, he became more and more immobile. My dreams consistently monitored his physical deterioration and would frequently provide me with suggestions for comforting and soothing his physical condition. I ultimately passed these on to him as he had done so often for me in my youth and young adult years. During the last year of his life I was intuitively aware of a rapid growth in my psychic abilities. It was as if he were passing the torch to me.

My father died January 26, 1983, yet, in the depths of my soul, I am absolutely certain he remains with me even today continuing to guide me along the path that he had trod so many years before.

Although I credit my father with the gift of my psychic ability, for 46 years it lay dormant. Had it not been for the interest, support, and innovative ideas that constantly flowed from my husband's creative mind, I would probably have remained an effective counselor and continued in the comfortable and secure niche I had carved out for myself. However, my husband continually prodded me to take the next step in our psychic progression in spite of, and often overruling, my occasional objections. He encouraged me to attend the conferences sponsored by the ARE on dreams, ESP, prophecy, diet, and nutrition. The information I acquired and new friendships that were forged as an outgrowth of these conferences not only have proved personally valuable, but were an integral part of my psychic development without which each ensuing step would not have been taken.

It was at his insistence that we contacted Roger and Nancy Pile, co-directors of the Center for Nonphysical Sciences, and traveled to Chester, Connecticut, for an intensive three-day course specifically designed to teach us practical uses for our "untamed psychic skills." And there is little doubt in my mind that without my confidence in the hypnotic expertise of my husband and the benefit of his rational and scientific approach to the phenomenon of psychic readings (described in the latter pages of this book), I never would have summoned up the courage to venture into the mysterious domain of the trance state. If one believes in partnerships and soul mates in life, my husband and I truly exemplify this concept.

So why am I writing this book? All my family and friends who know me intimately will attest to my extreme shyness and desire for privacy in my personal life. Why, then, should I risk this to write such a self-revealing portrait? It is my firm conviction, judging by my own experiences of the past three years and those of others who now have become close friends, that I am not alone in my psychic odyssey but, like Ruth Montgomery, have "companions along the way."

It is for you who read this that I am writing my story. If I can teach you the importance of recording, interpreting, and acting upon the information received in dreams and instill in you the realization that answers to many problems truly lie within the self, then you will have become a better person for having read this book.

It was not an easy decision for me to share my private life and thoughts with the world. However, the spiritual content of more than 5000 recorded dreams and the level of valid psychic information that has been channeled through me during the psychic reading process have convinced me that the psychic is truly of the soul. As such, it should be given the place of respect and reverence it deserves in both scientific and religious circles. If, by subjecting my dreams and psychic work to the intensive scrutiny of society, I can accomplish this dual purpose, then the long hours of preparation and soul searching required to complete this work will have been fruitfully spent. A quote from Harmon Bro's book *Edgar Cayce on Dreams* might annotate more completely my intent for publishing this book: "No life was fully lived which was not lived for others."[3]

You will note as you delve further into this book that the format is divided between my own personal experiences and discussions of various theories and constructs. The latter section is a direct outgrowth of my own research and survey of the literature over the past three years. By dividing the book in this fashion I hope to provide the reader with a more in depth appreciation of the subjects than would have been possible through the singular presentation of my own experiences.

2

An Investigation into Psychic Readings

Nobody escapes himself.
Harmon Bro, *Edgar Cayce on Dreams*

By early fall 1981 I had grown accustomed to the fact that future events pervaded my dreams almost nightly. For the past several months, upon awakening, I had not only kept a written account of my dream images but had made a concerted effort to describe and affix a date to all events of a seemingly precognitive bent. I also felt that I had gained enough confidence in the validity of my precognitive dreams to share the information contained in them with my family, relatives, and friends, especially if their theme revolved around business issues, health advice, or warnings of favorable or unfavorable conditions that loomed on their personal horizons. *This was the ultimate test for me: the sharing of my private visions*. These disclosures not only required my psyche to deliver up its inner most thoughts but also subjected me to ridicule if my predictions proved incorrect. Fortunately, the source or sources of my information viewed the future with considerable accuracy. Therefore, the rewards I secured for my interpretations were numerous expressions of sincere gratitude interlaced with only an occasional taunt. At this point, I felt I had finally achieved a successful transition from the status of a confirmed skeptic to that of a true believer in the concept of guidance.

The peaceful plateau upon which I was resting proved to be only a temporary respite in my psychic journey, however. The imaginative and continuously inquiring mind of my spouse was already formulating more challenging tasks for us unbeknownst to me.

"Honey," he inquired one morning, addressing me in the most affectionate of voices, "what would you think of my hypnotizing you in an effort to see if you can receive the same type of precognitive information in a trance state that you pick up in your dream episodes?"

Shades of Franz Mesmer! This was the least appealing proposition my husband had ever presented to me. I vividly recalled seeing pictures in the psychology textbooks I had studied of this master hypnotist bedecked in his swishing black cape "mesmerizing" his patients who were seated in tubs with metal rods surrounding them. (At that time the metal rods were thought to assist in the magnetizing procedure of hypnotism.) I must admit to some overexaggeration here, but, in truth, the idea of having someone else exert power over my mind, even my husband whom I trusted implicitly, was extremely frightening.

"Thanks just the same, darling," I retorted, matching his syrupy tone, "but I prefer my dreams to being in a trance state. I feel safer there."

"I don't believe you truly understand the nature of hypnosis," Jim continued politely. "You will not be in my power at all. I will act as a guide for you. You can determine the depth of your trance and bring yourself out of it at any moment. All hypnosis is truly self-hypnosis. You will be in control at all times. We can even set up a tape recorder, if you are afraid of what will be said, and record the session." I was summarily unimpressed.

Let me retrace our steps a little. My husband had attended several training conferences sponsored by the American Society for Clinical Hypnosis and, in the past year, had begun using the techniques he had been taught in his counseling practice. He had developed into quite a skilled hypnotist. I marveled at his recountings of how precisely, under hypnosis, some of his clients could recollect traumatic events of their childhood that they had effectively blocked out of conscious reality. These suppressed traumas were still exerting a negative influence on their present-day emotional lives until, through hypnotic regression, the crucial issues were squarely faced and dealt with effectively. It was my husband's considered opinion that these hypnotic self-confrontations usually reduced the time his clients spent in therapy by half. In spite of the confidence I had in my husband's professional abilities, the unknown elements connected to the trance state caused me anguish.

"All right, wary wife," Jim responded. "Just let me know when you are ready to participate in our joint enterprise." His smile was one of unconcealed amusement that grew out of a knowledge acquired from a close association of 24 years of matrimony. He was well aware that it was only a matter of time until my intellectual curiosity would override my need for security and our experiment would commence.

It has always been my policy when starting a project to investigate all aspects thoroughly before embarking on it. This venture proved to be no exception. I had noticed several books on hypnotism on the third shelf in my husband's study. I was particularly anxious not to give any indication that my position was weakening so quickly. Thus, I would patiently wait until Jim left for work each day before poring over the contents of one textbook after another in an effort to master some of the elemental concepts of hypnosis. I often retreated to the far corner of our pool deck when reading the material. I find this to be one of the most relaxing spots around our home and the one that provides me with the most positive vibrations. In such pleasant surroundings my feelings of insecurity began to diminish, and, as I continued to digest one chapter after another, the idea of experiencing the trance state appeared less threatening. Statement after statement attested to the principle that all hypnosis was truly self-hypnosis. There was relatively little danger connected to the process if a subject undergoing hypnosis was in the hands of a competent hypnotist. I was particularly encouraged by the section on self-hypnosis in the publication *Handbook of Hypnosis for Professionals* by Roy Udolf. One of the advantages he cited in using self-hypnosis was that it developed in the subject "a sense of self-mastery and control and an ego-building feeling of independence."[1] This statement struck home. If I could enter and exit the trance state safely and still maintain complete control over all my thoughts and actions, the necessary reassurance I had been searching for had been located. I was now ready to risk the next step in my psychic progression.

"Jim, dear," I confessed one evening as we were finishing supper on our patio, "I have been reading several of the books from your library on hypnotism. After much deliberation and carefully weighing all aspects of the question, I am in complete agreement with your proposition and would be willing to participate in such an experiment."

His eyes danced at the prospect. "Great!" he exclaimed. "Let's get started immediately." He had known victory was his before the first shot was fired.

"I must insist on taping the session," I continued, trying to salvage some dignity from the ashes of my defeat.

"No problem at all," he remarked, and, before I had a chance to clear the first dish from the table, he was already arranging the recording equipment for our initial psychic reading session.

If there was ever a reluctant clairvoyant, it was I. My husband's enthusiasm was counterbalanced by all the foot-dragging activities I could invent, but the moment of truth was finally upon me and I was soon to learn the errors of my ways. I settled back in our comfortable chair and waited.

"Relax and take several deep breaths," Jim began.

I complied.

"Now, imagine a beautiful scene in which you are comfortable and enjoying yourself. Relax and let the sun warm you. Visualize this and experience it to the fullest." His voice seemed further away now. I immediately saw myself beside my pool, safe and secure in a place of familiarity.

"Now, I am going to count down from ten to one. With each number you will find you are more comfortable and relaxed than you have ever been in your entire life." (This sounded good to me because I am usually in a state of hyperactivity.) I decided to go with the feeling.

"Ten, nine, eight, seven." Jim's voice faded more and more, and with each count I began to feel my body become lighter and lighter.

"Six, five, four." I was almost buoyant by now.

"Three, two, one!" I felt as if I had left my physical body behind. This was the most pleasant sensation I had ever known. Suddenly, colorful scenes began to flash before my eyes. At first, they looked out of focus but gradually the visual images sharpened. My husband's voice interrupted my concentration. "Return to your tenth birthday and describe the scene."

Immediately, I saw myself two feet smaller in a pink silk dress with embroidered rosebuds. I was standing before a birthday cake with ten candles. My sister stood beside me, and my mother was poised to cut the cake. I could see my cousins, aunts, and uncles seated around the table singing "Happy Birthday" and waiting expectantly for me to blow out the lighted candles. I described the scene in detail to Jim. The voice I used seemed to belong to me but the discourse I gave was formed in whispered syllables. The pace of vocalization had slowed to a crawl.

"Do you recall having a dress like that when you were younger?" Jim inquired.

"Absolutely," I replied emphatically. (If you could imagine how emphatic one becomes in the depths of a trance!)

"Now, I want you to go forward in time," Jim's voice directed, "and see if you can envision any significant future events that either of us will encounter in the next several weeks. In that way we will be prepared for their occurrence."

Did he really expect I could do this? Before another thought entered my mind, I saw myself driving my blue station wagon out of our driveway and up a snowy road. Suddenly, my tire hit a patch of ice. I swerved and ended up in a ditch. Then a second scene appeared in which I was talking to my sister, Arlene Helmus, on the telephone. I listened while she enthusiastically related how my niece Kris had received a special honor at college for her academic achievement.

Jim excitedly made notes and readjusted our recorder to be certain the volume was high enough to capture my hushed tones.

"What can you foresee in my future?" In the next instant two more distinct sets of events flashed before my eyes. In one I saw Jim and myself at the Hotel Roanoke greeting a good friend at dinner time. The second in the series revolved around antique furniture. Jim was seated on an outdated couch. He immediately arose and walked over to a desk where a lady wearing a floral blouse was working and bent over to ask her a question. Neither of these scenes made any sense to me, but again I informed Jim of the scenes pictured.

"That's enough for tonight. I'm bringing you out of your trance." I heard Jim's voice more strongly now, but the theater of the future had become so enthralling to me that I wasn't sure I wanted to return to reality yet. All the while, I could hear Jim counting upward.

"One, two, three, four, five." I became alert and more aware of being in my Shellbank living room once again.

"Six, seven, eight, nine, ten." I opened my eyes and through somewhat blurred vision beheld my husband's triumphant face.

"You were a fine hypnotic subject." His voice quivered with emotion. I noted the calm, serene exterior that usually surrounds my husband had given way to the sense of joy that often accompanies a successful accomplishment.

"Now we'll have to wait." He rewarded me with a hug. That reward was more than ample for all the imaginary trials and tribulations to which I had subjected myself in the weeks preceding my initial excursion into the mysterious yet unbelievably fascinating world of psychic readings.

Several months went by without any confirmation of the foreseen events. Then, one Monday morning, I raised my window shade to survey a familiar scene. A snowstorm had begun while we slept, and there were already more than four inches of sparkling white crystals blanketing the earth.

"Aha!" I thought."Drive carefully as you proceed up Shellbank Road or you will end up in a ditch."I did just that, never exceeding 10 miles an hour. In spite of all my precautions, however, as I rounded our curve to drive onto the main thoroughfare, my right front tire skidded on a patch of ice and our blue station wagon veered out of control. In the next instant Robin and I landed sideways in a ditch. Upon opening the door and studying our predicament, I concluded the car was firmly entrenched and would be impossible to dislodge without a wrecker. Robin and I retraced our steps homeward to place the call.

The question connected with this incident continued to haunt me. Could I have done anything more to avoid the accident? A careful review of the events leading up to the skid revealed no different course of action other than the ones I had already chosen to take unless, of course, I remained at home, which was out of the question. I therefore concluded that the function of the ditch premonition was one of preparation rather than prevention.

The following Friday the telephone rang as I worked at our dining room table completing the educational reports of the children whom I had evaluated that week. Upon answering it I was delighted to hear my sister Arlene's voice on the other end of the line.

"Guess what, Joan." There was an element of excitement in her tone. (I had the distinct feeling I knew what was coming next.) "Kristen has been presented with the Panhellenic Award for the freshman with the highest grade point average at Davis College. We are so proud of her achievement. She wanted us to call you immediately. It just happened yesterday."

Needless to say, I shared my sister's sense of pride in my niece's accomplishments. Kristen had always been an extremely mature and conscientious student who set a high standard of excellence in all her academic endeavors. Through this honor she had been properly recognized for her diligence.

"Tell Kristen she is highly deserving of this honor," I replied. We then talked of other family matters and, after 20 minutes of sisterly gossip, I placed the phone on its receiver. I sat in stunned silence on the side of my bed. A few short minutes before I had witnessed prediction number two enter reality.

Predictions three and four followed closely on the footsteps of number two. My husband had been appointed chairman of a special committee to evaluate a college for accreditation by the Southern Association of Colleges and Schools. This entailed a four-day trip to Tennessee for the evaluation procedure. We consulted a map and found that it was approximately a two-day drive between Williamsburg and our destination. We decided to combine business with pleasure and stop overnight at the Hotel Roanoke in Roanoke, Virginia.

Over the years Jim and I have toured extensively throughout Virginia in connection with his professional responsibilities as a practicing psychologist. Early in our travels we had the good fortune to attend a meeting located at the Hotel Roanoke. From that time to this our family has had a continuing love affair with the hotel. Fond memories of epicurean delights savored in the quiet elegance of the Regency Room flooded my mind. This haute cuisine was frequently followed by a late-night dip in the azure blue indoor pool providing the necessary ingredient for a peaceful night's slumber. These pleasurable impressions served to intensify my desire to revisit this captivating place.

After making arrangements for our daughter, Robin, to be cared for and packing our belongings in our blue station wagon, we began our journey. The trip through the mountains of Virginia provided us with colorful panoramic scenes of the surrounding countryside. As was frequently our custom, we parked our car at the top of Afton Mountain to reexperience the breathtaking aerial view. From our vantage point we observed dozens of miniature farms positioned like squares on a patchwork quilt as far as the eye could see. This is one of the rewards one enjoys when residing in Virginia.

We arrived at the Hotel Roanoke in midafternoon, and after my husband had registered at the desk, we took the elevator to our room and unpacked our bags. As we dressed for dinner, I was struck by the feeling that this scene had an air of familiarity about it.

"Do you remember my psychic impression regarding dinner at the Hotel Roanoke?" I remarked. As I turned from the mirror, it was immediately obvious by the look on Jim's face that he was well aware of a sense of déjà vu.

"Whom do you think we will see?" I continued.

"Finish powdering your nose and we'll find out," he called as he hurriedly walked toward the door.

We rode the elevator down to the main lobby and looked around. No one we knew was in sight. We entered the Regency Dining Room and were seated in a quiet candlelit corner beside a heavily draped window. The waitress took our order. I leaned back to listen to the melodious strains of a 1950s vintage song rendered by the three-man combo across the dance floor. The pressures of the workaday world seemed unreal in this tranquil atmosphere. I closed my eyes. Upon opening them again, I glanced toward the entrance to the dining room. A tall gentleman was busy confirming his reservations for dinner.

"Do you see who I see?" I motioned to Jim.

"Henry Hecker, of all people!" Henry is one of the finest audiologists in our area. Jim and I have maintained a close working relationship with him for a number of years, referring to him clients whom we suspect have audiological dysfunctions. Henry spotted us, waved a greeting, and continued with his party to dinner. Later, we learned that he was attending an audiological conference at the hotel and was scheduled to give a presentation the following day.

"Prediction number three," Jim smiled smugly.

We left Roanoke early the next morning and resumed our drive to Tennessee. After making sure I was settled comfortably in our motel room, Jim proceeded to attend the evening meeting of his accreditation committee. He appeared around eleven o'clock pleased with the selection of coworkers and their willingness to participate in the evaluation process.

The next day I divided my time between report writing and sightseeing, returning to the motel around four P.M. to rest before dinner. I must have dozed off because an hour later I was awakened by a gentle nudge.

"Guess what I saw today," Jim reported. "Your antique couch. The college had a collection of valuable antiques bequeathed to them by a wealthy benefactor. Several of them were selected to be used in the president's outer office. I sat on the couch while I waited for the schedule of morning appointments. After several minutes had passed, the president's secretary called me over to give me the list, and as I bent over her desk to see the assignments, I noted she was wearing a floral blouse. The 'third eye' strikes again!" he added teasingly.

Our batting average the first time out was four hits out of four predictions.

Jim was far more confident in my psychic abilities than I was at this point in time. It would take one more year of weekly hypnotic trances accompanied by extended periods of self-questioning before I would accept the validity of my psychic readings.

My husband's mind works like a precise, orderly computer. He reasoned that if it were within the realm of possibility for me to divine events for the two of us, then the next step in our psychic progression would be to investigate whether or not I could read the future psychically for close friends and relatives. Since the closest relatives we had were our own children, Jim selected them as the subjects for our next experiment.

Permit me to digress here and introduce you to my offspring. One of the many blessings I have received during my lifetime is the gift of two marvelous children. Jimmy, my son, aged 24 as of April 30, 1984, is a second-year law student at the University of Richmond Law School. He was a dean's list student during his four years of college at James Madison University, and his name appeared in *Who's Who in American Colleges and Universities* during his senior year there. In addition to being highly disciplined academically, he displays an inordinate desire for service to others. This characteristic was reflected in his election to leadership offices in both his fraternity and the Student Government Association at JMU. I feel that his choice of professions is a further manifestation of this personality attribute.

My daughter, Robin, is a carefree spirit of 17. A senior at Walsingham Academy in Williamsburg, she emulates her brother scholastically by frequently achieving honors in many of her academic subjects, but the similarity ends there. She is extremely athletic and appears to me to be the embodiment of energy, dividing her interests between cheerleading, swimming, and jogging. She is proud of the fact that she was a peer counselor for her fellow students this year. With a swish of her long blonde hair and her ever-present smile she darts from one activity to another leaving father and mother at the homestead to serve as social secretaries for the numerous telephone calls received during her absence. Measuring only five feet three, she is our "Little Robin Bird," — our "joie de vivre" personified.

I feel compelled to furnish my readers with specific details of my children's personalities so that they may gain a more personal understanding of the events I am about to describe. At the time of this writing my son was a senior at JMU and Robin was a sophomore at Walsingham Academy.

We proceeded as we had in our first psychic reading session. Jim selected a simple induction method, and again I felt as if my consciousness was separating from my physical body. It was the pleasantest of sensations, but before I had a chance to immerse myself too deeply in these delectable feelings, a series of movielike images was again being projected onto my visual field. Amidst this conglomeration of mental scenes, I perceived Jim's distant voice continuously offering guidance.

"We are currently doing a reading for Robin Joan Windsor of One Hundred Thirty Shellbank Drive, Williamsburg, Virginia. Describe in depth what you observe giving me any and all impressions that will prove beneficial to her both in her current life and in the future."

Immediately, a single mental picture became clearly focused in my mind's eye. Robin stood before me on a beach talking to a young man whose face was unfamiliar to me. I was certain his name began with *D*. Drew perhaps?

A second psychic image replaced the first. I gasped as I witnessed Robin lose her balance and tumble into the water from the side of the swimming pool. I knew she was not in danger physically, however.

A third and final mental picture came into view. Robin was busily engaged in cleaning tables although her surroundings were clearly not those of a restaurant. I relayed my impressions to Jim.

"Relax, now," his voice directed. "Clear your mind of all past information. See if you can focus your attention on James Laurent Windsor of the same address. Give me any and all impressions you receive concerning his present and future existence."

Once again the "movie screen" lit up and Jimmy appeared on the set with a lovely blonde. The face was unfamiliar, but she was dressed in a red and blue uniform with an *R* on the front of it. She was laughing at a joke Jimmy had told and appeared to be basking in his company.

This picture blurred. Apprehension gripped me. I had the distinct feeling that Jimmy was afflicted with an illness. It appeared to be centered on his eyes and a hospital was involved. "Great!" I thought. "Who needs this!" However, I reported my observations to Jim and released the final tableau.

The impact of the last impression had lightened my trance so that, in a matter of seconds, I emerged from my altered state. Jim had recorded all my new predictions. Now we would wait patiently to see what if anything developed. As a precautionary measure we telephoned Jimmy at college and warned him to monitor his health carefully. He assured us he would.

Two of the five events observed blossomed into reality shortly. In late spring of 1982 Robin went on a church retreat. She was a member of the cleanup committee at supper and "bused the tables." On Saturday of the retreat she and a male companion engaged in a shoving match and she fell into the swimming pool clothes and all. She came up laughing! The beach scene with "Drew" happened later in the summer when I attended an ARE Conference at Virginia Beach. The 16-year-old son of another of the conferees became a good friend of Robin's, but his name was David, not Drew.

Jimmy's blonde girlfriend was named Lisa. He met her at the University of Richmond in the fall of 1982. The uniform was a cheerleading outfit. This scene took place several months after I initially observed it.

Unfortunately, I must report my premonition regarding Jimmy's illness was not a figment of my imagination either. In April of 1982 we expected Jimmy home for spring vacation. We were late in returning from work and found his car already parked in our driveway. We opened the back door and were delighted to see him seated at our kitchen table.

"Hi, parents." He greeted us with enthusiasm but made no move to give us "bear hugs" as is his usual custom.

My motherly instinct told me something was amiss. I looked him straight in the eye and said, "What's the matter?"

He grinned sheepishly and replied, "I had a fall last night

and seem to have hurt my ankle." With that announcement he produced a swollen ankle the size of a bowling ball from its hiding place under the table. "It doesn't hurt much." His voice belied his words. "I just can't walk on it."

We quickly drove him to the Williamsburg Community Hospital where the physician on duty X-rayed the injured joint and reported he had suffered a hairline fracture. This necessitated his wearing a cast for six weeks.

I discussed this incident in depth for one reason: to make the point that psychic impressions are not always 100 percent precise. I had foreseen the situation accurately, but the injury was to his foot, not his eyes. It is my opinion that I was probably picking up his dazed condition resulting from the force of the fall when I focused on the eyes instead of the ankle. This error increased my awareness of the fallibility of psychic impressions. A good rule of thumb is to approach a reading with the idea that *this is what a probable future might hold* rather than *this is what is.*

Having succeeded in procuring a satisfactory response to his second question, my husband now formulated a third proposal. Since I could apparently read successfully for friends and relatives close by, could I read psychically for them at a distance? The subject we selected for our third project was my sister, Arlene Helmus. Not only was she a relative, but she just happened to reside in Orinda, California, a continent away from our home in Williamsburg, Virginia. Any distance beyond that would put the person chosen residing in the Pacific Ocean. I was eager to share our ideas with my sister as she has been my confidante throughout life, and by now I was in dire need of another understanding soul besides my husband and partner with whom I could discuss our discoveries. I dialed her number, and after several rings she answered.

"I was just thinking of calling you but I waited this time for you to call," she laughed. We have a standing joke that when one thinks of the other, a telephone call usually ensues. This is another manifestation of the strong bond between us.

We exchanged small talk for a while. Then I took a deep breath and hesitantly inquired, "Would you still claim me as your sister if you knew I was psychic?"

There was a long pause at the other end of the line. This

was the sister who had always participated fully with me in everything we did from selling lemonade to our neighbors to marching side by side as majorettes in the William and Mary Band. This was also the sister whose father made "snow dream telephone calls" to her over the years as he had done with me. The long silence ended. "I always suspected you were," she giggled. "How else could you have known what I was always thinking and doing? Tell me all about it." I breathed a sigh of relief.

Now I was free not only to share our secret with my sister but to seek her opinion on matters that heretofore I could discuss only with Jim.

After supplying her with the background information on our past experiences, I outlined our current project. She readily agreed not only to participate but to provide us with the required feedback for confirming or denying the success of Jim's hypothesis.

Within two days of my telephone conversation, we scheduled Arlene's reading. Using the same procedures as before I entered the trance state more quickly. By now, I had some idea of the altered state of consciousness that it was necessary to achieve in order to begin a reading. Jim's voice directed my focus toward occurrences that might be within my sister's destiny for the next several weeks and again, in my mind's eye, I viewed a myriad of brilliant portraits depicting futuristic eventualities that as yet lay dormant in time and space. I relayed these impressions to Jim:

1. One of Arlene's three poodles appeared to have a health problem.
2. I saw Weldon, Arlene's husband, give her a small package that contained a vaselike item for the home.
3. A bouquet of flowers was pictured.
4. I felt there was a small element of danger for someone as he stepped into their sailboat.
5. There seemed to be a new pillow or bedspread in one of the bedrooms.
6. Arlene and Weldon had dinner guests. A lady wearing a blue dress was seated on Arlene's right at the dinner table.
7. Arlene was attending a meeting with a number of ladies present.
8. Arlene was witness to a huge fire or a building burning.

These impressions were recorded, and, after Jim had requested some guidance in personal questions of our own, I heard his now-familiar directive to reenter the world of reality.

We debated the most verifiable experimental design for our project and decided to withhold the list of predictions from our subject for several weeks. In that way the foreseen events would transpire without being tainted by Arlene's aspirations for success.

Approximately one month after the reading I telephoned my sister and gave her an account of our prognostications. She excitedly reported confirmation of the majority of my predictions although there were obvious deviations of time and interpretations of visual images.

1. Cinnamon, Arlene's oldest poodle, had had a benign tumor removed several weeks before with no complications.
2. Weldon had given Arlene a coffee cup with "Mom" written on the side for Mother's Day.
3. Arlene had presented Kris with a bouquet of flowers for singing in a college production.
4. Weldon had had a male friend accompany him to their sailboat, and, upon stepping aboard, he had slipped. He avoided taking a serious spill by catching hold of a railing.
5. Arlene had purchased a new bedspread for Dana. This was two months before I had done the reading so I had traveled back in time also.
6. The female dinner guest clad in blue had arrived on schedule but had seated herself on Arlene's left rather than choosing to sit on her right.
7. Arlene had not attended a ladies' meeting but planned to attend one in two weeks.
8. The most astounding happening of all, and the one that amazed us both, was the fact that Weldon witnessed the effects of an explosion and a resulting fire in the tunnel connecting Oakland with San Francisco in which several cars had been incinerated. The disaster was of such great magnitude that it had been televised nationally. I remembered seeing pictures of the catastrophe broadcast on our local TV station. Arlene described to me how she had driven through the tunnel later and shuddered in horror when she observed the blackened walls. Although there were slight alterations in the pictured observation, because of the emotional impact

connected to the disaster, it was one of the most prominent events in Arlene's life during these few weeks.

We were sufficiently impressed with the reading to conclude that Jim's theory concerning doing readings for friends and relatives at a distance was correct.

I now realized that to become more proficient in doing the readings, it was essential for me to practice on a daily basis as much as possible. In order to do this I learned to place myself in a deep trance by using the techniques of self-hypnosis and subsequently discovered that I could do "short readings" on my own and then record the impressions I received afterward. The continuing experience with these "short readings" provided me with a method of determining the accuracy of my predictions and gave me confidence in my abilities and their correct usage. Needless to say, this was not an easy period for me, but I had the unfailing support of my husband and my sister, and their enthusiasm and excitement supplied the necessary energy to spur me on.

I must at this time mention two other people who played significant roles in my psychic journey. One is Dr. JoAnne Squires, with whom I have maintained a working relationship in my business over the past 12 years. The other is Mrs. Betty Hall, my secretary since 1979.

JoAnne is a professor of psychology at Christopher Newport College. She has been serving as consulting psychologist for Learning Development Services since its inception. She possesses a keen intellect and a highly analytical mind. We have been close friends since we met some 15 years ago. I do not recollect a cross word exchanged in that entire span of time with the exception of one luncheon at which we discussed the success of the Reagan administration and two hours later were as far apart on issues as we had been at the beginning of the debate. As the precognitive dreams and the study of the psychic became more and more an integral part of my life, I turned to the two others in my circle of friends in whom I had implicit trust.

My intuition told me that if I shared my experiences and psychic premonitions with JoAnne, my reward would be an analytical evaluation of the data compiled coupled with constructive ideas for future psychic progression. And so every Friday noon for more than one year we met at the Trellis, a gourmet restaurant for natural-food enthusiasts, and partook of a delicious repast while reviewing the past week's incidents. Our conversations centered on her work at the college, our children, matters of physical and mental health in which we both shared a deep interest, and the mysterious world of the psychic. I would often furnish her with one of my "short readings," and on consecutive Fridays she faithfully presented me with her responses and comments regarding the accuracy of my prophecies. I foresaw her making three overnight trips during the spring and summer, previewed her daughter, Anne, in a yellow-and-black truck that was purchased at college, and provided her with several valid health suggestions. In return I received confirmations or denials of the accuracy of the items listed. Each of us derived immeasurable benefits from these Friday meetings, but there is no doubt in my mind that I was the greater beneficiary.

Betty Hall came to work for me in May, 1979. She is the wife of Lt. Col. Gary Hall, who was stationed at Fort Eustis, Virginia, at that time. He is now retired, and they remain in this area.

At the time I employed Betty, I had not the slightest inkling of the important role she would play in my life for the next five years. We liked each other on sight, and the relationship that developed has been one of friendship rather than that of an employer-employee nature. I began to share some of my precognitive dreams with her when the information I received concerned her family's health. Initially she was skeptical, but as time wore on and Jim and I became more and more immersed in our psychic work, she had an opportunity to observe the authenticity. Her role then switched. She began to act as my conscience chastening me when I became overconfident in my successes and rushing to my aid when I threw up my hands in despair upon learning of incongruities and misinterpretations of the information. The questions she made me ask myself were always pertinent and to the point.

"Where does it say in the Bible you should foretell the future?"

"What is your approach to the calamities you foresee?

Should you make people aware of them and, if so, how?"

"How would you handle visions of tragedy within your own family?"

"Be objective! Say what you see! Don't shy away from unpleasant events or you will lower the accuracy and usefulness of the readings!"

"How can these readings be best used to achieve the maximum good for others?"

"Most of all be true to yourself and your own values!"

Each of these remarks became ingrained in my mind and remained there being inwardly debated until a satisfactory solution was conceived that was consistent with my ethical, moral, and religious philosophy of life. Betty, being the kind of person she is, is unaware of the immensity of her contribution to our psychic work. It is always a source of amusement to me that whenever I attempt to thank her for her encouragement, she looks at me quizzically and asks, "How?"

One of the principles upon which the psychic is based is that whatever gracious or malevolent deeds are rendered to others return to the perpetrator tenfold. As you sow, so you reap (Galatians 6:7-8). I have repeatedly observed the truthfulness of this axiom, but the anecdote I am about to relate serves as an excellent illustration.

In the spring of 1982 Betty's daughter-in-law, Patricia Hall, became afflicted with an excruciating pain in her right calf. She was unable to obtain relief from traditional medical therapies, and her malady persisted. The entire course of events encompassed approximately six weeks, during which time I was keenly aware of Pat's distressing situation through daily conversations with Betty. At the end of the six-week period Betty hesitantly approached me with a proposal.

"Do you think a reading on Pat's ailment would provide us with some answers?" she inquired.

"I have no way to be sure," I replied, "but, if you feel Jim and I can be of service, we would be more than happy to request information from our source. But remember, there are no guarantees. Do you think Pat would agree to the suggestions given?"

After almost a full year of working in the psychic field I

knew with certainty that the success or failure of a psychic reading is strongly dependent on the client's belief in the process.

"She has nothing to lose," Betty declared. "She is in constant pain and, I feel, would be open to any form of treatment that might afford her some relief."

I agreed to her proposition. During supper that evening Jim and I made plans to conduct the reading the following night. Before falling asleep I sought guidance through the dream incubation process as well as the future reading. I felt it could do no harm to receive as many ideas as possible. The dream presented to me contained precise recommendations for healing Pat's leg. I entitled it "The Out-of-Tune Piano" and recorded the following symbolic material:

THE OUT-OF-TUNE PIANO

There is a piano that is out of tune. One of the strings has lost its tension, and poor vibrations produce a flat note. It needs adjusting to go back in place.

To my understanding the strings and keys of the piano represented the spinal cord and spinal column of Pat's back. The resulting discordant notes represented the poor nerve energies or vibrations caused by one area of the spinal column's being misaligned. The pain was referred to the leg producing a flat note. (I had the flat note symbolizing Pat's pain in her leg one night in another dream.) Therefore, realignment of Pat's back would remedy the physical disorder.

The advice offered in the dream was suggestive of chiropractic adjustments. The reading conducted the subsequent evening concurred with the healing prescription outlined in my dream. This was not surprising because the information communicated through both the dreams and the psychic readings appears to flow from one common source. I had some misgivings, however. I had had absolutely no contact with chiropractors throughout my entire lifetime.

I recalled one conversation with a female colleague in my husband's psychology department. She suffered from cystic fibroid disease of the breasts as I did. She had recommended Dr. Genevieve Haller, a chiropractor and nutritionist who resided in Virginia Beach. Being in excellent health at the time of the conversation I filed it away in my brain under "Future Health Treatments" and turned my attention to other things. Now Dr. Haller's name reappeared in my consciousness and I recalled how sympathetic she was to the Edgar Cayce regimens. I wrote her name on a slip of paper and placed it in my briefcase, thinking to give it to Betty after I had summarized the contents of the piano dream and my psychic reading.

Betty was elated by our source's advice and carried the slip of paper to her desk to copy Dr. Haller's name and address. As she studied the paper, she mentally recalled the name of Dr. William Scanlan, a local chiropractor. His office was five minutes from her door. She asked me if I knew anything about his practice. I had to admit that, while I could vouch for Dr. Haller's competence because I had respect for Jim's colleague's opinion, I knew virtually nothing about Dr. William Scanlan except that I had heard his name mentioned favorably among local ARE members.

Betty decided to make one appointment with Dr. Scanlan because of the proximity of his location. If his treatment proved unsuccessful, they would then consider driving to Virginia Beach to seek Dr. Haller's assistance. Betty telephoned Pat to inform her of the fruitfulness of our psychic inquisition, and Pat made an appointment with Dr. Scanlan for that very afternoon.

At eight P.M. I received an alarming phone call from Betty.

"Pat's leg feels worse now than it did before she went to see Dr. Scanlan." Betty's voice contained a note of desperation.

I despaired with her, feeling that I had been the main contributor to the expansion of Pat's discomfort. While my guilt was growing by leaps and bounds, my inward voice was busily engaged in impressing upon my psyche how imperative it was that Pat continue with Dr. Scanlan's treatment program. I theorized that perhaps the condition had to get worse before it improved. (This assessment later proved correct.) After attempting to allay Betty's fears, I encouraged her to have Pat schedule another appointment with Dr. Scanlan. Pat agreed, and, to her great surprise, this session turned out to be less painful than the previous one, and the torturing pain she had endured for more than two months began to subside.

During the second office visit Dr. Scanlan reviewed Pat's X-ray with her pointing out the skeletal misalignment present in her spinal column. His professional opinion was that it was this misalignment that was responsible for Pat's painful affliction. A continuing series of chiropractic adjustments over a period of five months finally put an end to her misery. Pat is currently in perfect health and returns to Dr. Scanlan for a periodic "tuneup."

How did an incident such as this benefit me? In July of 1982 I developed another cyst. This time, however, its location was such that the castor oil treatment was not as effective as it had been on the preceding occasion. With the failure of my initial attempt to heal it facing me, I again requested guidance from my source to effect a cure. I recorded the following two dreams given in response to my plea.

SHRINKING THE CYST
(July 25, 1982)

A lady has a cyst. A lovely oriental-looking lady with healing hands says it can be shrunk.

AN APPOINTMENT WITH GENIE
(July 25, 1982)

I see the name Genie *written on an appointment calendar among other names.*

A short reading done in connection with these dreams indicated it could be drained by surgery or treated nutritionally.

I reexamined my dreams and realized the name Genie written on the appointment calendar referred to Dr. Genevieve Haller, the chiropractor-nutritionist recommended to me. I never would have considered visiting a chiropractor had it not been for the astonishing recovery I had witnessed in Pat Hall's case, although I have become convinced in recent years that nutrition plays a large part in maintenance of one's bodily health.

An appointment with Dr. Bell confirmed that surgical methods could be used to drain the cyst, but I opted for the chiropractic-nutritional approach instead, following my inner promptings.

During my preliminary visit I received a thorough examination. Upon its completion, Dr. Haller pointed out the five weakest areas of my entire body. These coincided exactly with the few minor physical disorders I had ever been bothered by since childhood. The results of my hair analysis furnished her with a profile of my nutritional deficiencies. She then outlined a program of diet and vitamin supplements accompanied by weekly chiropractic adjustments, which, if adhered to, would alleviate my suffering.

Thus I became the willing patient and she the miraculous healer. By the end of September my cyst had shrunk to half its original size and I had under control a borderline case of hypoglycemia that in the past had precipitated wide mood variations. In four short appointments she had also cured my daughter of back problems that had plagued her since the age of 10. As I studied her face one day, I realized she looked amazingly like the lady with the healing hands from whom I had sought succor in the dream "Shrinking the Cyst." *I had truly been rewarded tenfold*!

I would like to take this opportunity to clear up any misinterpretations that may result from a lack of understanding on the part of some readers. In no way am I advocating that everyone switch from medical to chiropractic treatment. Indeed, competent medical diagnosis and treatments are mandatory if one is to continue to possess excellent physical well-being. My own physician is an outstanding example of this fact, and many of my professional referrals as a counselor come from pediatricians, who are among the finest people I know. There are, however, alternative procedures that can be considered when traditional medical treatments fail.

By the spring of 1982, thanks to the support, understanding and love freely given by my family and close friends, I was gaining confidence in my abilities and was also beginning to perceive the world of the psychic from a more spiritual point of view. Over a period of eight months I had acquired a large psychic library, and, as I continued to read page after page, statements leaped forth from their hiding places as if they had been written exclusively for me. Among them were the following:

"What has been one's 'stumbling block' . . . can be made his very 'stepping-stone' towards love and aid to others, because of deep sensitizing action."[2]

"We all learn only by experience. We come to have faith or understanding by taking one step at a time."[3]

"It is for the individual, by understanding himself and his fellow-man, to find his own reason for existing, to shape his own destiny — with the help of a living God."[4]

I now genuinely began to believe that the psychic was of the soul.

3

A Visit to the Center for Non-physical Sciences

> "I will bring all things to thine remembrance" that are needs be for thy soul, thine mind, thine body development.
>
> Mary Ellen Carter, *Edgar Cayce on Prophecy*

During the summer of 1982 I had finally arrived at the point where I had mastered the basic techniques connected with successful psychic readings and felt comfortable doing them. Jim had taught me extremely well, and I was reeducating myself through a continuing diet of books pertaining to psychic development. What we needed now was a master teacher to bring refinement and order to our primitive techniques. It has been said that when one is ready, such a teacher arrives. It was so with us in the persons of Roger and Nancy Pile.

I am firmly convinced that nothing in this life happens by chance. Therefore, persons who enter our lives during the transitional phases of our existence are, in reality, mentors whose duty it is to assist us in the rearrangement of our code of values so that we may meet more effectively the challenges presented to us. Because of this I am certain that there was nothing accidental about the discovery and subsequent purchase of Sandra Gibson's book *Beyond the Mind*.

I have previously confessed to being a chronic bookstore browser. The spring shopping trip to Miller and Rhoads department store in Richmond while my husband attended a Mental Health Board Meeting proved to be no exception. As I reviewed the unfamiliar publications that had been added to their stock since my previous inspection, my gaze fell upon her work. A note on the cover said that this was a beginner's handbook for psychic development. I leafed through the pages reading snatches of paragraphs here and there. Gradually, I came to the pleasurable realization that the description of Sandra's psychic experiences paralleled mine almost exactly. Without hesitation I bought the book, and being the voracious reader that I am I consumed its contents in two days. The section describing her method of doing psychic readings was immensely valuable, but what would prove to be of infinitely more value in our future development was the directory of facilities for psychic instruction listing the Center for Non-Physical Sciences in Chester, Connecticut.

The center was codirected by Roger S. Pile, Sr., and Nancy J. Pile, both of whom appeared qualified to teach psychic education courses. Roger offered instruction in healing and psychic counseling for business, and Nancy was a deep-trance medium who did psychic counseling as well as teaching a class in parapsychology at a local college. Sandra Gibson knew them personally; she had received instruction from them and had devoted several pages of her book to their philosophy and activities. Other examples of psychics and mediums were sprinkled throughout her text, so the Piles were by no means her sole resource, but, of all the people Sandra mentioned, it was Roger and Nancy Pile's names to which I was inexplicably drawn. There were at least a dozen facilities listed in the psychic directory, so after conferring with Jim on the advisability of writing for information, I selected several whose programs most nearly met the criteria Jim and I felt to be of prime importance for our future growth and development. I wrote letters to each requesting brochures describing their fees, courses, and central focus.

It had become my nightly custom when faced with an important issue to request guidance through the dream incubation process. The process of choosing a master teacher from a group of unfamiliar names seemed awesome, and I was well aware I needed spiritual direction. I therefore made an earnest appeal to my guiding sources to chart my course appropriately.

The dream I received showed a green wooden house situated by a stream. I was almost certain the residence was in Connecticut. I entered an account of the vision in my dream journal and left space for future confirmation or rejection of its accuracy.

Within two weeks the packets containing the brochures and course descriptions began to arrive. One of the organizations described a well-organized plan for a home-study course, but I had already decided I needed personal instruction. Another institute offered courses taught by highly qualified instructors. The subject matter covered was exactly what I required, but their prices were exorbitant.

Eventually, the pamphlet from the Center for Non-Physical Sciences arrived accompanied by a personal letter from Roger Pile. Included in the offerings were courses entitled "Health, Healing, and Well-being" and "Psychic Development." These sounded intriguing, and the center's rates were within our budget. (I learned later that Roger prices his readings and courses reasonably so that cost will not be a prohibitive factor when clients wish to avail themselves of his services). Jim and I were impressed by his intellectual yet spiritual approach to counseling and psychic readings. He wrote:

Our method is to use a psychic or mediumistic "reading" to get to the heart of the problem as quickly as possible. The information comes from the core of the person, the very soul, if you wish, of the client or sitter and is transmitted to him/her by the psychic verbally so that it is brought into consciousness, thus effectively by-passing the ego defense mechanisms. Only that information that the sitter needs to know at that particular time will come through. Usually, the sitter already knows the information deep within and the psychic only serves as reinforcement and confirmation.

One rule we have is that the sitter must be willing to help him/herself. He must take on the responsibility and charge of his own direction in life. It is up to the sitter to make the decision and take the action of implementation — the two essentials to change and growth. We offer appropriate techniques for self-discovery and coping, but we will not allow ourselves to become a crutch. If a client becomes dependent and unwilling to change direction, then we will promptly drop him/her until such time as that client decides to adopt a more positive/constructive attitude. Our role is mainly that of a guide.

Since we get what we ask for, I always ask my clients, "Why are you asking for this problem or problems — or series of problems?" It has been a very effective way of getting the client to see the cause-and-effect relationship between his problems and the direction he is headed. Negativity begets negativity as loving begets loving. We must first and foremost love ourselves, however, before we can possibly love others. I speak of love at a "being" level. [1]

Roger's and Nancy's philosophy was compatible with the ideals Jim and I had employed in our counseling practices for the last 15 years. Consequently, we concluded that much could be gained from enrollment in their psychic development course as well as the sharing of ideas with one another.

From the pamphlet enclosed with Roger's letter we realized that it would be impossible to enroll in their regularly scheduled classes due to the distance barrier. By chance, however, Jim and I had planned a twenty-fifth wedding anniversary trip to Ames Farm Inn, a charming and secluded resort situated on the shores of Lake Winnipesaukee near Laconia, New Hampshire. I had made periodic treks there since I was a child of seven, and when I acquired a husband and children, they learned to love the inn as I did.

The drive from Virginia to Lake Winnipesaukee usually takes 17 hours. It was obvious from the map that Chester, Connecticut, was a good overnight stopping point before continuing our journey, so I composed a letter to the Piles inquiring about the possibility of a compact three-day course designed specifically to speak to our areas of interest. Almost immediately, I received a positive response agreeing to my proposal and outlining the course of instruction. We were directed to bring our tape recorder so that we could tape the sessions and replay them in the future when we had more time to digest the essence of the lectures.

We busied ourselves making plans for the trip, which was scheduled for the first week of August. An air of expectancy permeated our beings, but this was mixed with some degree of consternation. The sequence of events seem to have fallen in place exactly as if fashioned by some master planner (probably with considerable help of my unseen advisers), but we did face the prospect of spending three days discussing psychic matters with two people who up until two months ago had been total strangers and whom, as yet, we had not met face to face.

Always up to the challenge of the moment, my husband suggested we do a psychic reading connected with our visit to the Center for Non-Physical Sciences. "It will serve two purposes," he said. "First, it will provide us with some input concerning whether or not this is the proper step to take. Second, we can determine whether or not you can do readings at a distance for persons about whom we know very little."

I was in total agreement with his idea. I settled into my favorite gold recliner, which I now thought of as my "trance chair," and prepared myself for a reading. With Jim serving as my ever-present guide, pleasant sensations of heightened awareness enveloped me and I felt myself transported to another domain. Jim directed me to focus my attention on Roger and Nancy Pile, and, on July 25, 1982, I gave the following readings for these two extraordinary souls:

READING FOR ROGER PILE

1. A large mahogany desk occupies much of his study.
2. There are many bookshelves there.
3. Roger is in his fifties and has white hair.
4. He is extremely accurate psychically.
5. He provides instruction in picture readings.
6. He will suggest books to read about diet, yoga, psychic readings, and meditation.
7. Roger's house is by a stream with a tree on the right.
8. There seems to be redwood picnic furniture in the back of the house.
9. The house is one story with green-and-white wooden siding.
10. White shutters adorn the windows. The house is situated on a corner.
11. Roger possesses healing hands and is a good teacher.
12. He will teach us to reach inside ourselves.
13. He emphasizes revisualization exercises for healing.
14. I see trophies for running.

READING FOR NANCY PILE

1. Nancy has light curly hair and an engaging smile.
2. She is five foot seven and of medium build.

3. She is an excellent cook and enjoys culinary activities.
4. Nancy exhibits superior mediumship ability.
5. Many of our most urgent questions will be answered by her if we prepare a list beforehand.
6. Nancy lectures at a local college teaching a course in parapsychology, which includes meditation training.
7. Mental health activities interest her.
8. A reading will be done for us that will give us directional guidance.
9. We correspond with the Piles after we leave.
10. Nancy works in her garden and grows large-sized produce.
11. Suggestions are given to Jim by her for creativity.
12. Nancy leans toward holistic health ideas.
13. A bone in her finger appears to have a hairline fracture that has healed.
14. Her personality is pleasing and her laugh lilting.

As the reading ended, the guiding forces stated unequivocally that our visit to the Center for Non-Physical Sciences would be a rewarding adventure instilling in us an even greater respect for the psychic and enabling us to attain new understandings in our spiritual evolution.

After finalizing our vacation preparations, on Tuesday, August 3, we departed for Chester, Connecticut, stopping overnight to visit my father in Rahway, New Jersey, before continuing on to the Center for Non-Physical Sciences. We had no difficulty in locating the town of Chester but found it necessary to stop in the center of town and ask directions to Deep Hollow Drive. According to a local resident we were about one and one-half miles from our journey's end. We followed his instructions to the letter and without further delay arrived at our appointed destination.

"Do you think you will be able to recognize the house if you see it?" Jim asked as we drove down Deep Hollow Drive.

"I'm not sure," I replied uncertainly, "but I'll tell you if I see one that resembles it."

We drove further along and rounded a curve.

"There it is!" Jim exclaimed excitedly, pointing to a green

and white two-story house. "I recognized it from your description." He pointed to a structure on our left. The house was almost a duplicate of the one I had viewed psychically except it had two stories instead of one. White shutters were attached to the windows and a large pine tree flanked its right side. As we turned into the driveway, I saw Nancy's small vegetable garden about 10 feet from our car.

The front door opened and a tall white-haired man emerged and strode toward us extending his hand in greeting.

"You must be the Windsors from Virginia. Welcome to the Center for Non-Physical Sciences. I'm Roger Pile. Nancy and I are delighted you could come." His voice was warm and friendly, and his eyes danced as he talked. I had pictured Roger as a man in his fifties from my reading, yet his youthful appearance and unbridled vitality made me doubt the accuracy of my initial physical impression.

"Nancy is in town running errands and will return shortly," he continued. "Come in and let's get acquainted." He ushered us into the house and motioned toward an Early American couch, inviting us to make ourselves comfortable while he prepared iced tea. Returning to the living room with our refreshment, he seated himself opposite us and began to fill us in on his background.

He had been a successful businessman for many years. Eight years before, he had grown disillusioned with the demands of industry, feeling there was something more to life than the mere acquisition of material possessions. An acquaintance suggested he seek a reading from a well-respected psychic. This reading and his friendship with the psychic changed his entire existence. He discovered he had untapped psychic abilities of his own and began to develop his transpersonal consciousness. What started out to be an avocation soon became a full-time vocation, and he and his wife, Nancy, set up the Center for Non-Physical Sciences to meet the ever-growing demand for his services.

The center currently offered instruction in healing, coping with stress, psychic development, mediumship, and meditation. Having taught a course in parapsychology himself, Jim was delighted at the prospect of discussing his ideas with Roger, and the two became immersed in parapsychology issues. As I sat back listening quietly to their animated conversation, I sensed an immense amount of energy surrounding Roger. I often noticed this in other dynamic personalities, but the energies he emitted appeared to fill the room.

"Hi, folks." A pleasant salutation interrupted my train of thought. I looked toward the door to locate the source of the greeting. Nancy Pile entered the room. Her physical appearance conformed to the specifications the reading had assigned to her except that she had long brown hair. (She cut it short during the time span between our initial visit and our return trip from Ames Farm Inn.) She apologized for being tardy and immediately joined in our conversation, interjecting her own unique thoughts on psychic topics as our discussion flowed along.

The characteristics that most impressed me about Nancy were her engaging smile and that lilting laugh. No wonder that part of her personality had made such a profound impression upon me during the July 25 reading. I noted with amusement that she often bantered with Roger, poking fun and lightening the mood when his comments became overzealous and he took himself too seriously.

"Let's get down to business now," Roger suggested and led us into the adjoining room where the Piles hold their seminars and workshops. As we entered, I noticed several trophies on the mantle over the fireplace.

"Did you earn them for running?" I inquired hesitantly.

"No, I won them in swimming when I was younger," Roger responded. (Wrong sport, I noted mentally.)

Through the screen door at the rear of the house I could see a stream rippling over rocks sunken below its surface. Noticing the focus of my attention Nancy observed, "That stream is peaceful now, but in June we had a flood and it became a raging torrent carrying away everything in its path and causing extensive damage to our neighbor's properties. Luckily, we sustained only minor losses. We must have been protected somehow." (I recalled my May flood dream, which is mentioned later in this book, and wondered if there were any connections.)

Jim and I seated ourselves opposite Roger and Nancy, and Jim set up our tape recorder while Roger passed us our three-day course schedule and a list of books on his recommended reading list. The subjects covered corresponded to those I had foreseen earlier. I was familiar with only one quarter of the publications and would enjoy delving into the remaining three quarters in the months to come.

Roger began our series of lectures with information on body communication and spiritual healing, after which he discussed sources of psychic energy and the methodology and philosophy of psychic readings. His scope of knowledge was so diverse and far-reaching that it would be impossible for me to include Roger's lectures in their entirety. Therefore, I have selected some highlights from our three-day seminar, which seem to me to be representative of the variety of subjects covered.

ON BODY COMMUNICATION, ILLNESS, AND SPIRITUAL HEALING

Everything in the world is composed of energy. Our bodies operate on energy so that there is a normal flow of energy through the auric field. Our bodies know they are finite and our souls are immortal. Therefore, it is in our best interest to maintain optimum physical health.

Emotions belong to the body. These include anger, resentment, and hate as well as optimism and love. These negative emotions create fear in our bodies which create blockages in the normal energy flow. When this happens, our bodies send out an SOS message for assistance in reestablishing metabolic balance and harmony. A progression of bodily symptoms seems to provide a "physical barometer" for determining the amount of deterioration that has already taken place. This ranges from a mild shaking and chronic headaches to organ involvement (i.e., ulcers, heart attacks) and bone disintegration. If the progression is allowed to continue unabated, death is the eventual outcome.

Psychic healing removes these blockages caused by fears. The psychic healer provides an abundance of psychic energy that changes the vibrations of the body and sends healing to the cells. It would be wise for the psychic healer first to evaluate the person through a psychic reading in order to determine what problems his client is trying to avoid. These are responsible for the energy blockages. Once the cause is determined and there appears to be a willingness upon the part of the client to change and take responsibility for his life, the degenerative process can then be reversed. At this point the psychic healer becomes a healing channel, and through the bond formed between his client and himself, physical and spiritual healing occur and the normal flow of energy resumes once again.[2]

HEALING WITH THE WORD

Counseling is a form of psychic healing. It heals the spirit, which is often the most important healing of all.

Counseling involves the positive energy called love. Within the counseling relationship this positive energy is utilized to heal the client's despondent spirit. The desire on the part of the counselor answers the need on the part of the client to be helped. The energies for the healing are provided by the counselor, but it is up to the client himself to perform the work required for the healing to take place.[3]

SOURCES OF PSYCHIC ENERGY

The following are abundant suppliers of psychic energy. One need only to tap the source.

1. *Evergreens: The needles of evergreens store the sun's energy. If a person finds his energy level at a low ebb, a long walk in a pine forest is very soothing. One can also "hug a pine tree" if he doesn't care what his neighbors think.*
2. *Energy from the Sun: A walk in the open with palms upturned so one's hands become energy receptors is an excellent mode of energy replenishment.*
3. *Wood: When building a house or selecting a new home, be certain the interior contains one or two rooms entirely of wood (for example, a pine-paneled den). Such rooms are a continuing source of vitality.*
4. *Walking Barefoot on the Beach: The process of reflexology is involved here. The sand acts as the masseuse sending positive vibrations to all portions of one's body thereby establishing balance and harmony.*
5. *Deep Breathing Exercises: The most beneficial pattern of breathing is that of a four-twelve-eight count. Breathe in for a count of four, hold the breath for a count of twelve, and then breathe out on the count of eight. This might be done seven times. This breathing pattern tends to build up a supply of psychic energy which one can then call on as needed.*[4]

ON PSYCHIC READINGS

There are no limits to one's psychic learning except those one imposes on himself. You are the sole authority for yourself.

The desire to know and the desire to help are prerequisites for a good psychic reading. This is true for both the psychic reader and the recipient alike.

Fear shuts all psychic doors. The key to excellence in psychic readings is relax and allow. The more of yourself you put into the reading, the less reliable it becomes. All knowledge is within you. Trust yourself.[5]

PSYCHIC PHILOSOPHY

Why We Should Develop Our Psychic Talents

Our psychic abilities (all of us have them) are not gifts. Although not all of us possess the same abilities and the ones we share are not shared in the same degree, they are as much a part of our being as the five physical senses are, except that they lie dormant because we don't use them. Why? We are afraid of them, of using them, because most of us allow others to run our lives and are dependent upon others for our direction. If we were to use these abilities, we might become independent, and be forced to make decisions and take direction of our lives—something to be avoided.

We use our five physical senses to live, learn, and grow at the physical level; we use the nonphysical or psychic senses to exist, learn, and grow at the spiritual level (a level we cannot see, feel, or touch yet know is there). It is time we unified both levels thus bringing the new heaven and new earth together within ourselves. If we do this, we will become balanced, and in harmony with all Creation—sharing all its power and glory.

Developing our psychic abilities, therefore, is a good opportunity to develop ourselves into a whole being, at peace and in harmony with our environment because we will then control that environment without games, manipulation, or effort!

As in all things, balance is paramount. Becoming totally spiritually focused is as unproductive as being totally physically oriented. We exist in both worlds and, therefore, must develop and use all our senses, physical and nonphysical. In so doing, we will discover (to our utter amazement) what beautiful and creative souls we really are! If we, then, are willing to trust and believe in ourselves, willing to understand and accept ourselves, willing to love (not dislike) ourselves, we will reap peace, joy, and other rewards beyond even our wildest dreams. Remember, we are all children of the Father, each of us carrying the seed of Divinity within us. Do we let that seed lie dormant and unnourished, or do we give it love and much attention so that it grows in time to its full potential? The choice is ours![6]

For the remainder of the three days the four of us delved deeply into each other's psyches, mentally noting similarities and differences between our current philosophies of life and psychic understanding. The Piles offered us instruction on subjects such as the human aura, spiritual healing, the process of reincarnation, higher dimensions of consciousness, the concepts of mediumship, psychometry, and picture reading.

On the final morning of the three-day course I was required to give a psychic reading from a picture I held in my hand. Roger served as guide and instructor, pointing out certain inefficiencies in my trance induction and supplying suggestions for refinement of unpolished techniques I had used in the past. Gradually he revitalized my confidence in myself, initially by frequent encouraging comments during the reading and ultimately by offering his genuine approval and respect of the abilities he perceived to be developing.

Then Nancy Pile entered a trance state and, through a psychic reading, offered us the following advice concerning our current developmental status:

NANCY PILE'S READING

What is happening has been a transitional period in which consciousness has gained not only in depth but in breadth. It has been a reconfirming of concepts already held and an opening to concepts that are new. The first reaction is one of great discomfort trying to shrug off the mantle which has been placed upon you. So I would speak to you about what now is supposed to accomplish.

Now is the time when you become acquainted with this process. Now is the time to become acquainted with yourself enough to accept and be patient. I smile at the phrase "Be patient" as it is one we have heard often. Being patient with oneself is not an easy task.

As soon as the concept reaches consciousness, one wishes that it were magically brought about in one's own mind but it does not work that way because it involves a changing of habitual actions. Since they have built up over a period of time, it also takes a period of time to rearrange them into new patterns and new habits so you must give yourself enough time to adapt.

This is the forming of a new pattern of thought which will be receiving more energy the more you think of it so that when the time comes for you to put it into psychical reality, you will have clothed it with energy so that it will be real and it will be easy to step into. It will seem almost familiar but, at this point, the feeling is nowhere near familiarity and therefore nowhere near comfort. My point is, now is the time to evaluate and think about it, so be patient with your own hesitancy. That is healthy.

Now, Joan. You have not given yourself the privilege of this hesitancy. You have designed yourself to be aware of all these new possibilities and put them into practice almost simultaneously. This is your style and it is fine for you except that it will lead you to question yourself a great deal. This self-questioning is part of your pattern. It is part of the reason you have incarnated. The lesson you are to learn through this lifetime is a self-evaluating process without self-flagellation. You are taking steps toward doing that in that you are risking giving credence to your impressions and so a great deal of growth has come to you in a very short period of time. Your only problem with this is adjusting to it and making some sense out of it. At the moment you are sorting through and trying to formulate your own code from all that has happened to you. That is good, but once again my message is be patient with yourself in this. That is what the time is for. It is an evaluation time as well as a time of growth.

Both of you are extremely people-oriented, but this is becoming more on a mental/spiritual plane. Therefore the focus of service has altered somewhat from what you have done previously. The communication of ideas is extremely important here. What is happening with all your questioning of this process is formulation of a new way of looking at the world for the two of you and this is the process you will share with other people.[7]

The reading ended here, as did our time with Roger and Nancy. The finality of our goodbyes, however, was tempered with a feeling of unrestrained optimism for, as the Piles' figures receded into the distance, Jim and I were both well aware that this was only the beginning of a new and rewarding friendship with these two kindred souls.

4

The Hollis Readings

> First the dreamer must change and grow. Then he must find a way to share his growth in unassuming service to those closest to him in everyday life.
>
> Harmon Bro, *Edgar Cayce on Dreams*

In retrospect, the summer and fall of 1982 seem to have been a period of continuous psychic training. These months were spent attending ARE conferences, poring over subject matter that one year prior to this time had been entirely foreign to my life style, and forging friendships with those who not only shared my updated philosophy but were the possessors of complementary abilities. Up to this point I had been the prime dispatcher of psychic information. As a result of these new relationships I now became the recipient of novel psychic knowledge that heretofore had been unavailable to me.

I had the privilege of becoming acquainted with Mark Thurston and Harmon Bro, whose literary works I have so liberally quoted throughout this book, and found to my delight that they were even more personable and stimulating than I had pictured them mentally.

The conference entitled "ESP and Prophecy" afforded me the opportunity to attend lectures given by Albert Bowes, a practicing psychic from Florida, and Charles Thomas Cayce, the grandson of Edgar Cayce and the current president of the ARE. I was impressed by Albert Bowes's sense of humor and the wisdom contained in his address "My Experience as a Professional Psychic." According to Bowes:

One's psychic ability is a gift to be shared with others.
Every reading is unique because everyone is unique.
Each reading should be started with a prayer.
People don't ever grow up. We are all children learning and growing.
The feeling of exhaustion that accompanies unhappiness stems from the fact that unhappiness takes effort!
One should live his religion or one shouldn't believe it.
Be proud of your differences. Truth always endures.[1]

I found Charles Thomas Cayce's speech to be informative and thought-provoking. In "Problems on the Path of Psychic Development" he presented his ideas on the various sources of psychic information (the reader will find these slightly different from those discussed in the chapter "Psychometry and Psychic Readings"). Five sources were touched upon:

1. *One's Personal Subconscious:* This encompasses dreams and is related to personal experiences in this life.
2. *One's Personal Unconscious:* This is related to past life states. Extended periods of contemplation or repetitive contemplation can bring such psychic experiences into consciousness.
3. *Extrasensory Perception:* This includes telepathy (mind), clairvoyance (events) and precognition (the future).
4. *The Collective Unconscious:* This source can be contacted in a dream or trance state.
5. *Miscellaneous Sources:* Discussions of problems with the dead in the dream state may be real.[2]

Charles Thomas then went on to point out that motivation and self-discipline are essential for psychic development. He proposed recording one's own experiences, participating in a small group for psychic enhancement, and devoting a regular time each day to spiritual work. One's accuracy could be increased if the psychic were calm and contented with his own life, but without faith and trust in oneself and one's source, little progress could be expected. His closing remark in his talk "Synchronicity and Divination" made a lasting impression on me: "There is no simple form to foretell the future. Each person needs to experiment until he learns what works most effectively for himself."[3]

The week of September 19-25, the ARE offered a conference entitled "How to Use New Age Healing Techniques." By enrolling in it I felt I could both maintain my own physical well-being more efficiently and incorporate the holistic health procedures and suggestions I acquired into my counseling practice.

The featured speakers for the week included Dr. Norman Shealy, director of the Shealy Pain and Health Rehabilitation Institute in Springfield, Missouri, and my friend, Dr. Genevieve Haller. I was well aware of Dr. Haller's competence as a chiropractor and nutritionist, but I read with interest Dr. Shealy's qualifications. He was a neurosurgeon who also had earned a Ph.D. in psychology. His clinic treated patients with chronic disorders through biogenics. This included "self-help through suggestion, becoming conscious of one's body, taking responsibility for one's own health and well-being and using the imaginative forces of the mind to build health."[4] Given the circumstances of the past year this approach was extremely appealing. I made the necessary arrangements in my work schedule and began looking forward enthusiastically to the conference.

The night before I was to attend I received an important message during meditation. My source informed me that I would meet a "psychic friend" there who would prove to be invaluable to Jim and me in both our short- and long-term psychic research. I would have expected that such a person might be more likely to have made his or her appearance at the previous "ESP and Prophecy" conference, but after more than one year of accurate tips I decided it would be wise to heed my unseen guide's message and see if I could locate such a person.

Monday's lectures included Dr. Shealy discussing "Nutrition: Eat Right to Think Right", and a nutritional workshop with Dr. Haller. Tuesday morning Dr. Shealy demonstrated exercises for improving physical health in his morning address, and I marveled at an acupuncture demonstration given by Roger Jahnke. The Tuesday afternoon meeting came to a close. By this time I had met several interesting conferees, but none of them seemed to fit the description of the mysterious "psychic friend." Wednesday morning passed uneventfully, and I began to feel less confident that such a person existed.

On Thursday morning I parked my Aspen in the parking lot before the conference building and started toward the stairs. Several paces ahead of me I noticed a petite auburn-haired girl whom I judged to be in her early thirties. She carried books on acupressure and reflexology along with her notebook. She turned her head, and I noted that her features were incredibly like those of my sister-in-law, Florence Mathis, although her appearance was more youthful. Impulsively, I called to her and she stopped and waited. As I drew closer to her, I realized that she had attended the conference all week but was always seated on the far side of the room.

"Have you enjoyed the conference thus far?" I asked.

"Tremendously," she replied. "I am especially impressed with Dr. Shealy's approach to holistic health." She pointed to the books she carried. "I bought these for a friend of mine. She is very interested in these subjects."

We opened the door and entered the lobby. "Are you sitting with anyone in particular?" she ventured hesitantly.

"No one at all," I responded, delighted to find such an amiable companion with whom to share the morning lecture.

We entered the auditorium and took seats near the front. Dr. Shealy was just beginning his remarks on "Self-regulation: Avoiding Burnout." I listened intently to his address as the majority of my husband's patients suffered many of the symptoms he described. His ideas could be used in treating them.

"Fear is always at the root of all our life problems. We fear a loss of life, health, love, money or moral values. If a person can identify what the fear is, he can handle it better."

Dr. Shealy listed three recourses to deal decisively with such fear:

1. *Assertion:* Confront the issue. This may involve a compromise.
2. *Divorce with Joy:* Make a list of the good and bad points involved, and if, after meditation, the bad points far outweigh the good, then cut the ties.
3. *Accept and Forgive:* True forgiveness may bring about a change in another person.

Dr. Shealy proposed seven measures to be used when combating physical burnout:

1. *Sleep seven to eight hours per night.* One can lick insomnia by:
   - **(a)** Avoiding caffeine after three P.M.
   - **(b)** Drinking only two cups of coffee or tea per day.
   - **(c)** Avoiding sugar. Sugar interferes with good tryptophan metabolism.
   - **(d)** Avoiding all sleeping pills. No sleeping pills give a good night's sleep.
   - **(e)** Shunning Valium.
   - **(f)** Shunning barbiturates.
   - **(g)** Exercising well.
   - **(h)** Taking a tryptophan supplement 3 to 10 grams 30 minutes before bedtime as well as 100 to 200 milligrams of B complex.
   - **(i)** Using meditation and biogenics 30 to 45 minutes per day.
   - **(j)** Not drinking alcohol within two hours of bedtime.
   - **(k)** Using electrosleep in severe cases.
2. *Do not smoke:* You are harming not only yourself but everyone in your vicinity.
3. *Drink alcohol in moderation:* Two drinks per day might include one 11 ounce glass of wine or 12 ounces of beer.
4. *Maintain body weight within 10 percent of the ideal.*
5. *Exercise adequately:* Use aerobic exercises such as the ones previously demonstrated.
6. *Minimize fats and salt in the diet.*
7. *Practice some form of self-regulatory mental exercises at least 30 minutes per day.*

His presentation ended with the comment "Never go to bed with a grudge inside or beside you."[5]

The meeting at ARE adjourned at noon, and my friend and I crossed Atlantic Avenue to the Marshall's Hotel dining room. After making our selection from a variety of appetizing dishes, we carried our trays out to the patio to enjoy a leisurely lunch by the ocean. There was never a lull in the conversation.

I learned that her name was Elizabeth Hollis; she was 30 years of age, and resided in Charlotte, North Carolina. She was married to John Hollis, a businessman, and had a four-month-old daughter named Caroline. She had graduated from William and Mary with a major in French and then had earned her master's degree in counseling from Old Dominion University several years later.

"You won't believe this," I commented, "but I graduated from William and Mary as a French major and also have an M.Ed. in counseling and guidance." She shook her head in disbelief.

We continued our comparison, finding many other areas of common interest. I learned her husband was a pilot. My husband had always been fascinated with flying but had never found the time to acquire his license. I described my counseling business to her, and she in turn told me of her position with the Bell Telephone Company. She was currently on a leave of absence, however, because of the birth of her baby.

"Do you have any interest in astrology?" she asked.

What I knew about astrology could be written on the head of a pin.

"I know very little about it," I confessed.

She then confided that she had always had a deep interest in the subject since childhood and often prepared charts for her family and friends. The information was often extremely accurate, but she was well aware she knew more about her client than was available through normal astrological channels.

As we continued to discuss her theories regarding her astrological charts and their relationships to the personalities of her clientele, Elizabeth's tone became more animated, her eyes glistened, and the air of formality that exists between strangers evaporated, revealing her delightfully piquant sense of humor.

"Perhaps you're psychic," I ventured half-jokingly waiting for her reaction.

"I never thought of that," she replied. "Do you know anything about psychics?"

Taking a deep breath, I began a résumé of the previous year's events. Again, she shook her head in disbelief.

"What would you think of our exchanging astrological charts and psychic readings for our immediate families?" I offered. "That way we could cross-check each other's work, and

I could also determine how psychic you are." She agreed immediately.

As we exchanged addresses and other information necessary for the readings and charts, I noted that the two hours allotted for lunch were almost at an end. During that time our conversation had proceeded at such a rapid pace that we had hardly had time to pause for breath.

"It's odd," Elizabeth mused. "I usually am rather shy with people, yet you and I never seem to lack for conversation. Have I known you somewhere before?"

I assured her that I had never set eyes on her before today and yet she seemed vaguely familiar to me also.

"Perhaps it was another life," she said laughingly as we rose to return to the afternoon session.

Dr. Haller presented a workshop on "Body Language and Health Problems" from two to three P.M., which we agreed was most informative. Then, with the activities of the day concluded, we parted ways, and I headed toward Williamsburg contemplating how excited Jim would be when I related the day's adventures to him. Was Elizabeth Hollis the psychic friend of which my source had foretold? Time would tell.

Within a week's time a letter arrived from Elizabeth describing how she had begun working with her dreams and how fascinating and enlightening she found the process to be. The photographs I had requested for her readings were also enclosed. I studied John Hollis's unfamiliar face intently wondering what type of personality resided behind that unabashed grin. Her letter ended with a promise that our astrological charts would be forthcoming.

Another week lapsed with Monday through Thursday speeding by so rapidly that they seemed to blend into one another. Then, late Thursday afternoon on the way home from work, I opened my mailbox to find a large brown envelope postmarked Charlotte, North Carolina. I was elated. I returned home and, after depositing the assortment of material I had collected during the past nine hours on the bed, I hurriedly tore open the envelope to examine its contents. Was it truly possible for Elizabeth to describe our personalities accurately after simply being given each family member's time, place, and date of birth? The answer was not long in coming.

JOAN RUTH WINDSOR

She is practical, hardworking, and conservative and is capable of great self-discipline. Matters of health are among her central interests. There is a possible tendency to hold things in mentally, physically, and emotionally. This contributes to the cysts. It is important for her to learn to express emotions healthily and let go of harmful mental processes.
Unconventional mental faculties exist. She possesses creative abilities. She experiences adventures of the mind. These are unusual ones which she wants to analyze and intellectualize about.
There is much religious and philosophical probing with an intense desire to search for the true meaning of life. [6]

The personality the chart discussed accurately matched the self-concept I held as well as comments made about me by my family and close friends. Although I hated to admit it, even the unflattering traits were characteristic of me. I read on:

JAMES CLAYTON WINDSOR

Charming, outgoing, and talkative describe this gentleman. His nature is warm and generous, and he likes appreciation. He can be proud and playful, but he has his dignity.
Jim is likely to have unusual partners in marriage and business.
He has many "New Age Concerns." He directs energy toward higher education, philosophy, and religion. He inspires others to more ethical behaviors and actions and tries to live this philosophy himself. He is a lifelong student with high goals which he is likely to reach. [7]

My husband's personality leapt from the written words before me as if I were reading from the pages of a well-worn book. I felt I also was acquainted with his unusual partner.

The astrological charts Elizabeth completed for Jimmy and Robin were equally precise. (The reader will recall the descriptions of my children from Chapter 2, "An Investigation into Psychic Readings.")

JAMES LAURENT WINDSOR

He is practical and ambitious—a steady worker with lots of ideas. His orientation toward life is similar to that of his mother but less complex. He enjoys good verbal

communication and is extremely apt in oral expression himself. Is he a joke teller? [Absolutely!]
He exhibits good managerial ability and expects people to do their best. He has quite a sense of responsibility.
He communicates easily with his sister.
He has lots of energy to use. He has the capacity to complete much work of a transforming nature.[8]

ROBIN JOAN WINDSOR

She is warmhearted, outgoing, and friendly. Her appearance is magnetic in some way. She directs her energy to several things at once rather than any one thing for an extended period of time. Her mood changes frequently. She likes to be with other people and communicate with everyone. She may overdo this.
She is quick to learn with a sharp intellect. She is curious about everything and everyone.[9]

As I laid the four charts aside, I marveled at their authenticity. And as I reviewed them in more depth, I was relatively certain much of the information Elizabeth had included in her astrological readings originated from psychic sources.

With the receipt of Elizabeth's materials it now became my turn to "perform." Jim was unusually delighted with the terms of the Hollis-Windsor exchange as he detected an additional advantage inherent in the agreement. I had spent several hours conversing with Elizabeth at the ARE conference in Virginia Beach. Our conversations had focused on our work and psychic and health subjects, so she was not a complete stranger to me. The only facts I knew about John Hollis were that he loved to fly and had an engaging smile. Therefore, Jim made the assumption that this would be an outstanding test of my ability to do readings for total strangers.

On October 16, 1982, I seated myself in my comfortable gold recliner and prepared myself for a reading. I gazed with rapt attention at John's picture grinning back at me as I held it in my left hand. Were there any additional tidbits of information about him from Elizabeth lurking in the dark recesses of my subconscious? I drew a total blank! Suppose the same thing happened during the reading? A shudder rippled through me. *This was the ultimate test of my capabilities.* Drawing several deep breaths I began to relax and acquiesced to Jim's familiar directions. Our source obligingly furnished us with the following readings:

JOHN HOLLIS

Physical Health

John wears black-rimmed glasses occasionally. I am uncertain whether these are for vision or not.
He has tremendous lung power and great endurance. This comes from swimming and playing sports. He is very sports-minded.
He works out and perhaps lifts weights. He may play handball.
He injured his finger one time during a sports event.
He has a tendency toward weak ankles when he runs and jogs.
He likes to work on cars. I see him with a small blue foreign car with the hood up. He seems to know a considerable amount about motors.
He is a well-balanced person who is in harmony with the world.
He feels "shut in" at times. This is the reason he likes to fly because it is so open and free.

Future Events

He is going to make a trip cross-country on business.
I see him in his office. It is in a high building with lots of glass.
He has a big desk with a wooden top.
There are unusual pictures of birds or animals in his office.
There is a dinner party for a promotion.
We may become good friends over the years.

ELIZABETH HOLLIS

Physical Health

There is a tendency toward her throat tightening up and sore throats when she has a postnasal drip.
Eating peaches and foods high in alkalinity would be of benefit.
Later this year she will have a toothache in the lower left part of her jaw.
She is generally in good health except for minor difficulties.

Personality and Current Events

She is a happy soul and has lots of compassion for people.
We liked each other immediately because we had a lot in common—a similar orientation toward life.

She is very motherly. She would like to devote more time to her baby but feels she has to work.
With the type of abilities she has she would do well in some type of counseling, educational therapy, or play therapy.
The choice is up to her. She has a healing orientation.
Within the next six months she will make a decision that might be in favor of this course of action. She is not ready to do this yet.
She is a favorite of her father, a tall, gray-haired man who is partly bald.
She has a very close relationship with John.
They balance each other. She is an idealist and tests new ideas and they have a 'give and take' exchange. He is more analytical.
I see them in an airplane. They are going to Hot Springs to a hotel on business and pleasure.
I see Elizabeth at a beach holding her baby in the air. It may be one of the Carolina beaches. They may have rented a cottage or this was a friend's or a family cottage.
The Hollises' house is two-story with beige paint. There is siding on top and a sun porch in the rear.
There is a beige color throughout the house.
The sun porch has wide glass windows with tile on the floor with blue in it.

Future Events

John and Elizabeth will visit us before Christmas.
I see the four of us eating together while Robin babysits with Caroline on their visit here.
Elizabeth is a good subject for past life regressions.
Her astrological business will thrive in the future.

These readings seemed to be more copious than those completed up to this date. They also contained physical data accompanied by health recommendations, comments on personality characteristics and central life issues, and a variety of factual information that could be verified.

I organized the readings into a logical format. Betty typed them, and I mailed them to Elizabeth accompanied by a lengthy letter containing a commentary on her astrological charts. Again we waited impatiently for validation.

A week passed with no letter. Our apprehension grew. At the end of the second week I peered into my post office box and was rewarded by the sight of an overstuffed envelope in Elizabeth's handwriting. Hastily tearing open the seal, I eagerly devoured its contents. She wrote:

Just received your readings in the mail. I start with John:
His glasses are dark brown and he really doesn't need them as his vision is good. They are sort of habit. He often injured a finger at baseball and had a bad ankle which bothers him when he jogs. He played lots of sports in high school and we played racquetball for a while but he kept hurting his ankle so we quit.
He is a good son. He reads a lot about flying and history especially the Civil War and World War I and World War II. He is mechanically inclined, and we have a blue VW Rabbit which he works on occasionally.
He does like open spaces rather than enclosed—one reason why we built the sun porch with 10 seven-foot windows.
He works now in a five-story building with glass windows all around. His desk has several pictures of airplanes, one unusual one, and birds on the California coast.

I had at last met the "stranger" whose personality was hidden in the photograph. It was as if I were encountering an old friend well known but whose memory had faded with the passage of time. Elizabeth's voice echoed in my ears: "Another life perhaps?"

My consciousness returned to the written page. I continued absorbing Elizabeth's annotations.

I do get sore throats and had a dream about tightening in the throat and not being able to breathe. The next day I developed a sore throat, which I warded off with vitamin C and yoga. I shall also investigate alkaline foods in my Cayce material.
I've had a gradual worsening problem with sensitivity in the lower right molar which can be taken care of at my dentist's appointment at the end of November, I hope.
My stomach problems are very occasional and I think related to eating too much. This may apply more to John.
I'm not ready to make a decision about my career yet. We'll wait and see what the next six months bring.
My father and I are very close and really appreciate each other. He is gray and partly balding—not tall but he appears so because of being somewhat slender.
Your remarks about John the analyzer and Elizabeth the idealizer are exactly right.
I was very interested in the beach scene, because it is true for present, past, and future. We rented a cottage at Nags Head, North Carolina, in September and had both relatives and friends come to visit us there. A couple of weeks ago we visited friends in Carolina Beach near Wilmington, North Carolina. We will be staying at their house over Thanksgiving weekend to house- and dog-sit. We had friends who suggested we visit them at Hot Springs but we haven't finalized our plans yet.

The Hollis House

It is brick and split level (two stories) with beige siding, a sun porch on the back, and a fence surrounding the patio! The rug is beige throughout most of the house. The blues come in various photographs I have done or bought. The "walls" of the porch are big clear storm windows, with brown tile flooring—no blue, yet, believe it or not, I told John last night I wanted a blue or green rug out there. We put a beige and blue sofa out there too.

Future Events

We had thought of coming to Williamsburg either a weekend in November, one of the two before Thanksgiving, or stopping by on Saturday the fourth of December since we will be in Norfolk. Would either of those dates suit you?[10]

I was absolutely enthralled at the prospect of spending a day or two in the company of two such captivating people. (And I would finally meet John face to face.)

A flurry of letters and phone calls followed, and after much deliberation and consulting with family schedules we settled on December 11 as the date of their visit. I was thrilled and began making preparations several weeks in advance.

Elizabeth had expressed an interest in past life regressions in her most recent epistle. I discussed the possibility of such a session with Jim. He readily agreed to her request, surmising that since Elizabeth's and my personalities and orientation toward life were so similar she would in all probability prove equally suggestive. John had agreed to be a subject also but due to his analytical mind we both felt he would be less apt to reach a satisfactory trance state.

The night preceding John and Elizabeth's appointed arrival I turned on the eleven P.M. news and weather broadcast, well aware that December's rapidly changing weather can create hazardous flying conditions for light aircraft such as the one John flew. My heart sank as the weather forecaster warned of an approaching low-pressure area and went on to predict a severe winter snowstorm for Saturday morning—the first of the season.

"John won't fly in that," Jim remarked, reflecting on his own flying instructor's warnings concerning the dangers of air travel in inclement weather.

My conscious mind tended to agree, but somewhere in its deeper, more knowledgeable recesses, I believed that nothing short of the Apocalypse would prevent Elizabeth from keeping our rendezvous. This assumption proved correct. At three P.M. Saturday, December 11, undaunted by the ferocity of a blinding rainstorm that would later turn to snow, the Hollises' plane touched down on the small runway in Williamsburg, and I heard Elizabeth's excited tones at the other end of the wire saying, "Hi, this is Elizabeth Hollis and several other persons with me with whom you are not yet acquainted. We all have a voracious appetite. Can you accommodate us for dinner?"

Jim and I hurried to the Williamsburg Airport so that our guests would not be kept waiting long in such unfavorable circumstances. Within 15 minutes we entered the tiny waiting area where deplaned passengers remain until suitable transportation is secured. There, patiently waiting ensconced from the frigid winter temperatures, were John and Elizabeth and their infant daughter, Caroline.

Elizabeth extended her hands in greeting and turned to introduce us to her "other half." I would have known John anywhere even if he hadn't been standing next to Elizabeth. His face was still boyishly handsome and his brown eyes without guile. He stood a foot or more above his petite wife, and it was easy to see from his athletic physique why he would have excelled in sports in his younger years. The most magnetic feature about John, however, was his grin. No wonder that aspect of his personality had come through in such a forceful fashion. It was the central focus of his personality—expressing his joviality, healthy sense of humor, openness, and an all-encompassing love affair with life in general. If I had known nothing about John up to this point, I would have taken an instant liking to him on sight.

Elizabeth bundled up Caroline warmly in her pink snow-suit, and the five of us braced ourselves against the biting winds and made our way cautiously to our white Aspen because the ground was now beginning to be covered with ice. The conversation during the ride home centered on how to use the short time we had together most fruitfully. We decided that after dinner Jim would attempt a hypnotic age regression, first with Elizabeth and then with John, since Elizabeth seemed to be most intent upon discovering whether or not she had ever had another existence prior to this life time. We all agreed to keep open minds about the information received because none of us held any strong convictions regarding the validity of past life regressions at this point.

Over dinner, while our husbands discussed the joys of flying, Elizabeth and I shared dream interpretations, natural food recipes, and what types of subjects should be covered in a newly created parapsychology course Jim and I intended to teach at Christopher Newport College in the spring. Jim and I have been known to remain at the dinner table for several hours engrossed in such lively discussions as this, but the element of time was of prime importance this weekend, so after one and one-half hours of dinner-time chatter, we rose from the dining room table and adjourned to the living room. The firelight cast a warm rosy glow about the room, making it appear cozy and inviting.

"Would you like to go first, Elizabeth?" Jim said, motioning her to make herself comfortable in my golden "trance chair."

Elizabeth preferred our Early American couch and took a reclining position on it. I seated myself across the room in the "trance chair," and John sat cross-legged on the floor to Jim's left. I would find this session unbelievably intriguing. Prior to this night, I had always served in the role of "psychic receiver." Now I had a unique opportunity to observe the process.

Jim began using his usual hypnotic induction techniques, and Elizabeth obligingly went under within a matter of minutes.

"Return to your tenth birthday and describe the events of that day," Jim instructed. Elizabeth proceeded to describe a scene similar to the one I had envisioned at our first trance session. After instructing Elizabeth to clear her mind, Jim directed her to look beyond her current lifetime and pick a life that had the most significant impact on this lifetime. Immediately, Elizabeth began to describe a character named Rachel Dubois who lived in France in the eighteenth century. She saw an old lady sitting outside of a small wooden hut churning butter. Jim asked her to look at her home and describe it.

"There appear to be three to four rooms. I see the children's bedroom and our bedroom, a kitchen, and perhaps a living room - dining room area combined. I see blue shutters and bread baking in the oven."

Jim asked her about her husband. She replied, "His name is Raoul. We have to work very hard to earn our living. There is a war taking place. There is a lot of killing in the area and a lack of food even though this is a highly fertile area. The soldiers take the food and steal it from the children. Many children die. There is much famine and starvation. Raoul and I produce cheese and dairy products, which we subsist on. We sell most of what we make in town."

"How do you feel about yourself?" Jim asked.

"Tired! So very tired and old! I wish I could stop and rest for a while, but there is so much work to be done. I must continue." Elizabeth's voice was reduced to an almost imperceptible whisper.

"Now, move to the day of your death," Jim continued. "And give me any impressions you receive. How did Rachel die?"

"She just seems to fade away. She lies in bed with her daughter standing beside her. She has a disease like influenza, but she is bone-weary. She says, 'I'm ready to go,' and she leaves."

Jim brought Elizabeth quickly out of the trance, because occasionally scenes involving death precipitate deep emotional reactions. Elizabeth rubbed her eyes and sat up.

"Do you really suppose I lived as Rachel Dubois?" She shook her head in an effort to rid herself of the baffling scenes she had just witnessed and at times entered into completely.

"I'll tell you something that will interest you though," she added. "John and I have our refrigerator continuously stocked with yogurt, milk, and cheeses of all kinds. These are the staples of our diet, and we couldn't exist without them."

Now it was John's turn to participate in the experiment, but would he be able to bypass that keenly analytical mind in his search for another dimension of his personality? This was the question the four of us asked ourselves as John lay back on the couch and took several deep breaths to relax his body. Jim had the situation well in hand, however, and used an entirely different method of hypnotic induction on John than he had on Elizabeth. Because John was not anticipating this move, his mind was unprepared for such an action, and he immediately dropped off into a deep trance state within a matter of minutes. Elizabeth and I exchanged hopeful glances as Jim guided John back through his early years.

"Now I would like you to go back in time to another lifetime that has an important bearing on your current existence and give me any and all impressions you receive concerning this person." Jim's voice had a gentle yet commanding quality about it.

John reported that he envisioned a sailor standing on a ship docked in a New England seaport. The seaman had canvas breeches on with a striped shirt and a ropelike belt tied around his middle. When requested to describe his surroundings, he stated that he slept in a hammock below deck and was often annoyed by his shipmates playing cards till all hours of the night. Jim asked John to relate to us how this man's life ended. John replied he met with foul play and drowned after falling from the ship. Elizabeth and I sat in stunned silence trying to grasp the enormity of John's final remarks. John's story was truly one of the most dynamic and intriguing past life regressions Jim and I had heard to date. Its implications provoked a stimulating discussion that lasted through the wee hours of the morning.

Sunday we decided to communicate with our source through a reading to understand more clearly why such strong bonds appeared to exist between the four of us. The amount of time we had known each other could be measured in hours, and yet, to quote Elizabeth, "It was as if we were old friends becoming reacquainted."

No sooner had I achieved a trance state than the information began to flow. There seemed to be four past life ties. In the beginning we lived in Atlantis and knew one another as students in a temple or health center. A second set of incarnations placed us together in Egypt with Elizabeth interested in astrology and John having taken on the role of an architect. I was a practicing clairvoyant and Jim an herbal healer. A third past life connection centered on soldiering and religious orders in France in the early 1600s. The fourth and final in the series, and by far the most interesting, revolved around life in colonial Virginia in the middle and late 1700s. The reading identified one of us as a gentleman farmer named Nathaniel Henderson. The estate he owned was somewhat small in comparison to other wealthy plantations such as Carter's Grove, just three miles east of Williamsburg, or Westover, located midway between Williamsburg and Richmond on Route 5, but he was apparently affluent enough to possess a number of horses, which his wife Sallee delighted in riding. The reading further stated that Nathaniel Henderson was a member of the Virginia House of Burgesses and that this fact could be verified if any of us cared to take the time to consult such records. These were said to be housed in the Swem Library at the College of William and Mary. The reading ended here.

The remainder of our visit was spent with Elizabeth and me gossiping about a multiplicity of subjects that were of common interest to us both while John and Jim spent two hours trying to remove the ice from the plane so the Hollis family could fly home safely. This undertaking met with success by five P.M. Soon thereafter their plane lifted off the runway and took flight into a crystal clear December night heading homeward toward Charlotte.

But the story does not end there. John's business obligations made it necessary for him to be away from home for a short period of time during the latter part of February, and Elizabeth paid us a visit again. During her stay we decided it would be great fun to see if we could locate any proof of the eighteenth-century gentleman named Nathaniel Henderson. We were uncertain as to how to begin so, as soon as we arrived at Swem Library, we sought assistance from the librarian on duty. She accompanied us to the section where the Virginia reference materials were situated and proceeded to instruct us on the use of Virginia genealogy books. Elizabeth and I diligently set to work in our quest for any small bit of information confirming the existence of the plantation owner, but an hour and a half of intensive searching proved completely unrewarding.

Then, as I placed the genealogy book I had been using in its proper location on the third shelf, my eye fell upon a blue reference book entitled *The General Assembly of Virginia July 13, 1619-January 11, 1978: A Bicentennial Register of Members* compiled by Cynthia Miller Leonard. I removed it from its hiding place on the second shelf and, as I searched the index for the name Henderson, I motioned Elizabeth to join me. Together we found a listing for Henderson, N., and turned the voluminous pages of the book to page 130 to read:

"Members of House of Burgesses of Virginia"[11]

Sessions

May 4 to June 1, 1778
October 5 to December 19, 1778

Kentucky	Nathaniel Henderson

Was this coincidence, had I read this clairvoyantly, or was this truly suggestive of a previous colonial incarnation?

5

The College Psychical Research Project

Service to others is central to human destiny.
Harmon Bro, *Edgar Cayce on Dreams*

Section I

The evening of December 31, 1982, found me settled comfortably in my trance chair gazing intently at a series of 10 photographs. The subjects of the photographs I held in my hands were volunteers my husband Jim had recruited for a new experiment he had designed entitled the College Psychical Research Project. Our research over the past 18 months had provided us with the following psychic progression in connection with our readings:

1. Jim and I could receive personal information and guidance for ourselves upon request.
2. Successful readings could be done for family and close friends if they sincerely desired them.
3. Accurate readings could be secured for relatives and friends at a distance.
4. Accurate readings were possible at a distance for acquaintances with whom we had had little actual contact.
5. One psychic reading had been recorded with a total stranger as the recipient.

One question remained to be answered in my husband's mind: *Could readings be acquired for total strangers at a distance on a consistent basis?* Hence the College Psychical Research Project came into being.

Jim had inquired among his psychology students whether or not any of them were interested in participating in an experiment involving psychic readings. The terms that were set forth for such participation were three:

1. The subjects had to furnish a recent photograph of themselves.
2. They were to submit four questions of their own choosing to be answered in their readings.
3. They agreed to supply feedback on the validity of the information contained in their psychic documents.

Within a matter of days 10 students signed up for the project and we were ready to proceed.

It is not my intention in this section to discuss in depth the project's experimental design or the types of evidence for the existence of specific psychic phenomena derived from its results. I shall leave that to my husband's expertise in the latter portion of this chapter. I prefer rather to recount three of the most interesting readings accomplished by each coresearcher's confirmation or denial of their validity, so that readers will have a basis for comparing my initial attempts at psychic readings with the present state of the information being currently channeled. Such a comparison, it seems to me, exemplifies the growth of psychic development fashioned through love, understanding, and encouragement but, *first and foremost, through faith*!

To return to December 31, 1982, I studied the expression in the faces of our coresearchers in a vain effort to secure any clues as to their personalities. All, however, had armed themselves with engaging smiles and broad grins personifying contentment and successfully blanketing whatever private sorrows and burdens each had to bear. Would it be possible for me to peer behind these well-fortified facades and delve into the subconscious of each individual for the purpose of procuring the self-knowledge contained within? Could I provide them with information that would enhance their relationships with their loved ones and expand their own levels of consciousness?

With the introduction of questions to accompany the regular reading, a new dimension was added to my psychic tasks. It now became necessary for me to attune myself to specific issues concerning my subject's life instead of merely "reading" the pictures as they appeared before my mind's eye.

The questions submitted by the participants had to do with life themes that concern all of us from time to time. They centered on career choices, physical health, the success of their marriages, the well-being of their children, and financial matters, all of which were of prime concern to the particular individual seeking guidance. I determined I would not worry about whether or not the answer to specific questions would come and relied on a rule of the psychic taught to me by Roger Pile: "Everything that is necessary for the growth and development of the individual will be given." It seemed to me that if these people had a strong desire to know the answers to their questions, such answers would undoubtedly be forthcoming.

All these ideas surfaced in my mind one after another as Jim and I prepared to begin the first in the series of 10 readings for the College Project. I held the photograph of an attractive blonde coed in my left hand. Once again the psychic stream began to flow.

The following readings consist of psychic impressions with the paraphrased responses from the recipients. Accuracy usually improves with practice and when the recipient has faith in the process.

READING FOR MARY JONES

December 31, 1982

Emotional and Physical Health

1. She recently had her hair cut. This was right before Christmas. She had it curled and was pleased with the results. *Correct.* (She does often cut and perm her hair.)
2. When she was younger, she had trouble with her right eye. It was perhaps a muscle weakness or a slight astigmatism. *Correct.* (She still does have astigmatism in the right eye.)

3. She is subject to frequent colds and occasional sore throats. *Correct.* She has three to four colds a year; seldom does she have a sore throat.)
4. She may have fractured or hurt her right leg or ankle when she was younger and it was fractured and in a cast. *Partially correct.* (She had two deep cuts on her lower right leg that required stitches 20 years ago.)
5. She needs to go to the dentist and has been putting it off. There is a tooth that had a sensitive nerve, but she doesn't like to go to the dentist, so she hasn't treated it. *Correct.*
6. She burned her finger recently. There was a blister that had healed up. She was rushing and nervous because company was coming so she burned it by accident. *Probably correct.* (She often burns her finger because of "rushing when company is coming.")
7. In the future she may sprain her wrist. Be cautious!

Futuristic

8. She may have an occasional rash on her hands. *Correct.* (Dry skin more than an actual rash.)
9. This is caused by a powerful cleaner she uses when she does heavy cleaning. This is not used frequently, but if she changes from this harsh cleaner the rash will be eliminated. If she would use olive oil when this happens, it would clear this up. Vitamin E would help also. *Correct.* (Floor cleaning products adversely affect her hands.)
10. She has good digestion and appears to eat anything without any trouble. *Correct.*
11. She is generally a very level-headed person not subject to wide swings of mood. *Partially correct.* (She feels there are days each month in which her mood changes greatly.)
12. She has tried to ice skate with her children and appears to have her ankles wobble. This may be from the ankle that she broke. It would appear to be connected. *Incorrect.* (She has skiied and roller-skated with her children, and her ankles do get tired.)
13. She is generally in quite good health. *Correct.*
14. She is a nice person. *Correct.* (People around her seem to think so.)
15. She is well disciplined when she studies. *Correct.*
16. She outlines and uses red marker. *Partially correct.* (She always outlines but seldom in red — usually pen or yellow highlights.)

17. She does A, B, C, 1, 2, 3 and memorizes. She is a good student, B's and A's. She is not an A+ student but she does quite well. *Correct.*

18. She spoils the baby. The baby rules the roost and is very demanding, and she indulges this. Less indulgence would help. Ask her if she doesn't agree with this. (She feels she is *loving* and *firm*. Her "baby" is now five and not demanding, but he was *very* demanding as a baby. Indulgence? . . . She doesn't know.)

19. Their house has a chain-link fence around the outside. There is brown on it. *Partially correct.* (Her neighbors have a chain-link fence and one side borders their yard. Both the neighbors' and her house have brown on them.)

20. There is a garage in the rear. *Incorrect.* (Garage on the side of the house.)

21. The decor is Early American. *Correct.*

22. I see a colonial braided round rug. *Incorrect.* (She would like to have this some day.)

23. There is a rocking-type chair in the living room and a wooden rocker in one of the children's rooms. *Incorrect now.* (They did have a rocker several years ago.)

24. There are many plants around the house. She has a green thumb and grows plants well. *Correct.*

25. They have a small, square-shaped car. *Incorrect.*

26. The color is dark maroon or purple or rose-tinted. *Incorrect.* (Neighbor's car is maroon but very large.)

27. She likes to cook. There are lots of cookbooks around in the kitchen. *Correct.*

28. She frequently exchanges recipes with friends. *Correct.*

29. She may be a very good swimmer. *Correct.*

30. She may have won awards for this when she was younger. Some second and third places and occasional first places. *Incorrect.* (She passed the classes and received certificates but did no competitive swimming.)

31. I see a hospital connected with her somehow. Perhaps someone works there, but there is a hospital connected to her life. I am not sure what this means. *Correct.* (She is a nurse but not working now; her father was very ill last summer and fall and in the hospital.)

READING FOR ANNE WHITE

January 8, 1983

Physical Health

1. There appears to be some problem with a color rinse or hair product used on the hair. It creates a scalp problem or "allergic reaction." She may switch to another brand, but it would appear wise to discontinue this. *Correct.* (Redken shampoo and hair rinse caused an allergic reaction.)
2. She is subject to bloodshot eyes — redness of the eyes. *Partially correct.* (When she swims in the pool water without goggles, her eyes become extremely bloodshot; otherwise, she does not have a problem with redness of eyes.)
3. Tea bags like comfrey tea bags over the eyes would be very restful. *No answer required.*
4. In addition, doses of vitamin A — 20,000 units per day for three to four weeks — can be taken when the eyes become bloodshot or tired. It would be wise to begin with this treatment now and then stop and then resume treatment on the occasions that these occur. If she continues this treatment, her body will build up enough resistance that these attacks may be eliminated. *No answer required.* (Goggles prevent eye problems.)
5. She appears to have good sinuses, and the throat area is healthy. *Correct.*
6. She has two caps in her mouth. *Partially correct.* (At the time of the picture she had one cap; she is now in the process of getting another cap.)
7. She has a slight lisp especially in the *t* and *th* sounds when excited. She stumbles over words when she gets excited and has difficulty expressing herself. *Correct.*
8. There may be an old scar two to three inches on her right arm. She had stitches there. *Incorrect.*
9. She cut her arm on some kind of metal object. *Incorrect.* (She later reported a scar on the left arm.)
10. She has lots of nervous energy. *Correct.*
11. Her heart and lungs are very good. *Correct.*
12. She has a tendency toward a hiatal hernia when she gets older —not presently. *No answer required.*

13. She may have a tendency toward colitis later on also. *Partially correct.* (She now has colitis.)
14. She is high-strung but not like this all the time. *Correct.*
15. She may have had an appendicitis operation or one of another type. There is a scar on her abdomen from a minor operation. *Partially correct.* (She has a four-inch scar from major surgery — appendix removed at time of operation.)
16. She appears to jog. I see her in a blue jogging suit. *Correct.* (She jogs some although not regularly. She wears a blue jogging suit.)
17. She is about 15 pounds overweight and needs to lose this. *Correct.*
18. The exercise is good, but she needs to watch her diet in that there are too many types of food that she eats that contribute to the buildup of fatty tissues especially in her lower body. This is just a word of advice. *No answer required.* (She has lost ten pounds in the past few months with five more to go.)
19. She is a creative person who makes things with her hands. She sews and embroiders. She is quite good at this. *Correct.* (She sews now and embroidered as a teenager but doesn't now.)
20. There are pictures around the house that she has done. *Correct.*
21. She embroiders initials and all kinds of designs. Very creative with her hands. She often designs her own things. *Partially correct.* (She doesn't embroider now. In spare time she does work with her hands by painting, sewing, and decorating, and she does design costumes and flower arrangements.)
22. She likes to work in the yard. I see her in the front yard. She does the flowers and grass. *Correct.*
23. There appears to be a white fence. *Incorrect.* (No fences at all.)
24. She works on a vegetable garden in the back. She likes to grow things and has a "green thumb." This is part of her creativity. *Correct.* (Although she had a reputation for a "purple thumb" in the past, it appears in the last couple of years her thumb is turning green.)
25. She appears to be very talented at growing roses. Some are big enough to be prize roses. She could have competed in flower shows. It is unclear whether she has done this or not. *Do not know.* (She began growing roses last year.)
26. There is a doghouse in the back with a shingled roof and the name of the dog over the door. *Incorrect.* (They do not have a dog.)

27. The name is Daisy? Begins with a D. *Incorrect.*

28. The exterior of the house is white wood, one story, seven-eight rooms (seven rooms, one bath). *Partially correct.* (They live in a brick house with gold trim; seven rooms, two baths.)

29. It is near water. If you go out of the house and turn to the right and go back *quite a ways* there is water. It is like a creek, but it is some distance from the house. *Partially correct.* (They live on a creek about 50 feet from the house.)

30. They have a small rowboat. They put a boat in the creek and then go out to larger water. I see a rowboat and oars. *Correct. (How true!)*

31. I see a boy crabbing. *Partially Correct.* (A man — her husband — she feels like the psychic sees that she has a son; she wonders if she is actually seeing her husband, who acts like a nine-year-old when he "plays" on the water. Her husband has brown hair and bangs. She has two daughters.) (Later mentioned neighbor's nine-year-old boy who does some crabbing.)

32. He may be eight or nine and has brown hair with bangs in the front. He likes to crab in the creek, and he sometimes goes out further and his mother worries about him. *See number 31.*

33. His mother tells him to wear a life jacket. He often goes with friends. They have crabs a lot. *Correct* (If it is her husband, his mother does worry about him — reflecting on the life jacket — he does go with friends and they have lots of crabs.)

34. I see them eating on the kitchen table, and there are piles of crabs. This is a happy time for the entire family. *Correct.*

35. She studies hard. *Correct.*

36. She wears glasses when she studies. These are big round glasses — 20/50 to 20/60 vision. *Correct.*

37. These are reading glasses. She has trouble with near vision. *Correct.*

38. She is a B-C student. *Incorrect.* (She has an A average.)

39. She studies hard but is not systematic. She would do well to learn outlining procedures and systematic ways of learning. *Incorrect.*

40. She could do better if someone would teach her how to use A, B, C, 1, 2, 3, and colored pens for marking when reading. She could become a solid B student if she improved her study techniques. She might read books on how to study. This is given as a suggestion for her to follow. *No answer required.*

41. There is an older man in the house. *Incorrect.*
42. He has silver hair and partly bald. *Incorrect.*
43. He is in his late forties or early fifties. *Incorrect.*

Future Events

44. She will have trouble with one course second semester. It involves a language-type course. It requires the use of proficient language. *Partially correct.* (She is now taking English 102; not having trouble but realizes she has a vocabulary deficit.)
45. This is connected to the difficulty in concisely expressing herself. This shows up in the language course. If she gets some specialized help, this will improve. She will continue to have this problem otherwise. *No answer required.* (Good thought. She's studying in a word improvement book.)
46. She may be thinking about getting a car. I see a blue car in her thoughts. *Correct.*
47. She is now thinking about taking a vacation this summer. She is making plans for it in the next few months. *Correct.*
48. It is a cross-country trip. It involves a lot of travel. *Correct.* (She is going to Germany, Greece, and France for four weeks beginning May 14.)
49. She makes arrangements to stay at a hotel that is a nice place. It is tall and has three sections to it. It is 10 to 15 stories high. *No answer required.* (She can't tell yet because she doesn't have pictures of hotels.)
50. It has a peaked roof. *No answer required.*
51. The dining room is decorated in red, and she eats there. *No answer required.*
52. She is going with friends. *Correct.*
53. This is near a beach — small waves. *Correct.* (She is spending two weeks on Grecian islands.)
54. She will win a sum of money. *No answer required.*
55. It is like gambling. It may be in a contest or she bets. There is an element of risk involved. She knows she is going to do this. It does not come to her by accident. *No answer required.*
56. She takes a chance and wins several hundred dollars. *No answer required.*

READING FOR JANE SMITH

January 12, 1983

Physical Health

1. Watch when using coloring. It is not a good thing to dye one's hair. It predisposes one to problems that otherwise would not exist. It should be considered that these are harsh chemicals. A word of advice. *Correct.*
2. I suggest Auraglow for dry skin and lines under the eyes. Auraglow would benefit her skin as well as a lot of running to keep the blood circulating to her face. This would improve her complexion. *Correct.*
3. She has glasses and doesn't like to wear them. She wears them only when it is essential. She often squints to see phone books and recipes rather than put the glasses on. *Correct.*
4. She may have several teeth that aren't her teeth — a bridge or small plate? *Incorrect.* (About two years ago had braces — maybe this is what is seen.)
5. She is a very precise person in her speech. She chooses words carefully. *Correct.* (Somewhat.)
6. She is a very controlled person. *Correct.* (She never thought she was, but she must be. She'd been told this before.)
7. Everything should be done very orderly. This shows up in her whole personality, but speech reflects this whole personality. *Correct.* (Sometimes she doesn't like this trait in herself.)
8. She has a well-developed vocabulary. *Correct.*
9. When she was in Jim's class, she spoke and contributed a lot to the discussion. This does not mean she spoke often, but when she did, it was always to the point, well expressed and concise. *Correct.* (She isn't sure this is correct. Dr. Windsor would have to respond to this.)
10. When she laughs, it is rather controlled also. *Correct.*
11. She occasionally gives way to a good laugh. *Correct.*
12. At times she comes through as stern although she does not mean to be that way. *Correct.*
13. She is meticulous. *Correct.* (Another trait that she's not always happy with.)

14. "Well-controlled" describes Jane. *Correct.* (She's not sure. She doesn't know herself as well as she would like.)
15. She is a very nice person. *Correct.* (She likes to think of herself as being nice. This helps her self-image.)
16. She has good values and good morals. *Correct.* (Here again, she believes this to be true but maybe because she's so insecure.)
17. She has a very neat house and very clean. It is quite well kept. *Correct.* (She wishes that she could let some of this "neat house" syndrome go. If she has the potential, she would like to be creative.)
18. It has a garden. *Partially correct.* (They used to garden with friends — quite a large endeavor — up till a year ago. The psychic may be seeing the plants. They are everywhere in the house.)
19. Her husband is this way also. *Correct.*
20. They are compulsive people and like things neat and orderly. Their whole life is rather that way. *Correct.* (Too much so.)
21. Watch for small cysts. When you get controlled people, energies don't always flow as well as they should. *Cysts are a tendency of persons who constrict the flow.* This is a general rule. *Correct.* (Small cysts for 17 years — benign.)
22. If she develops any type of cysts, Carlton Fredericks's diet, use of vitamin E, 600 milligrams per day and the castor oil pack would help. Once a problem is given, a solution is necessary. *Correct.* (She has Carlton Fredericks's book. She has been taking 400 milligrams of vitamin E for one year.)
23. On her fingernails are white spots — a zinc deficiency. Thirty mgs of zinc per day for several weeks would help cutting back to ten mgs thereafter. A large amount ingested immediately will eliminate the deficiency and then taper off to a plateau. *Correct.* (She will try the zinc.)
24. There is a slight residue of scarring on the lungs. (Was she ever a smoker?) Perhaps it could be scarring from pneumonia. *Correct.* (She smoked three packs a day. She has not smoked for 10 years. She did not know about the spot on the lung but believes it is there.)
25. She has an overactive gall bladder. It may produce too much bile. This would cause a "sour system." This is not a severe medical problem, but this tendency exists. Her control may keep some in

her system instead of eliminating it completely. *Correct.* (She has had 10 or 20 gall bladder attacks over a period of five years.)

26. She may do exercises to keep thin. This helps to counteract some of the control and cyst problem. *Correct.* (Every day.)

27. It is recommended that she get a small trampoline and jump on it because it would increase the flow of blood to her head, face, and throughout the system. The present exercises are not sufficient to pump the heart and keep the blood flowing well enough. Aerobics and running in place would be good for her. *Correct.* (She has just started increasing her cardiac output by fast walking and running in place.)

The Smith House

28. In her living room is a large glass window. *Partially correct.* (Before she moved.)

29. There are many panes of glass and a sheer curtain in front of it. *Correct.*

30. There is a red brick fireplace and andirons there also. *Correct.*

31. There is a pair of bellows also. *Incorrect.*

32. The house has an Early American floor. This preference stems from a life in colonial America — perhaps when she was in this area before — several hundred years ago. *Incorrect.* (She has always wanted Early American decor. She plans in the very near future to remove all the rugs and have just the bare floors. Perhaps I'm seeing what she wants.)

33. There is one wing chair. It may be light green. *Partially correct.* (There are two winged chairs, but they are burnt orange in color. The green sheer curtains may make them appear green with the amount of light that comes through the window.)

34. There is also furniture with a floral print. *Partially correct.*

35. The dining room has an ornate chandelier. *Correct.*

36. It has fixtures that look like petals of a flower upside down, and it comes out in five or six different places. *Correct.* (Described exactly.)

37. On the end of each is a candle-type light. *Correct.*

38. There is a mirror in the dining room over the sideboard. *Incorrect.* (But here again the glass over the painting and the angle of the

light through the window may give the effect of a mirror. There is a sideboard.)

39. In the house there are glass doors, which have panes of glass in them that open on to a patio out back. *Correct.* (Exactly.)
40. She and her husband and family enjoy this patio and have dinners out there in the summer. *Correct.*
41. There are torches there and a barbecue. *Correct.*
42. Jane and her husband do a lot of gardening. *Partially correct.* (Used to — some now.)
43. This involves flower beds, neat rows of flowers, and well-terraced areas. This is a well-cared-for yard. *Correct.* (Most of the time.)
44. The grass is edged. *Correct.* (Most of the time.)
45. There is some sort of a swing in the yard. *Incorrect.* (She's always wanted one.)
46. The yard comes through a lot because they spend a lot of time out of doors. *Correct.*
47. One of their hobbies is working on the yard with fertilizer, grass seed, flowers, plants, etc. *Partially correct.*
48. They change the flowers in summer and fall. *Partially correct.*
49. They visit McDonald's and purchase a lot of different plants there. *Incorrect.*
50. They read seed catalogs also. *Partially correct.*
51. She likes to play cards. *Partially correct.* (Mainly for relaxation.)
52. She has a quick mind, and I see her winning often at bridge. *Partially correct.*
53. She will win in the future. (She hopes so, but winning is really not that important to her.)

The above three readings typify the nature of the information channeled throughout the entire project. Therefore, it would seem prudent at this point in the chapter to incorporate my husband Jim's analysis of specific psychical phenomena that were evidenced through the 10 readings. His insights and critical understanding of the supraliminal abilities being exhibited will afford the reader a more comprehensive overview of the aims and accomplishments achieved by the College Psychical Research Project than could otherwise be realized by the sole inclusion of the three readings themselves.

Section II
(December 31, 1982, to February 28, 1983)
Dr. James C. Windsor

The College Psychical Research Project was a research project only in the very general sense of the term. There were only 10 subjects, no control groups, no double-blind techniques, and no pages of impressive statistical data. The project was preliminary to more serious research. We sought, with William James, only a "general sense of dramatic probability." The results of the study, however, produced some impressive evidence, if not proof, that something was going on that conflicted with known principles of science. They also raised additional, intriguing questions.

Several different kinds of "extra" or "super" perceptions were used to produce the readings. Let me identify some of these phenomena and give examples of each.

Clairvoyance, the ability to perceive events or objects at a distance beyond the capacity of the five senses, was a prominent characteristic of the psychic impressions. For example, the following description of an apartment was given:

The place where she lives is a small apartment. I see a couch which is rather square and a dark brown color. The apartment is generally done in blue, yellow, or beige, and brown colors. There is an unusual lamp in the living room. It has two or three sections on top that curl together and come out. There is one base.

This was an accurate description of the apartment, especially the lamp, which was an unusual design.

The following quotes are similar examples of accurate perception at a distance (10-50 mile radius).

The tablecloth in the kitchen is checkered.

House has a small porch and three steps with an iron railing.

The dining room has an ornate chandelier. It has fixtures that look like petals of a flower upside down, and it comes out in five or six different places. (Joan is deadly on light fixtures.)

Even more intriguing than furniture and light fixtures are perceptions of physical characteristics of both the exterior and interior of the body. The following are examples of accurate information:

She has varicose veins in the legs, especially in the upper portion.

There is a deformity in the toes.

There appears to be gravel in the system. (True — gall stones.)

There is a scar on the right side of her head, on the scalp. (This was true. The hair completely hid the scar from view.)

There is a scar on her abdomen from a minor operation.

On her fingernails are white spots, suggesting a zinc deficiency.

One cannot help speculating what the future might hold in medical diagnosis if such perceptions could be perfected.

An interesting phenomenon that supports a mixture of clairvoyance and telepathy (reading another's thoughts) occurred when the perception was not of some object present but of one wished for. (This also gave the impression of inaccuracy.) The recipients of the following observations, for example, reported that the object described was not owned but desired.

She has a new blue car that is square in back.

There is some sort of swing in the back yard.

There is a large, oval colonial rug in the living room.

Retrocognition suggests some mechanism through which a person may get information from the past, information that is not in the present memory of the person undergoing the experience. This is especially hard for us to grasp, because we do not yet understand where or how such information is stored, much less how it is retrieved — over a distance. Retrocognition is demonstrated in the following quote from a reading for Ann:

"When she was younger, she had trouble with her right eye. It was perhaps a muscle weakness or a slight astigmatism." (Ann confirmed that her continuing problem with astigmatism began when she was 12 years old.)

From another reading:

"She had a blow to the right jaw at one time, and this knocked her jaw out of line." (The recipient confirmed that she had suffered a hard blow to the jaw that burst her eardrum. In a separate accident her jaw was knocked out of line. Both of these events happened 25 years before.)

An interesting retrocognitive twist is found in the following description of a house:

The kitchen has yellow tile. The floor has yellow and there are small circles and streaks and dividing lines.

There is a fireplace with a small wooden, brown mantel over it.

These statements accurately described not the current house but one lived in previously.

In another reading it was noted that *"there appears to be an upright piano that is not new."* (The recipient reported, "We sold the upright piano last fall.")

The difficulty of comprehending how one can know the future is compounded by our reluctance to accept the implications — namely, that the future is fixed and we have no control over it. Yet the history of precognition reaches back to ancient civilizations. Precognitive experiences are too numerous to ignore, so we were not too surprised when predictions of future events began to show up in the readings.

"She is not going to stay here long but will be moving out of this apartment in a short period of time. She is going to be in a wedding, possibly her own." (The young lady reported that she was moving out in three weeks to get married. This could be telepathic or precognitive.)

"She's playing softball. I see her with a bat and ball." (This athlete joined a softball team two months after the reading. Was this precognition or suggestion?)

Seeing the future with *any degree of accuracy* is a mind-boggling experience and shakes our confidence in the extent to which modern "scientific" theory is comprehensive. There is much we do not yet understand.

It is generally accepted these days that personality and health are intimately related. Comments in these readings, however, suggest a strong *symbolic* relationship as well. The following quote, for example, is from a reading for an obese young woman who had frequent bouts with dermatitis:

The hand rash is symbolic in the sense that she does not want to touch people. She avoids getting close. Not touching is the general trend in the entire personality. This makes her very lonely. She is rather heavy, and this shell keeps people away from her also.

This advice was given for a woman who had a variety of minor health problems:

There are all kinds of minor irritations. This would fit because she gets irritated with people. These irritations are reflected in little areas all over the body. She is like a crusader, and crusaders have battle scars.

Ruth had chronic intestinal problems. This advice was given:

Look into yourself for the answer to your health problem. It is connected to the relationship with your sister. The lack of resolution concerning the problem continually irritates the area that is affected. This problem is of long standing. The pain will leave if the relationship problem is resolved.

Similar to the above is the counsel given in another sibling-rivalry situation. These comments remind us that events and relationships early in life can haunt us forever if we don't learn to forgive and forget.

Fierce competition with a brother made her feel rejected when she was younger. Feeling sad, she ate more. She tends to carry this over into the present. This is not necessary. She is reacting to things that are no longer true. This is an overreaction rooted in the younger years. The solution is to realize that she has good skills of her own. She should forget about trying to compete with her brother. This would then eliminate one current source of stress. This might also help her drop some of the weight.

The following comment ties a specific personality characteristic to a specific condition:

Watch for small cysts. When you get emotionally controlled people, energies don't always flow as well as they should. Cysts are a tendency of persons who constrict their emotional expression. This is a general rule. (This lady had had trouble with cysts for 17 years.)

Finally, this bit of advice, given to a person who felt inferior, sounds a little poetic:

Think much of yourself, and people will think much of you. Think little of yourself, and the ant that crawls is a giant in comparison.

The College Research Project was an effort to be somewhat more systematic in our efforts to identify more precisely the nature of the phenomena with which we were dealing. We concluded the following:

1. Reasonably accurate psychic impressions could be given for persons at a distance. Approximately 75 to 85 percent correct information was typical.
2. The full range of psychic skills such as telepathy, clairvoyance, retrocognition, and precognition are used.
3. There are, without doubt, ways of perceiving other than through the five traditional senses.
4. Belief or confidence is a factor in determining the quality of the information given. Those who believe in the process and are receptive get better material than those who are skeptical.
5. Personality characteristics are intimately related to one's physical health not just generally but specifically. Getting our "head straight" takes on a whole new meaning.
6. We have just barely begun to understand the nature of consciousness and perception. The continuing search for a better understanding of "inner space" may be our greatest adventure.

Final Comments
Joan R. Windsor

Through the data and feedback extracted from the College Psychical Research Project we concluded that there is strong evidence to support the hypothesis of the existence of psychic bonds and communication between kindred souls. The project also enabled me to remove once and for all any personal doubts and insecurities I felt about my obligation to develop my abilities to the fullest. And, in accepting my soul's heritage, I entered into full partnership with my husband and our mysterious guides.

Why spend time interpreting our dreams and cultivating an interest in the psychic? Nowhere have I read it stated more clearly and concisely than in a statement by Ruth Montgomery in her book *A World Beyond*. She indicates that spending time to develop psychic abilities is a better investment than storing diamonds in a safe, for, she feels, psychic qualities are related to the soul and seek the core of the universe, which is the seed of life itself.

PART TWO

Expanding Your Own Personal Consciousness

6

Examining Your Dream and ESP Heritage

Progress has nothing to do with time, you see, but with psychic and spiritual focus.
Jane Roberts, *Seth Speaks*

Dreams from Antiquity, Primitive Societies, and the Bible

Evidence of prophetic dreams and dream symbology extends back in time to primitive humans. Our ancestors depended more on their own instincts than their rational minds.

In the process of becoming civilized, Carl Jung said "we have increasingly divided our consciousness from the deeper instinctive strata of the human psyche, and even ultimately from the somatic basis of the psychic phenomenon. Fortunately, we have not lost these basic instinctive strata; they remain part of the unconscious, even though they may express themselves only in the form of dream images."[1]

The evolution of an individual's personality toward more creative and mature modes of expression cannot optimally take place without the establishment of free-flowing communication between the conscious and the unconscious mind. This can best be achieved through dreams and altered states of consciousness. If we elect to pursue this exacting course of personal expression, then it behooves us to engage in a comprehensive study geared toward the historical and anthropological aspects of dream symbology and precognition.

From antiquity the belief comes to us that two of the chief functions of dreams are prognostication of the future and medical diagnosis. A dream recorded by Artemidorus of Daldis in the second century A.D. concerned a man who saw his father meet death in a flaming house. Several weeks later the father died of phlegnome (fire or high fever). This was probably pneumonia.

The therapeutic symbol of the Roman god of medicine, Aesculapius, is the snake. In ancient Greece a healing form of dream incubation was practiced. The afflicted were brought to the temple of Aesculapius in an effort to procure a healing remedy for their malaise while they slept. During the night harmless yellow snakes would crawl over the slumbering patients. It was hoped that with the coming of morning light a curative dream would have been received.

The snake has survived to modern times as the symbol of the physician. It is not uncommon for a person undergoing some type of therapeutic treatment for physical maladies to dream of snakes.

Whether in ancient or in modern times, precognitive dreams generally serve as benevolent friends warning us of circumstances advancing fast upon us — whether avoidable or unavoidable. One recalls King Croesus being told by the Delphic Oracle that he would lay waste a large kingdom if he crossed the Halys River. It was only after suffering a devastating defeat in battle did he come to realize that the kingdom described by the oracle was his own.

Oracular dreams seemed to be an integral part of the Japanese culture well into the fifteenth century. Those afflicted with seemingly insoluble problems made pilgrimages to holy sites for the express purpose of incubating a dream that would offer an insightful resolution to the dilemma. Among Buddhist temples famous for healing dreams was Hasedera, south of Nara. This temple was dedicated to the Bodhisattva Kannon. A quote from the fifteenth-century work entitled *Hasedera Reigenki* attests to the miraculous healing power of an oracular dream.

A man called Kiyohara Natsuno, for example, was horribly disfigured by leprosy and made the pilgrimage to Hasedera after all other attempts at cure had failed. After spending seven days in seclusion in the temple, he dreamed that a boy appeared from the inner sanctuary and said, "Your sickness is very difficult to cure because it is due to karma from a past life. But Kannon has nevertheless commanded me to heal you." The boy thereupon put out his tongue, which was very long, and licked the man all over his body. When the licking was finished, the man woke up in great astonishment, to find himself clean and cured.[2]

Islamic religious doctrines spring from the ancient culture of Arabia. In countries where Islam is the dominant religion (Africa, Persia [the modern-day countries of Iran and Iraq], parts of the Indian subcontinent, Indonesia, etc.) a multitude of pre-Islamic religious beliefs and practices continue to survive. In popular Islam there is almost universal acceptance among the common people of the portending of future events and decisions through the medium of dreams. These supposedly originate from supernatural forces. The dreams are received by the Sudanese fiqihs, religious leaders and saints of the surrounding areas, rather than by those who are unschooled.

The fiqih might be in a khalwah (a retreat for an ascetic, which would also contain a school for teaching religion) or a tomb of a departed saint. There, before falling asleep, he might reverently request guidance for the course of his future life. An example of such a dream was recorded by Abd Al-Rahman Wadd Ban Al-Naqa, a fiqih from a district north of Khartoum. "Abd Al-Rahman Wadd Ban Al-Naqa saw in a dream his grandfather flying between the Heavens and Earth, his own father flying behind him and himself behind his father. He recounted this vision to Sharif Abdullah who said to him, 'They have indicated to you that you should occupy yourself with exoteric learning.'"[3]

Ibn Khaldun, celebrated Islamic philosopher of history, explains dream visions in this fashion:

Dream vision is an awareness of the part of the rational soul in its spiritual essence, of glimpse[s] of the forms of events. While the soul is spiritual, the forms of events have actual existence in it, as is the case with all spiritual essences. The soul becomes spiritual through freeing itself from bodily matters and corporeal perceptions. This happens to the soul [in the form of] glimpse[s] through the agency of sleep . . . . through [these glimpses the soul] gains the knowledge of future events that it desires and by means of which it regains the perceptions that [properly] belong to it. When this process is weak or indistinct, the soul applies to it allegory and imaginary pictures, in order to gain [the desired knowledge]. Such allegory, then, necessitates interpretation.[4]

The Naskapi Indians are a prime example of a simple people who pay attention to their dreams in an effort to enter into a deeper relationship with the "Great Man." They live as hunters in isolated family groups in the forests of the Labrador Peninsula. "Dreams give the Naskapi complete ability to find his way in life, not only in the inner world but also the outer world of nature. They help him to foretell the weather and give him invaluable guidance in his hunting."[5] The Naskapi believe that lies and dishonesty drive the Great Man away from the inner realm, while kindness and love of one's fellow human beings provide them with a full life. In this respect these primitive people are closer to what might be labeled inner truth than modern people with all of their civilized ideas.

It is the role of religious symbols to give meaning to life. The Pueblo Indians hold the belief that they are direct descendants of Father Sun. The nurturing of such a belief bestows upon them a perspective and goal far exceeding their limited existence and encourages the personality to develop more fully. This is far superior to the myopic position rampant throughout our own civilization that portrays people as the underdog with no inner creed to which they pledge allegiance.

A discussion of the historical perspective of dreams and prophecy would not be complete without citing spiritually illuminating instances of clairaudience, precognition, and dream interpretation from the Bible.

In I Kings 3:5-14 the Lord appears to King Solomon in a dream saying, "Ask what I shall give you." Solomon, having no desire for wealth or power, speaks thus: "Give thy servant therefore an understanding mind to govern thy people, that I may discern between good and evil." The Ethereal Voice replies, "Behold, I give you a wise and discerning mind, so that none like you has been before you and none like you shall arise after you. I give you also what you have not asked, both riches and honor."[6] What better example of a clearly clairaudient dream with a message?

Another example of clairaudience can be found in I Samuel, 3:6-9. The boy Samuel hears his name called and runs to the priest Eli, thinking he has summoned him. Eli says, "I did not call, my son; lie down again." The episode is repeated twice more. Finally Eli comes to the realization that the Lord has called Samuel. He directs him to lie down again and, if he hears his name, to say, "Speak, Lord, for thy servant hears."[7]

The verses immediately following (10-14) are precognitive in nature and relate God's message to Samuel: "Behold, I am about to do a thing in Israel, at which the two ears of everyone that hears it will tingle. On that day I will fulfill against Eli all that I have spoken concerning his house, from beginning to end. And I tell him that I am about to punish his house forever, for the iniquity which he knew, because his sons were blaspheming God, and he did not restrain them. Therefore I swear to the house of Eli that the iniquity of Eli's house shall not be expiated by sacrifice or offering forever."[8] The events happened as predicted.

There are no more convincing illustrations of importance of accurate dream interpretation than those presented in the book of Daniel, Chapters 2 and 4. In Chapter 2 the Babylonian king, Nebuchadnezzar, has a dream and finds it impossible to recall the substance of it. Deeply troubled by his inability to summon the dream into consciousness, he commands that all the astrologers and magicians in Babylon be brought before him for the purpose of recalling and deciphering its meaning. Failure to comply with his edict means execution. The Hebrew prophet Daniel desires to save his life as well as the lives of his friends Hananiah, Mishael, and Azariah. Thus he enters a trance state to reveal its significance. *He counsels King Nebuchadnezzar that the dream has been given for the sole purpose of enabling the great ruler to comprehend his innermost thoughts.* The profundity of Daniel's statement should carry a special message for the readers of this book. If through personal dream study and interpretation we are able to achieve some semblance of self-knowledge and self-actualization, how much more joyous the lives of each and every one of us would become.

In Chapter 4 King Nebuchadnezzar experiences a second, more frightening dream. Once again Daniel is brought before the king and given the following dream to interpret:

I saw, and behold, a tree in the midst of the earth, and its height was great. The tree grew and became strong, and its top reached to heaven, and it was visible to the end of the whole earth. Its leaves were fair and its fruit abundant, and on it was food for all. The beasts of the field found shade under it, and the birds of the air dwelt in its branches, and all flesh was fed on it.

I saw in the visions of my head as I lay in bed, and behold, a watcher, a holy one, came down from heaven. He cried aloud and said thus, "Hew down the tree and cut off its branches, strip its leaves and scatter its fruit; let the beasts flee from under it and the birds from its branches. But leave the stump of its roots in the earth, bound with a band of iron and bronze amid the tender grass of the field. Let him be wet with the dew of heaven; let his lot be with the beasts in the grass of the earth; let his mind be changed from a man's and let a beast's mind be given to him; and let seven times pass over him. The sentence is by the decree of the watchers, the decision by the word of the holy ones, to the end that the living may know that the Most High rules the kingdom of men, and gives it to whom he will, and sets over it the lowliest of men."[9]

Daniel, realizing the significance of the dream, is alarmed but provides the interpretation nevertheless. The tree is King Nebuchadnezzar, a high and mighty ruler. It is the decree of the Lord that his kingdom will be taken from him and he shall dwell mindlessly among the beasts of the field until he comes to the realization that it is God, not he, that rules the land. At this point his kingdom will be restored to him. All comes to pass as prophesied, and King Nebuchadnezzar reigns once again over his subjects a much wiser man.

It is essential to differentiate between a dream and a vision. "Our dream state occurs when we are physically asleep and in an unconscious state. A vision occurs when we have a dream while awake or in a semiconscious state."[10] Paul was guided to Macedonia by a vision in the night. The entire book of Revelation was vouchsafed to John by an angel in a vision. In all, there are at least 70 passages in the Bible that refer to dreams and vision.

In conclusion, let me mention two biblical quotes that contain promises of God psychically speaking to man if man will only open his heart in complete surrender and joyfully receive His Word. The first is located in Joel 2:28. "And it shall come to pass afterward, that I will pour out my spirit on all flesh; your sons and your daughters shall prophesy, your old men shall dream dreams, and your young men shall see visions."[11]

The second, among my favorites, specifically cites dreams as a means of Holy Communication. It is contained in Job 33:14-16. "For God speaks in one way, and in two, though man does not perceive it. In a dream, in a vision of the night, when deep sleep falls upon men, while they slumber on their beds, then he opens the ears of men."[12]

Are these promises not inspiring enough to prompt you to focus your attention on dreaming?

Twentieth-Century Pioneers in Dream Explanation and Interpretation

The education of modern-day dream students would not be complete without an examination of the theories and contributions of Sigmund Freud, Carl G. Jung, and Ann Faraday. We are eternally indebted to these people for recognizing that the dreaming mind provides us with valuable insights about our lives through the use of symbolic picture language. The progression began with Freud's belief that the dreamer used symbols to disguise primitive sexual and aggressive drives. These were extremely unpleasant and therefore were repressed by the dreamer in the conscious state. Dream philosophy has evolved to the point where current experts in the field such as Ann Faraday maintain that dream symbols concisely reveal the truth to the dreamer rather than concealing it. How did such an evolution come about?

Freud held the general assumption that dreams did not occur by happenstance, but were rather the subtle expressions of feelings, emotions, and problems with which the conscious mind was attempting to deal while asleep. A graphic picture of a son enjoying the sex act with his mother would awaken feelings of horror and revulsion in the dreamer. However, when the subconscious disguises the idea as merely taking a ride on the back of a cow, the slumbering mind continues to indulge in the fantasy.

Freud agreed wholeheartedly with eminent neurologists of his time that neurotic symptoms such as hysteria and certain types of pain were related to some conscious experience and may, in fact, be symbolically meaningful. For example, episodes of vomiting may signify an inability "to stomach" a distasteful situation. Pseudo-paralysis of the legs is suggestive of the hysterical plea — "I can't go one step further." Freud eventually reduced the dreams of his patients to certain basic patterns and used them as a starting point in psychoanalysis for determining the unconscious problem of the patient. "Freud made the simple but penetrating observation that if a dreamer is encouraged to go on talking about his dream images and the thoughts that these prompt in his mind, he will give himself away and reveal the unconscious background of his ailments, in both what he says and what he deliberately omits saying."[13]

The core of Freud's theory was that *dreams were out to deceive us* and only through lengthy discussions with trained experts could one face the unconscionable truth he was trying to avoid.

Among Freud's disciples was a young psychiatrist named Carl Gustave Jung. He eventually broke with Freud, objecting vigorously to his dream deception beliefs. He theorized that concealment is an attribute of the waking mind and has no place in the deeper recesses of one's psyche. He also dismissed Freud's notion that all dreams originate from early childhood experiences. He held that specific universal patterns within the unconscious mind spring forth in myths, stories, art forms, and dreams. Such patterns formed what he termed a "collective unconscious" which was the property of all mankind.

According to Jung, the collective unconscious consists of universal thought-forms or archetypes. The collective unconscious contains the "wisdom of the ages" and this is often communicated through dreams by archetypal representations. These types of dreams not only reveal problems, but also contain their solutions.

The basic task of the individual is a full differentiation and integration of personality or individuation. This requires self-knowledge. Self-understanding is gained through the exploration of the *persona* (the sum total of all social roles), the *shadow* (the undesirable aspects of personality), the *ego* (the center of only a portion of the psyche), the *anima* (feminine aspects of the man), and the *animus* (masculine aspects of the woman).

The anima of a man undergoes changes throughout his lifetime as does the animus of a woman. For a man there are four stages in a growing relationship with the opposite sex:

1. The Seductress who can tantalize a man.
2. The Romantic woman who captures a man's passions.
3. The Virgin simple, innocent and capable of great love for only one man.
4. A Spiritual Guide — a source of stability, comfort and great wisdom.

The animus of the woman also undergoes stages each portraying man in a characteristic masculine role:

1. The animalistic male who is powerful and sexually attractive.
2. The Lover or romantic man who has power over her emotions.
3. The action man — competent and authoritarian.
4. The Wise Old Man capable of spiritual guidance and inspiration.[14]

In a healthy relationship the anima of the man complements the animus of the woman working together harmoniously. A fixation at any one of these archetypal personality representations throws the personality off balance. For example, the more the animus appears in a woman's dreams, the more urgent the message is to develop the masculine and intellectual side of her nature. A multitude of dreams depicting the anima should prompt a man to take similar action in developing his feminine traits.

In cases of irreconcilable emotional conflicts in one's life a dream image may emerge from the unconscious providing the dreamer with a higher point of view from which this conflict can be transcended. Jung called this aspect of dreaming the "transcendent function."

In his introduction to *The Secret of The Golden Flower* Jung discusses this concept. He theorizes that the most important of life's problems are probably unsolvable and, therefore, must be outgrown. This process seems to consist of advancement to a new level of consciousness whereby the sense of urgency that surrounds the issue is lost, and the entire question is observed from a different vantage point. Although the feelings of panic and frustration that accompany the conflict continue to rage, once having arrived at this elevated level of consciousness, instead of being enmeshed in its furiosity, the personality stands "transcended" and, having risen above the tumult, can view the conflict as a detached observer.

This transcendent function could also emerge in waking fantasy from remembered dream material or even under hypnosis.

Before leaving Jung's theories, we should examine his position concerning ESP. He termed this concept *synchronicity*. It is based upon the principle that an inner unconscious wisdom connects a physical occurrence with a psychic event, so that, although the happening appears to be a product of coincidence, it can in fact be physically significant. The significance of the meaning is frequently symbolically indicated through dreams that occur simultaneously with the event.

The phenomenon of synchronicity was clearly recognizable again and again in my life in connection with the appearance of recurring cysts. Its initial impact reverberated throughout the drama surrounding the almost miraculous healing of the first cyst with the application of a castor oil pack. The reduction of the second cyst, achieved by means of a series of "coincidental meetings" and "healing dreams" that led me to Dr. Genevieve Haller, subsequently left an indelible imprint of the doctrine upon my mind.

I also observed an excellent example of synchronicity in my life when writing the earlier section of this chapter, which focused on biblical interpretations of dreams. I had become extremely busy with my counseling business and had not had much time to locate the exact material I needed to complete this section. While I was sitting in my office musing on where to look next, "by chance" Kevin Riley, a precognitive dream student of ours, stopped by to show me some books he had just checked out for a term paper he was composing. The subject was *Dream Interpretations from The Bible*. The publications were just what I had envisioned several moments before as my mind had reached out in time and space to search for the desired information. *Coincidence or synchronicity*?

Dr. Ann Faraday, a psychologist trained in Freudian and Jungian analysis and Gestalt therapy, became disillusioned with the limitations placed on dream interpretation by these theories. Working with exploratory dream study groups of her own she formulated a promising new approach to unraveling the puzzling symbology of dream language.

In her book, *The Dream Game*, Faraday states that thinking by pictures and ideas associated with them is one of the most primitive avenues of thought, dating back to the dawn of history. Even in our everyday speech today we employ pictures translated into verbal metaphors, such as: "raining cats and dogs" or "soothing ruffled feathers." Dreams make use of these visual images and associations of ideas by projecting them on the screen of the mind to convey the desired messages.

Faraday maintains that although dream symbology often appears quite illogical from a rational viewpoint, it is readily understandable, if one would but take the time and trouble to unravel its messages in relation to thoughts of the heart.

Eight common dream themes are cited by Dr. Faraday because they picture common experiences we all share. These include dreams of falling, flying, appearing nude or scantily clad in public, taking an examination, losing teeth, losing valuables, finding valuables, and sex. She points out, however, that although similar feelings are shared, these themes may connote entirely different meanings to each person depending on current life experiences.

Faraday is known for her emphasis on puns, slang language, body langauge, and all sorts of colloquialisms. It is her opinion that this aspect of dream interpretation has been long overlooked. Examples of dream puns being shown the dreamer are "too big for his britches," "eating himself silly," and "ironing things out." The dream pictures the situation exactly.

Although many dreams seem banal or possess an air of

triviality, the serious dream student would be wise to take to heart the philosophical stances of Carl Jung in regard to this issue. In his opinion trivial dreams give the impression of being observed and weighed down with such a multiplicity of seemingly irrelevant details that they often leave the dreamer completely befuddled. However, if the dreamer is willing to surmount these obstacles and patiently set about the task of unraveling the illusive message woven within the mental fabric of the so-called "trivial dream," he will discover to his amazement *the subject in question is of the highest import*. Therefore, Jung encourages the dreamer to carry the dream about, letting it seep into the imagination, speak to others about it, and examine its aspects from all sides. Eventually, if enough meditation is applied, the hidden truth within is revealed.

In this chapter we have investigated the history of dreams and ESP and examined the theories and methodologies of early pioneers and current exponents in the field. Through presentation of this material we have established the basic foundations upon which one can build spiritually. The ensuing pages contain specific instructions and guidelines for the novice dream student to unravel the hidden messages so skillfully woven into the dream fabric and, "story by story," begin to construct a dream "manor" which reflects his own unique philosophical stance in life. Once completed, the visionary mason now possesses the key to unlock the inner door and, crossing the threshold, finds himself face-to-face with the Christ Spirit portion of his soul that dwells within the heart of each and every one of us. Thereafter, he need never be alone.

It is with this goal in mind that we now embark on our mystical dream pilgrimage.

7

What Is a Dream?

> There are "Universal Forces" that the individual can contact, according to his need and his training to use them. These forces can provide him with boundless information, and with relevant patterns of guidance. They are in effect the creative currents of the divine itself, moving through human affairs like some great unseen Gulf Stream.
>
> Harmon Bro, *Edgar Cayce on Dreams*

For the past 34 months a good portion of my time has been devoted to the study and interpretation of the phenomena of dreams. I have read numerous books in the field penned by leading authorities on such subjects as telepathy, clairvoyance, recognition and precognition in dreams, business guidance, personal guidance, and visionary dreams. I have attended workshops led by Stanley Krippner, dean of faculty at Saybrook Institute in San Francisco, and Robert Van de Castle, director of the Sleep and Dream Laboratory at the University of Virginia Medical School. I have enrolled in week-long conferences designed to teach basic methods of facilitating dream recall, understanding dream symbology, and interpreting dreams properly so that maximum benefits can be realized when applying them to current problems and issues. My husband and I have traveled to Connecticut to participate in an intensive three-day program of instruction encompassing such intriguing subjects as auras, reincarnation, psychometry, survival after death, and psychic healing. One of the main focuses of these sessions was dream interpretation. We came away with considerably more knowledge than we had before arriving but also with a feeling of astonishment that these techniques we had just mastered could be *functionally* used to offer guidance to ourselves and service to others in our daily existence.

Needless to say, there has been considerable sorting and sifting out of extraneous material for which there seems to be little use or factual basis as we pursued our research for universal truths and practical usages of the psychic in general and dreams in particular.

Since 1967, when my husband and I first joined the ARE, we have been incorporating the ideas and philosophies of Edgar Cayce into our lives.

Born March 19, 1877, 3 P.M., Hopkinsville, Kentucky, Edgar Cayce was brought up by a farming family steeped in Southern tradition that followed the Protestant faith. At age 21 Cayce lost the use of his voice as a result of a severe throat ailment. When medical practitioners were unable to cure him, hypnosis was tried but failed to restore his voice.

Subsequently, Cayce was permanently cured by utilizing suggestions he received while in a self-induced trance state. The answers which came through him indicated that a source existed that could be tapped for information to cure anyone's problems — and Edgar Cayce had the key to contact this source in order to help himself, and later others. Based on this idea he began to help many persons who were unable to find cures for their medical problems from the medical establishment of that day.

By the early 1900s, Cayce, with the help of his family and wife, Gertrude, was helping hundreds of persons by giving readings while in an altered state of consciousness. His biographer Thomas Sugrue mentions in *There Is a River* that by the time of Cayce's death in 1945, he had given over 14,000 readings in the fields of medicine and health, religion and philosophy and allied cures for mind, body, and spirit. Thousands of people from all over the world have been able to read about his work and use portions from the readings that are available to the public.

In the 1920s, the Cayce family settled in Virginia Beach and established an organization which later became the Association for Research and Enlightenment — now known as the

ARE. Cayce's readings are now available to the general public through the library in Virginia Beach, Virginia.

Those who use the Cayce material refer to different readings by their case number. This protects the persons who sought readings by using a numbering system in lieu of the recipients' actual names.

To this day the Edgar Cayce Foundation, which is the custodian of the readings, does not divulge the name or number of any person who had a reading. There is an alphabetical and numerical list kept in the vault of the Edgar Cayce Foundation Office.

Numbers 261 and 262 are the most famous of the readings, representing a body of information known as the "Search for God" material.

After lengthy discussions, in-depth research, experimentation, and the recording, analysis, and application of 5000 dreams, I have concluded that the best approach to working and analyzing dreams successfully can be found in the literature published by the Association for Research and Enlightenment. In the writing, experts such as Mark Thurston, Harmon Bro, and Elsie Sechrist have gleaned from the Edgar Cayce readings the ingredients and methodology essential for accurate and informative dream revelations. I have also based much of the material in this book on the ideas and philosophy of this extraordinary clairvoyant.

Let us begin with the first question that should come to mind when studying the subject of dreams: *How is a dream created?*

According to Edgar Cayce there are four primary sources of dreams.

1. Physical — Our own subconscious.
2. Mental and Emotional — The subconscious of another with whom we may communicate.
3. Spiritual — The Superconscious.
4. God.

One remembers from physics that the force is an energy that has a particular direction. Cayce says dreams are created by a correlation of these forces interacting with each other to form meaningful relationships. For example, in the projection of a dream the mental force could react with the physical force in depicting how holding a grudge against an enemy could result in a physical illness for oneself. The dream might go something like this: "You see your 'enemy' driving his car in front of you on the road and think you will sideswipe his automobile. After you have made several dents in his fender, you notice your car is overheating and the radiator is about to explode." *Interpretation:* Deliberate aggressive acts and harbored ill feelings are resulting in high blood pressure, which may eventually lead to a stroke.

A dream may also be created by direct projection of one of the forces into dream awareness. This can be illustrated by mental forces projecting the following dream:

"You are working on a business proposition and the mail arrives. There is a contract already signed for the project. This makes you feel as if you do not need to work as diligently on the details since you think your goal has already been accomplished." *Interpretation:* This may not be a precognitive dream, but rather one telling you not to make hasty decisions regarding important matters.

Elsie Sechrist, in her book, *Dreams: Your Magic Mirror,* provides us with a delineation of the types of dreams that originate from the various levels of the mind. From the upper level of the subconscious come physical dreams caused by conditions surrounding the dreamer. For example, you dream you are at the North Pole wearing a bikini and awaken to find you have left the window open and it is 25 degrees outside and snowing.

From a deeper level of the subconscious come dreams of body assimilation, tissue regeneration, and elimination as well as warning dreams concerning diet, physical exercise, and the general state of bodily health.

Dreams that emerge from the mental or emotional level are corrective dreams usually concerned with friends, enemies, diabolical acts, animals, arguments, and other daily stresses. Dreams of encouragement probably surface from this level also.

It is through our superconscious that we experience dreams of telepathy, clairvoyance, precognition, retrocognition, and spiritual direction. Many inspirational and creative dreams emanate from this realm. For example, an inventor, while in the dream state, might conceive of a workable design to finalize the invention that has been an enigma to him for months.

At the highest level of dreaming the superconscious provides dreams, visions and revelations through which we ascertain firsthand the very meaning of life itself, the nature of our Creator, and the interrelationship between God and humanity. These types are visionary dreams and are rare, but when they do come, it is an intuitive experience that leaves us with a feeling of mental and physical rejuvenation.

The Cayce readings specifically define sleep as "that period of time when the soul takes stock of what it has acted upon from one rest period to another."[1]

One of the most mind-boggling statements found in the Cayce readings concerns precognitive dreams and their manifestation in the dreamer's existence. The source of Cayce's information directs the dreamer to be aware that "any condition ever becoming a reality is first dreamed."[2] *That is, nothing happens unless one is initially aware of it through the dream process.* This statement, if nothing else, should make each of us run to purchase a dream journal posthaste and faithfully record our nightly dreams in the hope of being forewarned of a future disaster or receiving a stock tip through which our fortunes could be secured.

How then do we go about remembering and recording our dreams, and for what purpose? One could probably spend several hours listing a variety of reasons that would undoubtedly validate the importance of dream recollection. In the interest of time and space, and after considerable forethought, I have condensed the number to a few that I feel express the basic tenets that our dreams can serve to enrich our lives.

Purposes for Recalling Our Dreams

1. A dream can delineate the strengths and weaknesses that comprise one's personality.

2. Business and occupational guidance can be obtained.
3. Information of the physical condition of the body is contained in dreams.
4. Suggested treatments for bodily imbalances and illnesses are present in healing dreams.
5. Dreams offer ideas and inspirational thoughts that incite creativity.
6. Many dreams contain clues that clarify the course to be followed when making important decisions.
7. Occasionally, the dreamer is provided with glimpses of past life episodes.
8. Records of our dreams often reveal telepathic communication.
9. We frequently dream of events and information that can be of assistance to others in finding solutions to their problems.
10. Dreams furnish us with ESP experiences and enhance psychic development.
11. Some dreams are designed to clarify "foggy dream situations" that have presented themselves on previous nights.
12. One of the most exciting aspects of recording dream experiences is to identify future trends and thereby avoid or take advantage of foreseen events or advice.
13. Local or world events may be reviewed or observed clairvoyantly while sleeping.
14. Through dreams we are taught lessons in spirituality. The application of such lessons in daily life enhances the fruitfulness of our spiritual progress.
15. One of the prime reasons for recalling our dreams is that they serve as the true link between ourselves and our Creator.

Suggestions for Enhancement of Dream Recall

Many people think they are incapable of remembering last night's dream in the cold light of dawn. Often, the inability to recall your dreams is a matter of inspired subliminal blocking. The dreamer is unwilling to remember what he or she is unwilling to change. Recurrent dreams that remain the same year after year are indicative of such resistance. Dream recall can be facilitated through the following techniques and ideas suggested, in part, in "Dream Recall Techniques and Approaches" (Edgar Cayce Foundation):

1. *It is essential to develop an inquiring mind.* Reading books on dreams, studying dream theories and symbols, and discussing your dreams with friends can improve the quality and number of dreams recalled per night.
2. *Retire early in the evening.* Getting a full night's sleep provides ample time for the completion of three to five dream sequences. The longest dream session is at the end of our sleep period. If we cut ourselves short, we reduce the likelihood of superior dream recollection.
3. *Learn to wake up in the middle of the night.* The best time to recall a dream is immediately after it happens. How can one learn to do this?
   (a) Drink two cups of water before retiring and you will wake up for obvious reasons. Gradually, the mind will train itself to awaken, and the "water trick" will no longer be necessary.
   (b) Setting an alarm at a particular hour in the night serves the same purpose.
4. *Give yourself a presleep suggestion.* A statement such as "It will be easy for me to recall my dreams upon awakening" repeated numerous times before falling into slumber often results in additional dreams recollected. Note the increase that occurs when this technique is applied.
5. *Keep your dream journal and a pen beside your bed.* If you awaken in the middle of the night and do not want to wake your spouse, or you yourself do not want to take the time to write down the entire dream, a few key symbols will often bring back the entire dream sequence upon review in the morning.
6. *Review your previous night's dreams before going to sleep.* This might enable you to incubate dreams that will explain those for which you have been unable to find an interpretation. It may also serve to promote a continuation of a series of dreams that are taking place.
7. *Upon awakening remain entirely still.* The Cayce readings say specifically that dreams are best recalled before the body regains its physical equilibrium.
8. *Begin with the last scene you remember in your dream and work backward.* If you gradually review the dream sequence in reverse order, the

majority of events that were envisioned before will fall into place almost automatically.

9. *Ask yourself to what part of your life the dream is referring.* Does it deal with health, your family relationships, your studies, your work, your diet, lack of exercise, a future trip? Don't quit until you are fairly certain you have located the appropriate category dealt with in the dream scenes.

10. *If you can't decipher the meaning of a dream, request a similar dream that will improve the clarity of the problem one.* Such a request is usually complied with the ensuing night or soon thereafter. Keep an "eye open" for the clarifying response.

11. *Work on your dreams daily.* Progress in dream interpretation can only be made by studying them in a systematic fashion. A word of advice, however: If you cannot understand confusing dreams, put them aside for several days and then return to them. Often, the precognition events will have occurred providing you with the precise event the dream depicted, or additional information or guidance will have been received thereby supplying the dreamer with new insights.

12. *Observe recurring themes as well as serial dreams.* These types of dreams frequently convey messages relating to progress or failures on the road of life.

13. *View dream interpretation as the learning of a new foreign language.* Dream symbols should be thought of as the forgotten language of the subconscious. Internalization of common dream symbols and increased awareness of one's own personal associations make interpreting dreams eventually as easy as speed-reading an exciting novel in spite of the numerous plots and variations of themes involved.

14. *Dreams are almost always about you, a unique soul, although some relate to family members, associates or public happenings.* Recall, record, review, and rejoice in your own individuality.

15. *Give thanks to your Creator by praying and meditating daily.* You will be truly amazed at the improvement of the quality and reception of your future dreams.

16. *Action is required for true dream interpretation.* Determine what action is required of you and then take personal steps to comply.

8

Dream Interpretation

Dreams were a natural and appropriate vehicle in which the answers to prayer might be given.
Harmon Bro, *Edgar Cayce on Dreams*

Dreams have proven to be the safest method of communication between the self and other dimensions of consciousness. By the mere act of suppressing one's conscious awareness for a period of seven to eight hours we become heroes and heroines of dramas in which situations and emotions far surpass those conjured up by the conscious mind in the waking state. Our imaginations paint portraits of ourselves experiencing the thrill of winning an Olympic gold medal, receiving an award for a highly acclaimed literary work, or rescuing damsels in distress from the clutches of the most evil of villains. In contrast, we may find ourselves as victims of inalterable circumstances of fate. These condemn us to exist for one interminable night as the humblest of peasants barely able to eke out a meager living for his family, a prisoner on a slave ship beaten and starved almost beyond human endurance, or a pitiful semblance of humanity burdened with a gross physical deformity, pitied and shunned by all who come in contact with him.

Why do these images spring from the depths of our unconscious? What magician can invoke such awe-inspiring or terrifying creatures? *More importantly, what does each characterization mean to us, how can we understand and gain inspiration from such experiences, and how can we be certain our interpretations have validity?*

Information channeled through Edgar Cayce explains the purpose and perpetrator of such evocations:

Sleep is a shadow of that intermission [of life] or that state called death. — In sleep one is more aware even though the body physical is asleep. This, the sixth sense, is a part of the subconscious, which is the spiritual self ever on guard before the throne of the Creator itself. — There is ever, when the body is asleep, that other self that communes with the soul of the body, see? The sixth sense goes out at night to those realms of experience related to all levels of consciousness, all time, and to its own criterion *or standards, developed through the ages. As a result, through such comparisons and judging in sleep, peace or understanding may come. The more spiritual minded individuals are easily pacified in sleep or when awake. Why? Because they have set before themselves an ideal, a criteria upon which they rely completely.*[1]

What, then, are the methods to be employed for accurate interpretation of our dream epics? Through use of these interpretations, to what degree can we be assured of receiving gainful and revelationary insights from our nightly journeys? Listed below are 15 important standards or rules of interpretation designed to enable the reader to decode the messages and unravel the mysteries that nightly flash onto the screens of our minds. Keep in mind that most people dream four to seven dreams per night. Therefore, even if only two or three dreams are recalled and interpreted, significant benefits can be derived from engaging in such activities. These standards have been carefully selected from numerous books I have digested, material from Mark Thurston's dream lectures, and ideas that have grown out of my own dream interpretations.

Fifteen Rules for Successful Dream Interpretations

1. *In working with dreams initially the interpreter should seek to discover the overall message presented.* The basic mistake of most novices is writing down all symbols and their meanings from a dream dictionary in an attempt to derive understanding from the dream's symbology. One should rather review the dream holistically and try to grasp the central feeling or idea that is woven into the material. Mark Thurston feels that the contents of daily life experiences are represented by various shapes — that is, patterns of behavior, of thinking, and of feeling. Thus, in using the theme approach, the dreamer should try to identify the basic overall "shape" of the

dream and then look for the areas of waking life it is describing. Does the dream evoke feelings of joy, apprehension, fear, love, ill health, inadequacy, seeking, terror, or inspiration? To what area of your life does it apply? Your home environment, work situation, health, relationships with friends, local happenings, religious life, or some future event as yet unknown to you? If the dream student can summarize the entire dream in a concise statement containing the major actions and feelings depicted throughout the fantasy, the lesson or purpose of the dream then becomes apparent. *Example:* An employee attends an office party. Many of his business associates have congregated when he arrives. As he removes his overcoat, he notices in horror he has forgotten to put on his clothes before departing from home and is standing before his associates in the altogether. This dream can be summarized in the following sentence: In my working life I feel *exposed* in my relationships with my coworkers. The feeling of the dream is one of an inability to protect oneself adequately.

When the basic message of the dream has been located, the next step is to analyze dream symbols and their relationships to the dreamer. *Note:* If there is more than one message in the dream, it becomes necessary to use this process several times.

2. *If a question was posed before the dreamer drifted off into slumber, is the answer contained in one of the several dreams recalled upon awakening?* Suppose you have worked for a company a considerable time and feel you are entitled to a raise. You formulate the question regarding the increase in salary and then proceed to dream that a new five-dollar bill has been placed on your desk when you arrive at your job the following day. In all likelihood this is a dream of encouragement suggesting that a request for an increment in salary will be met with a favorable response. Formulating questions localizes the issues one must deal with in life. This process invariably culminates in the reception of specific information or guidance essential for arriving at the most fruitful course of action to pursue.

3. *Dreams are often the embodiment of lessons for the soul's progress.* Lesson dreams appear to me to be among the first dreams we receive when we fall asleep. Carl Jung's archetypes can often be found in lesson dreams. These may be seen as separate figures that comprise the individual's personality. As previously defined, the *persona* consists of the social masks one assumes. The *ego* is the center of a portion of the individual's entire psyche. A person's

shadow is the personification of one's worst faults and weaknesses. The *anima* or *animus* is composed of whatever is of the opposite sex within the dreamer. The *animus* represents the masculine attributes in a woman's nature, which, when well integrated, will provide her with greater self-knowledge and discernment. Conversely, the *anima* is the pattern of all feminine traits within the man — that is, the emotional, intuitive, and instinctive side. When feminine traits are well integrated in the male, receptiveness, sensitivity, and warmth compensate for his aggressive qualities. Finally, the *ideal* or *true self* is the highest potential the individual is capable of attaining. The self starts as a formless figure seemingly somewhere in the future, but when the animus and anima achieve harmonious balance combined with other aspects of one's personage, the self then becomes a whole, real and unified personality functioning at its highest level. In interpreting lesson dreams, advice and instructions communicated from these archetypes should be internalized into one's personality or applied in one's daily existence.

4. *Does the recalled dream contain elements of precognition or clairvoyance?* Are parts of the dream describing events that could happen in the next week or the next month? Do portions of the dream deal with current issues that will be resolved in the near future? Is the material contained in the dream entirely foreign to us? Is the dream to be taken literally or is it presented in a symbolic fashion? All these questions should come to mind when searching for precognition or clairvoyance.

   The most frequent type of precognitive dream is the warning dream. This gives us an idea of what the future will hold if we continue to follow the same course we are currently maintaining. If one then makes practical use of the warning, one can perhaps make a decision that will decrease the likelihood of the foretold event occurring. Some people feel they are intuitively aware of precognitive dreams. I have often noted that the position of precognitive dreams are frequently among the last ones remembered *but* this is not a hard and fast rule.

5. *Is your dream retrieving long-buried memories from the distant past or even from a past life?* What are some of the clues to look for here?

   (a) Dreams of past events usually return to the scenes of our childhood.

   (b) Old persons and people long forgotten are among the main characters.

(c) Dates in history or ancient dwellings are often noted.

(d) The left side of a dream usually connotes the past.

(e) Ancient clothing, unusual costumes, and antique furniture are representative of the past or of a particular life.

6. *Is the dream bringing into focus a pronounced fear you are harboring in order to force you to face it and deal with it effectively?* Many of us repress those things of which we are most afraid. Facing a fear, understanding the basis for its beginning, and then determining to overcome it through specific actions will often bring about a cessation of such recurrent dreams. Dreams of test failures indicate the presence of test anxiety. The solution is to practice relaxation techniques accompanied by proper preparation so the test information is easily retrieved when the fear situation is encountered.

7. *Does your dream reflect a wish fulfillment or secret desire?* Many people lead rich fantasy lives and have desires so secret that they often keep them hidden even from themselves. In sleep, when the ego is no longer on guard and the id is freely able to express its utmost desires, tales of wish fulfillment are often spun. What may appear to be precognitive or guidance dreams may in truth be just a reflection of one's excursion into the somnambulistic realm during which Morpheus bestows upon the traveler his heart's desire. Wish fulfillment is an entertaining way to pass an evening, but a continuing dream pattern of self-indulgence reveals a limited capability for soul growth and self-actualization. One must be honest in analyzing one's talents and shortcomings, for it is only through continuing self-assessment and reevaluation that the desired qualities of the higher self are brought into actuality.

8. *Through the process of dreaming, information is often supplied that can be of great service to others.* An excellent illustration of this can be found in one of Edgar Cayce's interpretations of a dream brought to him by a lady called Frances. In relating the dream Frances recorded the following impressions: "They told me about my sister, that she had committed suicide, or killed herself."[2] Frances and her husband became apprehensive and phoned the sister, who tearfully admitted she had been entertaining such thoughts. Only the timing of the call had prevented her from putting her plan into action. Cayce believed that the dream was actually showing Frances the intent in her sister's mind.

Dreams that contain evidence of telepathic communications between the minds of relatives and friends should be seriously examined. Cayce's source states, "and the entity should keep a record of its dreams. For these are a means, a manner of expression that may be applicable in the experiences of being helpful to others; enabling the entity to warn others as well as self" (2346-1).[3]

9. *Is the dream representative of some local or world event?* Does the dream seem to carry powerful emotional overtones? Are you dreaming of an explosion in which masses of people are injured? Does an assassination of a living world figure occur? Are there natural forces that appear to be out of control as in an earthquake, tornado, or hurricane? Last May I dreamed of a flood several nights in a row. I could make no sense of the dream. On a trip to Connecticut in August, however, we learned from our friends that the lower part of their house had been entirely under water as a result of a flood that had taken place during the early part of June. Inquiries have demonstrated that the major disasters were often foreseen by residents of the area where the occurrence was to take place weeks in advance of the happening.

10. *Does the dream you are about to interpret have to do with health or bodily illness?* Dreams of this nature are easily identified if such subjects as diet, exercise, bodily functions, medicines, diseases, doctor's offices, and hospital settings are the central focus of the drama. Dreams about stopped-up toilets, bathtubs, furnaces, and preparation of food in kitchens fall into this category also. Most dreams about one's car are concerned with bodily illness or health, because you move about in your body the same as you drive in your car. Note the area of the car that is causing the trouble.

11. *Does the dream consist of a message whispered to the dreamer from "an unknown voice"?* This phenomenon is known as clairaudience. It frequently occurs in the period between regaining consciousness and becoming fully aware of your surroundings. A person is much less suspect if such messages are given to him while in the dream state than if he reports receiving directions from voices as he goes about his daily tasks. Many of these messages contain universal truths or precepts. An example of one would be: "Marriage is an agreement in which two people work side by side." If you wake up with sentences in your head, write them down immediately. They are truly gems of wisdom by which to guide your life.

12. *Dreams may be comprised of a mixture of information on separate issues and often even contain nonsensical sections.* One lengthy dream I recorded appeared to have three sensible sections and one nonsensical one. The sensible sections dealt with events surrounding my father's

death. In the middle of the dream I recorded a picture of cigars falling to the ground in a pile. I could not figure out their significance until one week later when my husband and I attended a movie. In one scene soldiers were smoking cigars and several landed in a pile on the ground — the exact picture I had seen in my dream. This may have been truly nonsense as far as that dream interpretation was concerned, or it may have represented the expression "ashes to ashes" regarding my father's impending demise.

13. *Dreams can be interpreted through the symbols and puns that are an integral part of them.* Books containing dream symbols are an essential companion for the procurement of accurate dream interpretations. Two publications that are invaluable are *Dreams: Your Magic Mirror* by Elsie Sechrist and *How to Interpret Your Own Dreams* by Tom Chetwynd. More important to the would-be interpreter, however, are file cards on which notations have been written regarding one's personal symbol associations. Flanked by these two helpmates, sensible meanings can be derived from a jumble of nonsensical symbols in a relatively short period of time.

The recordee will also find amusement in the fact that dream language frequently employs cliches and puns to express the basic messages. For example, the expression "losing your head" can be illustrated in a dream wherein the decapitated dreamer watches his head roll away. A half human, half feathered creature might suggest one's attitude is less than courageous in a particular situation. Therefore, he is *chicken*! Many a chuckle arises in the process of transcribing dreams.

14 *How do you deal with the small percentage of dreams that have no apparent meaning or understandable theme?* The answer is always: *Wait*! Sooner or later another dream or series of them containing a similar idea will be forthcoming, or the future event perceived will occur. When these are recorded, the initial dream will then seem exceedingly clear, and you will wonder how the meaning ever eluded you in the first place. There are two ways to speed up this process.

(a) Request an additional dream for purposes of clarification the following evening.

(b) Review any new information received during daily meditation to determine whether or not it pertains to the uninterpreted dream. Often, while in altered states of consciousness, new insights suddenly appear.

15. *Is it possible to be sure of dream interpretations?* The answer to this question can be found in the book entitled *Edgar Cayce on Dreams* by Dr. Harmon Bro. Dr. Bro feels, "If the function of many dreams is to move the dreamer forward in his total life and growth, then such movement is an important function of interpretation, as well."[4] If the interpretation tends to get the person focusing on important aspects of his life, the interpretation might be a good one after all. Dr. Bro offers three criteria for validating one's dream interpretations:

(a) Several dreams given on the same night should shed helpful light on one another. Successive episodes of the same dream experienced on different nights might expand the basic tenets of the initial dream. If the theme of a variety of dreams shows progression, then one is usually interpreting them correctly.

(b) "A dreamer may validate his interpretations by comparing them with his subjective impressions about the interpretations. A feeling of release from inner panic may signal a sound interpretation, however unpleasant the truth the dreamer must face. . . . new stances in life, may also signal that one has struck upon the essential message of the dream."[5]

(c) According to Harmon Bro, Cayce told his dream students to examine the quality of their lives. "If they were growing, if they were functioning effectively in their rounds of life, the chances were that they were understanding and working with, rather than against, the mainstream of dream contents."[6]

9

Dream Incubation

Cayce's readings were limited to the information and the guidance which an individual could constructively use; it was the same with the dreams.

Harmon Bro, *Edgar Cayce on Dreams*

Do you realize that you have a source of universal knowledge, or an inner guru to which you have access at all times, and that by the mere act of posing specific questions or requesting guidance regarding decisions in your life before retiring, this stream of wisdom can be contacted? Knowledge concerning health and medical treatment, business ventures, politics, new inventions and outlines for books, advice to the lovelorn, ideals for personal improvement, and perhaps even discourses from higher entities on universal laws (consider Jane Robert's *Seth* books) flows through this never-ending stream of consciousness that is made available to us all.

"Fantastic! Amazing!" you say. "How do I proceed to take advantage of such a wellspring of sagacity? This must be some kind of new scientific breakthrough ultimately achieved after years of research by the best minds of modern man. " Wrong! This river of wisdom has been with us since the beginning of time and each of us has the capacity to receive information from it through the dream state or in altered states of consciousness.

How can we best attune ourselves to take advantage of this kind of dreaming? *Through dream incubation*. Mark Thurston describes an "incubated dream" as a dream that either presents a unique solution to a problem or a design on which the dreamer has been working or awakens the dreamer in a state whereby his intuition prompts the desired answer to spring into consciousness. In incubating a dream we must either formulate in our minds a specific question for which we are requesting a response or set forth a clearly defined problem requiring a solution that currently eludes our grasp.

Let us take, for example, the dilemma many young housewives face after raising several children and, as a result, being absent from the job market for a number of years. Beth, as we shall call her, had earned a college degree in business and was employed profitably for four years at a salary of $35,000 before the births of her children. With the youngest one in kindergarten she now desires to return to the labor market and resume her career. However, during the interim period she has become interested in child psychology and is intrigued by the thought of educational counseling. She is not particularly eager to return to her old job, which was rather boring: she had worked entirely with computers and had had little contact with people. The advantages she sees in resuming her old job are that she returns to a high salary as well as job security. She is certain she can be hired again by the company for which she previously worked. In contrast, entering graduate school to complete a master's degree in educational counseling will not only cost her money but require many hours of study, thus reducing the time she can spend with her husband and children. What to do? With a dilemma such as this facing her Beth would be wise to test the dream incubation theory in an attempt to ensure that a future decision regarding her career would be the one most likely to coincide with the ideals and goals by which she has chosen to be guided in her daily life. Let us follow Beth through an eight-step procedure for dream incubation (rules for this outline are based on Mark Thurston's tape entitled *Dream Incubation*).

1. *Set and ideal or living standard by which you can guide your life.* Beth's main concerns in life are the welfare of her husband and children and helping others achieve their maximum potential for growth. If she had to choose two words that would embody these ideals she has selected for her life, they would be *love* and *service*. Therefore, these

are the measures she must use when making crucial decisions in her life that affect both her family and herself.

2. *Clearly define the problem for which you are seeking a solution.* The dilemma with which Beth is confronted is whether she should continue in a financially profitable job where minimal personal growth can take place or pursue a master's degree in educational counseling. The latter would place both a financial and a personal hardship on the family in the immediate future but in the long run contribute to Beth's self-actualization as a person. It would also provide essential services in a field in which she feels confident she can make a significant contribution.
3. *List both the negative and the positive aspects of your decision.* For Beth the negative aspects of continuing in her present career would be:
   - (a) Minimal self-growth.
   - (b) Little contact with people.
   - (c) Business trips away from her family.
   - (d) Working from nine to five daily.

   The positive factors connected to a return to her previous position are:
   - (a) A high salary.
   - (b) Pleasant physical working conditions.
   - (c) A supervisor who is positively oriented toward her.
   - (d) An excellent chance for promotion.

   Negative considerations for pursuing a higher educational degree are:
   - (a) Financial loss of her future salary in business.
   - (b) Additional expense of the educational program.
   - (c) Long hours of study that deprive her of the company of her family.
   - (d) Hiring a maid to help with the running of the household.

   Positive outcomes resulting upon completion of a degree in educational counseling are:
   - (a) Continued growth and self-actualization.
   - (b) Intellectual stimulation derived from counselors who have similar life orientation and goals.
   - (c) Provision of services to persons who, without this counseling, might never realize their maximum potential.

4. *Measure your tentative decision against the ideals you have set to guide your life.* After lengthy discussions with her husband and many hours of deliberation Beth decides to attend graduate school. The ideals of love and service appear to be consistent with the basic reasons for enrolling in graduate school and becoming an educational counselor. She therefore determines to make the necessary arrangements if she get a positive response from her dream incubation experiment.
5. *Request a dream that will provide you with feedback regarding your tentative decision. Attune yourself through prayer and meditation to your higher self or superconscious.* Before retiring Beth might "center herself" through a short period of meditation. As she drifts into slumber, the question foremost in her mind should be "Would it be best for me to embark on a new path in educational counseling or resume my old career?"
6. *Upon awakening write down* all *dreams even those that appear to have nothing to do with the question. Include any fragment of any idea.* The dream received may:

   (a) Give you a positive response or a precognitive dream, in which case it would be prudent to begin plans to implement your tentative decision.

   (b) Redefine the problem. If this occurs, you have not looked at all important aspects connected with the situation and should do so immediately.

   (c) Indicate you have made the wrong decision and therefore pursuit of this course would not be in your best interest.

   (d) Offer an alternative solution. It may astonish you that you have never thought of this particular outcome before.

   (e) Supply the dreamer with a partial solution. When your question is only half answered, information concerning the remainder of the solution should be requested on succeeding evenings.

   Beth awakens the following morning with this dream in mind. Her former boss comes into the computer room where she has been busily engaged in work. He praises her past performances and says he has a new position in mind for her. He is taking her to introduce her to her new job and coworkers when the dream ends. Based on this dream Beth surmises she probably would be better off returning to her computer position. (Keep in mind point e.) On the ensuing night, however, the dream continues. Her boss leads her into another office where she meets the lady who will supervise her new position. Much to her surprise it is Mrs. Hunt, the lady who has assisted her in planning her graduate degree program at the university for the past several weeks. Even more surprising is the appearance of a small boy from whom she has been running away in many of her dreams for the past several months. He says, "I am so glad you finally stopped running from me. I've been waiting for you to help me all this time." He runs up and hugs her. She feels herself responding to him.

7. *Measure again if the guidance and information received in your dreams meets the criteria of your tentative decision with relation to your ideals.* This would appear to be the case with Beth's two consecutive dreams. *Service* is unmistakably an element in the student's request of educational assistance. *Love* is symbolized by her affectionate response to the hug.

8. *Take positive action in applying the dreams you intuitively know to be direct positive responses to your requests.* Beth enrolls in the university at four P.M. the same day of the dream.

The dream incubation process can be used in making many decisions that affect your life as well as the lives of people closest to you. When one considers just how much our lives are closely knitted to those around us, it would seem almost mandatory to consult with the source of universal knowledge for confirmation and assurance that we are proceeding on the proper course set by the life pattern that is intricately woven into the fabric of our own being.

10

Types of Dreams

Dreams are of prime importance for the meeting of the ultimate creative force of a person with that other force which ever seeks to help him.

Harmon Bro, *Edgar Cayce on Dreams*

During the past three years I have recorded, interpreted, reviewed, and put into practice approximately 5000 dreams. This recording and interpreting demanded an intensive study requiring many hours of careful deliberation and soul searching before I intuitively felt that I had unraveled the hidden messages so skillfully spun into the cobweb of each and every dream. A side benefit that resulted from this continuous scrutiny was the emergence of a framework or classification within which the majority of dreams could be categorized. Again and again I would sense upon concluding its interpretation that dream 1 of the previous evening fit into the health and healing category, dream 4 carried with it an air of clairvoyance, and dream 5 was a message dream. As time passed, I began to write notations beside each title so that, when I reviewed it at a later date, I could note the "dream shorthand" I had devised, which would quickly remind me of the exact class of dream I had felt it belonged to at the date of interpretation.

According to my classification system almost all dreams I have received can be typed under one of 12 reference titles. This is not meant to be a rigid categorization to which all dream students should adhere but rather a general guide which enables the interpreter to create some semblance of order out of the entanglement, confusion, and frequent overlapping of themes that accompany the studious pursuit of this subject. The 12 basic classifications which presented themselves repeatedly were as follows:

1. Dreams of Healing and Physical Health.
2. Guidance and Creative Dreams for the Self and Others.
3. Business Dreams.
4. Telepathic Dreams.
5. Clairvoyant Dreams.
6. Precognitive and Retrocognitive Dreams.
7. Dreams of Local and World Events.
8. Dreams of Death and the Departed.
9. Past Life Dreams.
10. Lucid Dreaming.
11. Message Dreams.
12. Visionary Dreaming.

To simplify this method of classification even further it is my intention to offer a concise definition for each particular type of dream category and, under that category, to present a variety of vividly recalled dreams the elements of which exemplify the exact nature of dreams that are and should be included in such a classification.

1. Dreams of Healing and Physical Health

Dreams of this nature almost always identify the type of problem afflicting the patient, the area of the body affected, the reasons for the illness, and perhaps even the treatment to rid oneself of the disease. Cayce saw the mind and body as a single unit. To quote Harmon Bro, "the mind is cradled snugly within the body, and deeply affected by the endocrine gland function, as well as indirectly affected by diet, exercise, eliminations, posture and other considerations."[1] This is truly a realistic view shared by many physicians today. It therefore follows that a "dis-ease" of the mind will most assuredly, after a period of time, make its presence known through a physical illness if the original "dis-ease" remains unresolved. If this premise is correct, then dreams portraying future illnesses and disorders of the mind should be carefully reviewed in order to avoid serious health problems if at all possible. If the disease already exists, search for clues for its minimization as well as specified healing suggestions. Dreams containing diet, exercise, cars in need of repair, poor plumbing, houses on fire or damaged (note the room), hospitals, drugstores, and medical treatment invariably have to do with bodily health.

Several excellent examples of dreams revolving around physical health and healing are:

MY CYST

(August 3, 1981)

I am in my own house and I see a small fire in the basement. It is an oil burner and has red flames shooting out from it. I panic but realize it is not serious. I think I can put out the fire by applying hot oil to it and regulating the amount.

This first dream describes a method of healing the cyst, which was scheduled for surgical removal through the application of the castor oil pack. This dream was discussed in depth in Chapter 1.

THE SECOND CYST

(June 28, 1982)

A laboratory test has been done for me in another state. They have run tests and the physician has the results. I have an infection around a cyst and it needs treatment. The nurse asks me if I want an examination. I tell her I am too far away to come. She tells me that they will send me the proper diagnosis and prescription.

SHRINKING THE CYST

(July 25, 1982)

A lady has a cyst. An oriental lady says it can be shrunk and the pus drained out.

AN APPOINTMENT WITH GENIE

(July 25, 1982)

I see the name Genie written on an appointment calendar among other names.

DR. HALLER'S ELECTRICAL MACHINE

(August 5, 1982)

I stop by an old house to be treated by a chiropractor. She uses an electrical machine in her treatments.

ACCEPTING ILLNESS

(November 21, 1982)

I feel glad to be rid of my cysts. A physician discusses my case with me saying "You accepted illness."

These were a series of dreams recorded over a five-month period involving the prescribed treatment and subsequent healing of a second cyst. On June 28, 1982, I was warned of the possibility of a second cyst but ignored the offer of assistance until the cyst became a reality. By July 25, 1982, I was eagerly seeking advice for its removal. Chiropractic treatments and nutritional therapy for a period of several months accomplished this end as depicted through my dreams. At the end of the period I was told that I would not have been subject to these cysts had I myself not *accepted* them.

DAD'S ANOREXIA NERVOSA

(December 26, 1981)

I see a physician and his assistant. They have subdued a patient and are taking care of him on a bed. I see two little waif girls near Lincoln School. When I consult with the doctor, he says my Dad has anorexia nervosa.

This dream occurred when my dad visited me one year before he died. It does show how far in advance I was being prepared for the gravity of his illness.

REFLEXOLOGY HEALING

(May 14, 1982)

In reflexology when you pull each toe and manipulate the entire foot, the process is reflected simultaneously and healthfully in the whole being.

The dream presents the dynamics involved in reflexology when used as a healing tool. I have since used reflexology on my entire family for a variety of physical problems with highly beneficial results.

2. Guidance and Creative Dreams for the Self and Others

These types of dreams suggest that all subconscious minds are in contact with one another. If this is true, then a sincere attitude of caring and genuine concern for one's family, friends, and acquaintances should enable the receptive dreamer to receive information and guidance to be used to promote the general welfare of all such persons. Reading 2419-1 of the Cayce material states, "Make practical all such dreams in the material experiences with others. And know that if they do not produce creative influences and better association in thy home, in thy relationships with thy fellow men, something is wrong with same!"[2]

The following dreams were presented to others in an attempt to comply with the directive given by Cayce:

ATTENDANCE AT UNIVERSITY OF RICHMOND LAW SCHOOL

(March 19, 1982)

We are driving to Richmond and go by way of Sanston. I know this place because my cousin lived here while he attended the University of Richmond Law School. He felt it was an outstanding institution. The road is sandy. I am trying to direct the car.

My son had applied to both the University of Richmond Law School and William and Mary in the spring of 1982. I had a strong preference for William and Mary because this was my institution of higher learning. The advice given to me was "Stop directing the situation. The University of Richmond is a fine school for Jimmy." He eventually became a first-year law student there for the 1982-83 session.

NINA'S OPERATION

(September 8, 1981)

I see a small throat and jaw. I hear the words, "The operation will be soon." I see Amelie put her hand up to her left breast.

The events spoken of in this dream were of both a retrocognitive and precognitive nature. Upon calling my friend, Amelie, in Louisiana, I learned her youngest daughter Nina had just had a tonsillectomy due to complications resulting several weeks before. In late October of 1981 Amelie wrote me that she had just undergone minor breast surgery.

The following two dreams were offered to me in an effort to guide me toward a more accepting attitude of my abilities during the early phase of my psychic development.

THE UNATTRACTIVE/ATTRACTIVE PSYCHIC

(March 6, 1982)

There is a lady who gives readings and helps people get rid of bad dreams. She is strange-looking. Her face is painted and her hair is braided in blue circles. She counsels a lady who thinks she has lost her family in a car accident. "It was only a bad dream," she tells her. As I look at this counselor, she is transformed into a lovely woman with long golden hair. She has an assistant who is older than she is.

THE CLASSROOM BY THE RIVER

(April 21, 1983)

I am doing problems in mathematics on yellow ruled paper. I circle the ones that are right. There is a river flowing from left to right in front of me. The side of the classroom has no wall. There is a tree beside the river.

"The Unattractive/Attractive Psychic" charges me to change my self-concept; "The Classroom by the River" is indicative of the stream of consciousness that flows through me during dreaming or doing a psychic reading.

3. Business Dreams

Dreams can have practical value in business affairs. Many of the dreams Cayce interpreted contained advice for profitable business management. Some even contained tips for buying and selling stock to realize substantial profits. The maxims that held true in the crash of the stock market in 1929 are still in force today. These are true for big and small business ventures alike. Bro explains Cayce's view: "Souls are not judged by absolute standards. . . . They are judged by their fidelity to their own ideals, rather than their own understanding. They are not judged by their failures so much as by their willingness to get up and try again."[3] A comparison of a dream recalled by a business friend of Cayce's in July of 1929 and one of my own recorded on February 5, 1982, is supportive of the guidance available on request if faith exists in one's ideals and a willingness to continue in the face of adversity.

STOCK TIPS

Voice: "Hold only that which you are able to pay for outright. Saw Fleischman 82,83,82. Big bank failure which precipitated a good deal of trouble on the market. Saw Western Union at 160."[4]

The stock broker was assured by Cayce that he was receiving correct promptings to defend himself against the coming stock market crash and need only continue to act in "simplicity of faith."

In my dream of February 5, 1982, I appear to have been the recipient of similar advice. (This time of year our testing schedule is not quite as full as usual.)

INCREASED BUSINESS BY MARCH 1

(February 5, 1982)

I am driving down Route 1 toward the Landmark Inn. Suddenly there appears to be a great increase in traffic coming in my direction.

4. Telepathic Dreams and Out of Body Experiences

Night after night the slumbering mind of one individual appears to transmit basic information concerning important issues around which his life revolves at the present time. The mind of the recipient may also be an active participant in this process reaching out mentally to retrieve such information. The majority of such mind-to-mind communications is the direct result of close emotional ties that bond the dreamers together.

My friend Elizabeth and I keep in touch by writing letters every two to three weeks, and though she resided in Charlotte, North Carolina, we seemed to be in touch telepathically also. On the evening of January 26, 1983, she recorded a very confusing dream and wrote to me to see if I could explain it to her.

THE NEW YORK TRIP

(January 26, 1982)

John and I have come to visit you. I hug Robin and notice she has heavy makeup on which has gotten on my clothes. After greeting you we proceed to fly in a black helicopter to a place near New York. There is some sort of gathering there of friends and neighbors. All seem glad to see old acquaintances.

The same night I dreamed Elizabeth and John had come to comfort me. This was the night of my father's death and the following day we began a sad trip to New Jersey for the funeral. In the course of five days I saw many relatives and old friends with whom I had not come in contact for 20 years or so.

"ARE DREAM TELEPATHY"

(June 23, 1982)

Robin and I are going down a road and several boys throw snowballs at us. One almost hits me. Robin and I walk on.

During an ARE conference dream telepathy experiments were conducted for several nights. The dream occurred on the second night of the experiment. Interestingly enough one of the four pictures chosen for the telepathic experiment, although not the one transmitted, was of schoolboys throwing snowballs at girls.

An out-of-body experience is just what the words imply. Note how the phenomenon works in a dream entitled "The ARE Meditation Room."

THE ARE MEDITATION ROOM

(November 9, 1981)

I walk upstairs in the ARE library building and see a prayer room with kneeling benches. There are unusual windows in this room. There also is a meeting room on this floor. Purple appears to surround this room.

This is a precise description of the ARE Meditation Room although I had never seen it until after the dream occurred.

5. Clairvoyant Dreams

Clairvoyance is described in Webster's dictionary as "clear or acute perception of what is not ordinarily discernible." It is derived from French meaning "clear vision." According to this definition the clairvoyant dream is one in which the person dreaming is cognizant of events that are happening almost simultaneously even though he may be hundreds of miles away. This should be distinguished from retrocognition and precognition in that these terms refer to past occurrences and futuristic trends.

Several clairvoyant dreams were selected as illustrations of this phenomenon. The events or objects were observed almost within the same time span they became part of reality.

ARLENE'S VICTORIAN FLOWERS

(February 4, 1982)

I am waiting in the car for Arlene to finish her business. She has made ornaments. I look at one of them. It is in a silver vase with lace, ribbon, and red rosebuds. She seems to be trying to sell them.

I perceived the Victorian flower bouquets my sister was to market later about the time she began to design them.

THE TRIP TO REDISH KNOB
(October 16, 1981)

I am riding in a car. There is an old brick factory on the left. There seem to be several old wooden structures I visit. The floors are blue tile. This is high up.

This describes a trip Jimmy took with two fraternity brothers when my husband and I drove up to see him at James Madison University on October 16, 1981.

6. Precognition and Retrocognition

Precognition refers to a knowing or perceiving of the future beforehand. Retrocognition is a review of previously unknown events. *How are these perceptions possible?* The answer lies in the oneness of all forces, that is, all life is interrelated. The theory presupposes that "the universe is made up of one essential energy which can express itself in many ways."[5] If we wish for a better understanding of the psychic aspects of dreaming, this theory of oneness needs to be studied more in depth. Mark Thurston, in *How to Interpret Your Dreams,* lists three perspectives of oneness:

1. "*The Oneness of All Force:* Any expression of energy can be transformed to another expression which is more in keeping with our ideals."[6] We can change that which is distasteful to us and use it in more positive oneness.
2. "*The Oneness of All Minds:* The mental structure of each individual is so created that there is a natural avenue for psychic communication."[7] It is therefore natural for us to communicate telepathically.
3. *The Oneness of Body, Mind, and Soul:* This principle suggests that dreams are best interpreted with the Triad (body, mind, and soul) viewed holistically.

One final question might be posed regarding psychic ability in dreams. How does one receive the best psychic information?

The Cayce readings state unequivocally: "It is in the individual himself through an attunement to the superconscious."[8]

A TRELLIS LUNCH
(September 29, 1981)

I'm at the Trellis eating lunch with Phyllis Belden and another lady whose face I cannot see. The waitress asks me if I want tea. I order skimmed milk. I cannot decide whether to order a salad or a sandwich. I finally order a salad. There is so much noise I can't hear. Phyllis is wearing a bright red suit.

This was dreamed September 29, 1981, and brought into reality February 5, 1982. I had not seen Phyllis for two years before that.

SNOWSTORM IN WEST VIRGINIA
(November 19, 1981)

One side of the mountain on the way to West Virginia is clear. When we get to the other side, it begins to snow. The roads become icy and there is two to three inches of snow. We drive cautiously.

This was dreamed on November 19, 1981, and became an actuality on November 20.

THE ARE PSYCHIC MEETING
(March 15, 1982)

I am at a Psychic Development Meeting sponsored by ARE. A psychic, Albert Bowes, is introduced. He teaches us how to look in a small book for particular sentences. There is a red sweater on the wall to my left.

The events unfolded exactly as foreseen on April 17, 1982, except for the red sweater on the wall to my left, which turned out to be a red decoration below a light fixture.

The week of the ARE Healing Conference in September of 1982 necessitated five trips between Williamsburg and Virginia Beach. The following dream forewarned me to drive with care:

THE ASPEN SKIDS

(September 22, 1982)

I am driving the Aspen and notice the tires skidding. I must take care when I drive.

I followed the advice given and just missed hitting a truck by slamming on the brakes quickly because I had been alerted to the forthcoming danger beforehand. The date was September 24, 1982.

THE HOUSEBOAT SINKS

(October 12, 1982)

The houseboat is submerged in Deep Creek because of high tides. The roof has blown off. Jim begins to repair it.

Much to our chagrin, our houseboat filled with water during a late November storm in 1982 and sank to the bottom of Jamestown Yacht Basin. Its sinking cost my husband Jim untold labor to restore it to prime condition again.

7. Dreams of Local and World Events

"Thoughts are things" and "Mind is the builder." These statements were constantly reiterated in all of the Cayce Readings. If these premises are true, then groups of thoughts put together should begin to form our own unique reality. Taking this concept one step further, since each of us is a member of society, our own individual thought patterns should then form a composite that comprises the group consciousness of society based on the principles of interrelatedness of minds and oneness of force previously discussed in the precognition and recognition section. Society could therefore be changed by the reshaping of one's life, becoming involved in the activities of home, work, church, and community using these precepts developed on a national and worldwide scale. Therefore, anyone responsibly concerned in a movement for social change, social service, or social justice might well seek nightly guidance in dreams.

Dreams such as these are frequently charged with emotions. The first example concerns a dream Cayce had one year before his hospital opened at Virginia Beach.

THE CLOSING OF THE HOSPITAL

Was going over pictures of various things of Virginia Beach regarding the Hospital. Saw two trains; one was the champion, called the Pankhurst ________________.[9]

This dream dealt with a future crisis when the "pictures" or views of the board members on how the hospital should be run would greatly differ and each would champion his own principles. "The hospital closed four years later in a climate of acrimony, where board members challenged each other's living up to principles, and challenged Cayce."[10]

One of my own dreams is an excellent illustration of how one's mind works in participation in world events and changes.

THE ASSASSINATION

(October 5, 1981)

They were building houses on Seminary Avenue. They had only begun to put up the frames. One man is mad because he says the houses in the center of the road look like cracker boxes. He and other rowdy persons get into a green army truck and drive around hitting things. Then they jump out and shoot. The glass around one man shatters into thousands of pieces. The sheriff steps in and captures them. I see the man who was building those houses has now built himself a house at the end of Seminary Avenue near St. George Avenue and is at peace.

This was recorded 6:30 A.M. on October 5, 1981 — *the day of Anwar Sadat's assassination.*

8. Dreams of Death and the Departed

Dreams of death can be recognized by the presence of items such as a hearse, black clothing, the ace of spades, a spray of flowers, a stopped clock, a wide river, or attendance at a funeral.

Dreams of your own death and the demise of your friends or loved ones should usually not be interpreted as literal. Dreams of this sort usually symbolize the death of long-held ideas and attitudes accompanied by the awaking of new realizations and changes in the direction and advancement of one's soul. Dreams of death can also serve as warning dreams.

When going into trance on one occasion, Cayce felt he had encountered death — as a personality. He remarked, "You are not as ordinarily pictured, with the black mask or hood, or as a skeleton, or like Father Time with a sickle. Instead, you are fair, rosy-cheeked, robust, and have a pair of shears or scissors.

"He replied, Yes. Death is not what many seem to think. It is not the horrible thing that is so often pictured. Just a change. Just a visit. The shears or scissors are indeed the most representative implements to man of life and death. They indeed unite by dividing, and divide by uniting."[11]

According to comments made by Harmon Bro in *Edgar Cayce on Dreams*, dreams of the living dead come when:

1. The dreamer is ready to experience such contact without fear.
2. A person gives credence to the message communicated from the departed one and uses it properly.
3. "one is ready for dreams of the dead when he *soundly loves* and serves the living."[12] These types of dreams are almost always for personal reasons or personal growth or contain information or a specific act that would be of service to another human being.
4. The nocturnal traveler is as eager to give aid to the discarnate as receive it.
5. Personal griefs and guilts have been worked through and the individual has forgiven himself as well as the departed for past sins and imagined wrongdoings.
6. When one's own life is drawing to a natural close and he has begun a time of preparation for rebirth into a new dimension.

The dreams I received between the period of December 31, 1982, and January 26, 1983, were in preparation for my father's death. On December 31 I viewed the following drama:

THREE GIFTS

(December 31, 1982)

A secret patient is being smuggled into the hospital. I have makeup hidden in the bedsheets for the patient. I am a nurse in the hospital. A figure wearing a hood comes into the room and tells us it is 9:30. Then, the Head Physician enters and tells the patient to stay in bed and rest. He looks like a physician we know who is a specialist in otolaryngology. We walk down the hall away from the patient and he tells me he has three gifts for me. The first is a lifeless doll that looks like a Christmas tree ornament. The second is a wafer in the shape of a Christmas tree and the third is a cord that is tied to Life Energy which I cannot see but feel. He says I will need them in the future.

The dream occurred five days before my father entered the hospital for the last time. The time 9:30 means the end is drawing near. The gifts show the departure of this spirit accompanied by the promise of eternal life.

SURVIVAL

(January 26, 1983)

A father has taken his two children out boating and is lifting them into the water to learn to swim by themselves. They cling to the rocks. They know they have to learn to swim on their own if they are to survive.

A feeling of abandonment pervades this dream, but the necessity of surviving and ultimately leading a productive life in spite of the loss of one's parents is the primary theme.

DAD'S MARRIAGE

(January 26, 1983)

Dad is getting married again and my sister and I are bridesmaids. I see I am carrying a bouquet of beautiful flowers and I am wearing a cross. Dad is not able to stand up for the wedding. I see a small dark-haired lady about 25 years old at the altar. Dad says he wishes he could go away with her but this is a "frozen state" and I am not permitted to go. I say, "Go away with her" and wave goodbye. I think one of the nuns at Walsingham Academy has read me this bedtime story as I wake up.

This dream was received the morning of January 26, 1983. My father passed away at 11:30 that morning. I truly believe at the time of Dad's death my mother was there to assist in the transition. The petite dark-haired lady in the wedding looked amazingly like my mother in pictures I had seen of her at 25. I had no inkling that my father's demise was imminent.

Three of the most dramatic and spiritually inspiring dreams of the departed Jim and I have been privileged to receive were recorded during trips involving ARE business. The theme of each was the certitude of life after death. The message was brought to us by loved ones. The symbol of eternal life was the same in all three dreams. The significance of traveling on spiritual business out of Virginia carried the implication of "spiritually being in another state."

The first of the series occurred in California the night before Jim and I were to visit my sister in San Francisco. It was the second time I had seen her after my father's death. The drama unfolded thus:

DAD'S PERSONIFICATION OF ETERNAL LIFE

I have returned to my home in New Jersey and open my bedroom door. My mind is troubled because it is near Christmas and I haven't gotten my family's presents yet. As I open my bedroom door, I stop short in a state of shock. My father is sitting on top of my bureau. I can hardly believe he is alive and ask him if he is really there. He says, "Of course I am." He comes over to me and shakes my hand. His flesh is as solid as mine. He says, "I came to tell you not to worry about Christmas. It is more than giving presents. Christmas is about the Christ Spirit and all should center their thoughts on him."

The second and third dreams were shared by Jim and myself on March 30, 1984, after a visit to Cassadaga. Cassadaga is a spiritual camp 30 miles from Orlando, Florida. Forty or more psychics and mediums reside there and provide people with psychic or mediumistic readings. On Sunday at 2:30 we read that an All Message Service was scheduled in the camp auditorium. There persons in attendance might receive messages from loved ones who had passed over. The idea of attending was an intriguing one but, physically impossible, as Jim had to drive to Atlanta Sunday afternoon for a business appointment. We voiced our disappointment over this conflict before retiring and then promptly fell asleep. The dreams envisioned by us revolved around Bill Polis, the former dean of students at Christopher Newport College and a classmate of Jim's for three years at Colgate Rochester Divinity School in Rochester, New York. In 1978 at the age of 43 Bill died of a heart attack. Neither of us had mentioned him for months, so it was impossible for one of us to have influenced the other's thinking and triggered the dreams. The informational themes of the dreams complement each other.

BILL'S INSPIRATIONAL MESSAGE (JIM'S DREAM)

(March 30, 1984)

I am at a checkout *counter and look toward the door to see Bill Polis standing on a platform. My mouth gapes as I realize he is vibrantly alive. I turn to the customers behind me and ask if they see Bill standing there. As I turn back, Bill stands in front of me and* grips my hand tightly.

THE MESSAGE OF THE CASSADAGA MEDIUM (JOAN'S DREAM)

(March 30, 1984)

Jim and I are visiting a friend in the hospital. He doesn't seem to be seriously ill and kisses his family goodbye saying he will see them tomorrow. Then, as we leave, to our utter amazement, he dies. [This is exactly what happened to Bill.]

Now, we are attending an All Message Service at Cassadaga. The man next to me urges me to watch what the medium does. The medium, dressed in a long white robe, dips her hand in a container with some dirt from our friend's grave and writes the word NO on the wall.

Note the symbols that reappear in all three dreams. In each case the departed person or the medium in contact with the departed one stands *above* the dreamer representing a higher level of vibration. The idea symbolized by the solidarity of the grasp is "I have substance!"

The resurrectional message channeled through the Cassadaga medium should strike a joyous and resonant chord in the very depths of each and every soul: "*The grave is no obstacle (wall) to life eternal.*"

9. Past Lives Dreams

Have you ever found yourself while dreaming in an ancient dwelling garbed in clothing that appears to be in keeping with the dress of that period? Other people wear dated apparel also. An air of antiquity pervades the entire scene. Is this a memory of a movie you have viewed at one time, is it characters from the plot of a long-forgotten novel, or is it perchance a recollection of a past life theme from your distant past reaching far back in time to revive a long forgotten lesson or emphasize a talent or ability to be used during one's current lifetime? In *Edgar Cayce on Dreams* Bro states Cayce's philosophy in these terms: "one of the 'dead' who will live . . . is the dreamer himself. In dreams he may meet himself as he has been in other lives."[13]

The dream may take place exactly as it happened in ancient times, or the dreamer may find himself in a modern-day setting but the past theme will be duplicated. Is it truly important to distinguish between past life dreams as opposed to those that revolve around current situations? Cayce replied in the negative. The important aspects of dreaming are to better understand the self, conquer undesirable character traits, use God given talents and abilities to their fullest and so live by chosen ideals that one's daily existence will truly provide inspiration for the spiritual growth of multitudes.

"All serious dreams may be read as embodying some degree of past life themes. The life of the soul is woven of these many threads, however modern the present design."[14] *Decisive actions taken in response to the theme of the dream whether past or present should be the prime focus of all dreaming.*

The following dreams are presented in order to illustrate what the dream student might look for when trying to identify past life dreams.

THE OLD MONASTERY

(April 10, 1982)

I am in an old monastery with the name St. Mary's Church connected to it. It is made of white stone and I see tall white towers. The inhabitants are Catholic priests and nuns. I walk down many stone corridors. I know I have been there before as I know my way around. As I turn a corner, I see statues of musicians on the left. In the basement there are vaults containing the remains of priests of bygone days. This place is in a hilly section of France.

JIM'S OLD MONASTERY DREAM
(May 5, 1982)

I have just been in a meeting of college presidents. A friend and I walk across a field and up a hill into an old building. There are marble statues and long, winding corridors in the lower portion.

These twin dreams are of extreme interest to me because I had never described the interior of the old French monastery I had so often "visited" to my husband; yet in his dream the lower level of the monastery was an exact replication of the building I had envisioned.

A SOUTH CAROLINA PLANTATION
(November 5, 1981)

Jim, Robin, and I have gone on a trip to South Carolina. We are staying with an older lady who sits on the porch. As we drive by in our car, I see a beautiful white-pillared house on the left before a lake. It has Spanish moss on the trees. I feel I have been here before and am returning again.

I seem to have a special attachment to the south but especially to Williamsburg, Virginia. Does this stem from several past existences here?

One of the basic reincarnational postulates I have encountered time after time during my search to crystallize my own personal philosophy regarding this issue is the statement that husbands, wives, fathers, mothers, sisters, brothers, and close friends often reincarnate together. This may be to learn lessons, right past wrongs, engage in actualizing common goals, or just to enjoy each other's company once again.

Such may be the case with our neighbors and dear friends the Hunt family. Bob currently serves as associate director of placement at the College of William and Mary and has always worked in college administration, sharing this interest with my husband. Sylvia is accomplished in handicrafts, quilting, and fine embroidery. Many of her creations adorn our tables and walls. The children, Stacy and Roger, have been inseparable friends with my own two youngsters since the age of two.

It is of extreme interest to me that when one enters the Hunt residence, it is as if he is transported into the eighteenth century. The furnishings and decor throughout unmistakably capture the aura of the period. By far, the most impressive piece of evidence suggestive of reincarnational ties during the colonial period occurs every Christmas. Bob and Sylvia don colonial costumes and entertain visitors and hometown folk by performing popular dances of that era at Colonial Williamsburg's Groaning Board. My family and I have attended this function for years, and when I see Jimmy and Robin kicking up their heels in a fast-stepping Virginia reel with Sylvia and Bob, it is as if we are again re-creating and reveling in long-forgotten joys from a distant past.

A dream I had concerning Sylvia and her handicraft is reminiscent of those bygone days.

SYLVIA'S COLONIAL HANDICRAFT TALENTS

(January 4, 1984)

I am wearing a long skirt and arrive at Sylvia's house. I open the door and observe her completing a quilt that she has been working on for months. On the table beside her are hand-embroidered pillows and dresses that she has been working on periodically. I gaze at her in astonishment and see her dressed in a beautiful crimson gown of the eighteenth century. She wears a small white cap on her head with long auburn curls peeking out from beneath it.

A psychic reading given us in 1983 tended to confirm the validity of reincarnational ties between our two families.

REINCARNATION LESSONS

(October 23, 1982)

Someone tells me the key to many situations can be traced to reincarnation. There is a book about France, about the colonial period and about another life, but the colonial period is the most important. If I can find these books, I will have most of the answers. I begin a search.

THE BROADWAY DRAMA

(October 23, 1982)

There is a broadway play with Vanessa Redgrave. The play concerns how one person tries to deal with the philosophical questions of life. It is entitled "How Reincarnation Can Explain the Incidents and Problems of Life." There will be a short 10-minute lecture afterward to review the important lessons.

The theory of reincarnation is an intriguing one. I have dreamed so frequently of the ancient monastery in France and a colonial life in eighteenth-century Virginia that I have come to believe there may be some past life connections with these two places because of the deep ties to them that seem to exist within me.

10. Lucid Dreaming

Lucid dreaming is a conscious awareness that one is dreaming while events in the dream are still occurring. Incidents of lucid dreaming are relatively rare, but when we do "awaken" in the dream state and realize we are still dreaming, we have a unique opportunity. We should "respond optimally to the dream events and symbols, thereby gaining the maximum understanding available."[15] Since the events in the dream are generally determined by the attitudes, emotions, and understandings of the dreamer, "we should work with altering our *responses* in the dream to the characters and events around us. With this newfound objectivity we can use the will to select the most loving, constructive action to what is going on."[16]

For dream students who desire to do in-depth research on lucid dreaming and the techniques employed I recommend Scott Sparrow's book *Lucid Dreaming*, available from the ARE bookstore.

This is one of the lucid dreams brought to Edgar Cayce:

Dreamed that I was exercising in Kansas City. Walking up and down beside train taking me from Los Angeles to Chicago. I realized that I had left my overcoat in station and started for it when the thought came to me that the train might start. As I stood there undecided, the train started rapidly, and I started running for vestibule. I couldn't make headway (as is customary in dreams) and I seemed to say to myself, this is only a dream as I can't run. With the thought I was released and ran easily and caught the train (195-51).[17]

Although I am not ordinarily a lucid dreamer, there is one particular dream that seems to have been given to me again and again.

OVERCOMING FEAR OF FLYING
(Various times 1981-1984)

I feel very buoyant. Upon opening my eyes I realize I am flying high above the earth with the twinkling lights of towns far below. Immediately, I recall how deathly afraid I am of flying in airplanes. Then the realization comes that I am dreaming and in complete control of the situation. I soar higher and higher toward the stars.

For the past 20 years my husband has had to almost physically force me to get on planes. I can remember taking a four-day train trip to Las Vegas rather than endure a four-hour plane flight. With the increasing recurrence of this lucid dream my fear of flying has diminished to the point where I have begun to relish air travel. On our recent trip to Florida I even fell asleep on the plane. Now that's progress!

11. Message Dreams

Message dreams at times come to the dreamer to communicate inspirational thoughts and maxims regarding universal laws and truths. On other occasions these messages contain *verbal* instructions specifying how to handle life-threatening situations that have kept the individual under constant duress. Still other directives are issued that provide advice for realizing the maximum benefits and progress based on one's unique talents and abilities. For whatever reasons these gems of wisdom are given, the method is always the same: *clairaudience*. It is as if a voice speaks to the dreamer in a crystal clear fashion and upon awakening the recipient immediately recalls verbatim what has been transmitted. The tonal quality may be extremely loud and commanding, or the whisper may be barely audible, *but there is never any question regarding the content of the message.* And, if the journalist internalizes the essence of the messages, tremendous rewards are often realized.

Listed below are examples of the type of messages that have been described:

MA PAROLE

(August 31, 1981)

A voice says, "Ma Parole." I do not respond. The voice booms, "Ma Parole." I quickly jump out of bed. ["Ma Parole" means "my word" in French.]

ONE'S TREASURE (Given in French)

December 11, 1981

Your treasure of gold lies where you spread your heart around.

BALANCE AND HARMONY

(August 4, 1982)

Be willing to be supportive of each other while developing one's own abilities. This will result in balance and harmony.

HEART MESSAGE

(December 27, 1982)

Wear your heart on your head.

WISE DECISION

(February 3, 1983)

A wise one makes decisions and does not down them.

When my sister was uncertain whether or not she should market her handmade Victorian rose bouquets, she posed a question concerning the issue before going to sleep. She was startled by a loud voice chastising her in the dead of night with the message "Why shouldn't you use all your God-given abilities!" She did and now runs a thriving enterprise.

An in-depth presentation of messages is presented in the final chapter of this book.

12. Visionary Dreaming

Through the superconscious, visions, experiences, and dreams are received that provide us with a personal knowledge of God and an understanding of his laws, the true meaning of life, and the nature of our relationship with the Almighty. These do not come with the sound of blaring trumpets nor the crashing of cymbals but are experienced as the still small voice that speaks within. Afterward, there is intense intuitive awareness of the actual contact and a feeling of transcendence and inspiration that remains with us indefinitely.

These dreams do not always revolve around God as the central figure but may focus on a religious figure, a master teacher, a celestial being, or even Jesus of Nazareth himself. Some dreams contain essays on how universal laws work, the function of prayer, what causes illness, how healing occurs, and the nature of love. *Of special significance is the visionary dream that reveals the basic reason for our own personal existence.* Each soul has elected to return to the Schoolhouse Earth for a chosen purpose. If we are able to discover our raison d'etre through lessons and guidance imparted to us in the dream state, and our responses to those promptings are creative and inspired, we can then be assured that each day will be filled with joie de vivre that originates from the satisfaction of knowing we are accepting the tasks that our Creator intended.

The following four dreams are presented as examples of visionary dreams that are instructional:

THE HEALER'S TEMPLE
(October 1, 1981)

Jim and I are on a trip to a foreign land. We are going up a narrow road on which cars have to come by the corner of a building to travel on down the road. There are so many cars coming down the hill we have to park our car and walk. We climb the steps to an old temple which looks to be an Indian or Oriental design. Inside we see various displays. A green William and Mary cup full of diamonds spills on the rug. The tall man beckons me to follow him. He takes me to a hospital room and speaks of healing.

This is one of the most inspirational dreams I have ever received. Why? *It is this place to which I am inexplicably drawn whenever I elect to enter a trance state for a reading.* Since my initial visitation on October 1, 1981, the Healer's Temple not only has provided me with invaluable insights and guidance through the readings but has served as an unfailing source of strength, joy, and love that permeate the very roots of my existence.

WHERE DO DREAMS ORIGINATE?

(August 10, 1981)

I am waiting for fish to be delivered. These come in round baskets. I look up and see a warehouse where shadowy figures are assembling these fish allotments for distribution. I feel that this is the place where dreams originate. My partner and I are to distribute these fish as we see fit. This is today's allotment, which we are to use well.

Fish represent spiritual food.

THE TIME WARP

(August 5, 1982)

I am with a white-robed teacher who beckons me to come out of the Temple. He points toward the sky and shows me an arc or split that is called The Time Warp. There are illuminated clouds surrounding it.

WHAT IS LOVE?

(November 7, 1982)

I see a wrinkled old woman taking care of her crippled husband, who is in a wheelchair.

I see someone taking care of a baby.

A husband and wife grow independently in an atmosphere of devotion.

I see a blind lady with a seeing-eye dog. The lady comes to the curb and the dog goes across leaving the lady stranded. I see a bus rounding the corner as the lady starts across. I rush to her aid before she is hit.

One final point: God should not be set apart as a superior intellectual being far beyond the reach of us mortals but rather should be experienced as an integral part of our daily lives. His humor and encouragement are evidenced in this delightful dream brought to Edgar Cayce:

Then our maid came in and said: "You should be close to the front door, for God may come in. He will enter that way." and Ma paid little attention to her, but I perked up at once and started forward and then the maid announced the distinguished visitor —that "God" was calling upon us. I rushed out into the hall and towards the door. Halfway to the door I met God, and jumped for Him, throwing my arms around His neck and hugging Him. He embraced me. After that I noticed God's appearance. He was a tall, well-built man, clean cut and clean shaven, wearing a brown suit and carrying a gray derby hat. He had an intelligent look, an eye that was kindly but piercing. He had an expression that was firm and features clean cut. He was very healthy, robust, businesslike, and thorough, yet kindly, just and sincere. Nothing slouching, shuffling, maudlin, sentimental about Him — a man we might say we'd like to do business with. He was God in the flesh of today — a business or industrial man, not a clergyman, not dressed in black, not a weakling, a strong healthy intelligent Man, whom I recognized as the Man of today and whom I welcomed and was glad to see and I recognized in this fine upright Man — not the ordinary — but God. Then we passed by the liquor closet — it was half open. God looked in — I showed Him the half-opened closet. But, I thought, I forget He is not the ordinary Man he looks but God and knows all, so I might as well show Him all, as pretend anything. So I opened the closet wide for Him to see. I showed Him my liquor, particularly the "Gin" which I use for cocktails. "In case of sickness," I said to God. "You are well prepared," God replied sarcastically. We proceeded into the parlor where the radio was still playing and (137) and Ma amusing themselves with it. I wanted (137) and Ma to meet God, but they couldn't seem to recognize Him. "Of course they would not know Him," I thought. "How could they recognize Him, when they have not the faith that He did appear in the flesh long ago in Christ." . . . So they did not see, or at least pay any attention to Him. I sat down on the sofa to converse with Him. "You could work harder," He said. I almost started to reply, yet bethought me that God knew all — no use. I meekly assented. "You could hardly do less," He continued. (1900-231)[18]

11

Psychometry and Psychic Readings

What I tell you in darkness, that speak ye in light.
Matthew 10:27

Just as there are three *R's* in *readin, ritin* and *rithmetic,* there are three C's that serve as tools for the psychic: *clairvoyance, clairaudience,* and *clairsentience.* These do not refer to normal senses but rather to superpsychical sense perceptions. Clairvoyance has to do with "Clear vision"; clairaudience refers to "clear hearing." A strong intuitive feeling about a future event would fall under the classification of clairsentience or "clear sensing."

The term *supersenses* suggests that super perceptions do not use our ordinary five senses when establishing contact with our conscious selves but rather enter our sphere of awareness through the deeper levels of our minds. Such communications can be likened to radio messages continually being broadcast through the subconscious whether we are in the waking or the sleeping state. These emerge as innovative ideas, flashes of insight, or undeniable hunches to the ordinary person, but to the psychically sensitive individual, these are the mediums through which all time becomes present. Then, the veil of the unknown is drawn aside providing this keen-eyed observer with crystal clear images of long-buried memories, current joys or traumas, or future trends.

These images may not *always* possess the clarity that is

essential for a concise psychic perception, however. One of the reasons for this is "the stained-glass window effect." This theory originated with Mr. W. T. Stead, a journalist and social reformer. He noted, "Just as a stained-glass window imposes its own patterns and colors upon the white light which streams through it, so does the subconscious stain and distort all that passes through it to the waking self."[1] This statement suggests, then, that impressions of present and future events that come through the psychic's unconscious may occasionally become distorted, causing some predictions to be inexact and others to be invalidated. The recipient of a psychic reading should therefore realize that the information viewed through "third-eye vision" may occasionally reveal tendencies toward events rather than precisely defined occurrences.

A second reason for inaccuracies of psychic impressions is that there is a time distortion in the psychic realm. Events perceived may happen days, weeks, months, and even years after they have been seen initially. Thus the interpretation of the time element must be flexible.

A third factor with regard to imagery distortions is that some thoughts picked up by the psychic reader are truly "thought patterns" and nothing more. When this is the case, these may never manifest themselves in physical reality, and fall into the 10 to 30 percent of items that are categorized as "nonhits."

A fourth and final premise for consideration is the receptivity of the subject for whom the reading is being given. Since the majority of the material contained in a psychic reading is obtained from the individual, the more receptive one is, the better the informational quality of the reading. It has even been said that if enough energy is focused on a prediction, it can become a self-fulfilling prophecy.

Since it is now obvious that no psychic is 100 percent accurate, what are the criteria for judging the authenticity of a psychic reading? if a psychic's accuracy rate varies between 60 and 75 percent, the person should be regarded as exceptional. Sensitives whose reading percentages range from 75 to 95 percent are truly rare. Remember, it is amazing that anyone has the ability to "tune in" on another person's psyche. Many a skeptic finds these ideas difficult, if not impossible, to accept. If one is to become a serious student of parapsychology in general and psychic phenomena in particular, openmindedness is the key to educational progress.

Since we have now hopefully established that there are no absolutes in the psychic realm, let us turn our thoughts to other issues concerning psychometry and psychic readings. What exactly is psychometry? W. E. Butler, in his book *How to Read the Aura, Practice Psychometry, Telepathy and Clairvoyance*, defines it as the "power of reading the past through the use of some object as a center of concentration."[2] Psychometry is really clairvoyance in time, but the concentration upon the chosen object provides a specific focus for the clairvoyant's impressions.

Supposedly, every object has imprinted upon it a record of its entire history, and one need only locate a psychometrist to pick up these hidden vibrations and reproduce them as one would replay magnetic tape from a tape recorder. The psychometrist either holds the article in his hand or presses it to his forehead and proceeds to decode the impressions contained therein. The psychometric reading may have three levels. (1) The first revolves around the origins of the object and its initial history. (2) The secondary level is concerned with events following its inception up to the present. (3) The tertiary level describes the current conditions that exist as well as future tendencies. With constant practice one who is talented in the field of psychometry can read the vibrational memories written upon an object as easily as you or I can peruse a book.

Edgar Cayce, also a famous clairvoyant as well as a psychic diagnostician, did not need to use psychometry in his readings. He was able to tap into the subconscious mind directly. Cayce appeared to channel information from three sources. The first source of the Cayce readings was the unconscious mind of the person for whom the reading was being given. Edgar Cayce, while in an altered state of consciousness, set his conscious mind aside and by permitting his unconscious mind to take command was able to "tune in" to the unconscious mind of the individual being read. The unconscious mind, psychologists say, acts like a tape recorder similar to the psychometric object described above in that it records all memories from birth to the present. Cayce went one step beyond. He stated that not only did the person's unconscious contain all events and memories that have transpired in this life, but it remembered every past existence it has had as well. Further, answers to each and every problem or dilemma to be faced were to be found within ourselves if we would earnestly search for the solutions. A selection from one of his readings maintains, "Then, for this information to become knowledge or understanding, there must be application of self to those sources of material knowledge, yes — but with faith and trust in universal knowledge. For, as indicated by the Lawgiver, think not who will come from over the sea that a message may be brought: for, lo, it is within thine own self. For the mind and the soul are from the beginning. Thus there must come within the entity's own consciousness the awareness of how the application is to be made."[3]

Cayce also drew upon a second source of material for his psychic readings. To the student of contemporary psychology this pool of knowledge could be likened to Carl Jung's "collective unconscious." Each individual's mind is commonly linked to all other minds, forming a stream of universal consciousness that "flows like a river." According to the Cayce source, every thought and deed of the human race since time immemorial is contained within the Book of Life. This is most often called the Akashic Records. *Akasha* refers to "the fundamental etheric substance of the universe, electro-spiritual in composition."[4] Cayce felt his ability to read these records had developed over many incarnations. He did not consider himself unique in this respect, however, but insisted repeatedly that the Akasha were available to any person who took the time and patience to develop his or her psychic ability. His explanation was "conditions, thoughts, and activities of men in every clime are things, as thoughts are things. They make their impressions upon the skein of time and space. Thus, as they make for their activity, they become as records that may be read by those in accord or attuned to such a condition. . . . [These activities] go upon the waves of light, upon that of space. And those instruments that are attuned to same may hear, may experience, that which is being transmitted."[5]

Some psychics claim they receive many of their impressions from spirit guides who, because of the irrelevance of time in the after-death state, have developed superior retrocognitive and precognitive capabilities. In addition, these spirit guides appear to be able to consult with other benevolent souls on the cosmic plane who, in past lives, have been highly qualified engineers, authors, physicians or inventors. The purpose of these consultations is to use each soul's specialized knowledge and talents not only for the benefit of the psychic and the recipient of the reading but also for the educational and spiritual progress of mankind in general. In this way the soul of the discarnate entity supposedly enhances his own soul's advancement on the upward path. The Cayce readings tend to give credence to such claims. During a reading session Edgar Cayce was asked whether he could communicate with entities in the spirit plane.

He replied, "The spirits of all that have passed from the physical place remain about the plane until their development carries them onward, or they are returned for their development here. While they are in the plane of communication, or remain with this sphere, any may be communicated with."[6]

The above three sources are generally accepted as the three main avenues from which psychic communications originate.

What types of psychic readings are there? My own personal experience, and investigation of the subject, leads me to believe there are five general categories into which psychic readings may be pigeonholed.

1. *Health and Medical Readings:* The psychic who is able to diagnose medical problems and prescribe corrective treatment is a helper to many. Those who exhibit this healing gift appear to possess a kind of X-ray vision that enables the psychic healer to peer into the body, identify the diseased organ, provide a diagnosis for the ailment, and list prescriptive, nutritional, medical, or psychological resources to alleviate the condition. The sleeping Cayce was just such a visionary clairvoyant. After describing the existing condition present in the body, he proceeded to recommend treatments requiring osteopathy, naturopathy, surgery, drugs, exercise, and diet. His "Mind is the builder" philosophy was an integral part of his

physical readings. He felt that just as destructive attitudes could cause ill health, constructive healthy attitudes could result in good, or at least improved, health. The holistic orientation of many medical psychics of today is expressed in the following statement by Cayce: "For what we think and what we eat—combined together — make what we are, physically and mentally."[7]

2. *Personality and Counseling Readings:* These readings are generally confined to the personal relationships around which the recipient's life revolves and the emotional ties that occasionally strangle as well as unify individuals. Our own personalities are often reflections of how others perceive us to be, with our inadequacies as well as strengths of character exposed.

   The psychic who delves into the subconscious personality of the client for whom she is conducting a reading is frequently merely reflecting the mirror image known unconsciously to her subject, but which, for reasons of pride and self-deception, he has been unwilling to face alone. Unless the issues of life are squarely faced, long-term anger continually turned in on oneself surfaces as arthritis or a heart disorder, and suppressed feelings of hopelessness and helplessness can serve as a catalyst for a virulent cancer. Fortunately, many psychics who engage in this type of counseling have such "healing presences" that it may be a matter of a few appointments until the counselee is able to see his way clearly and formulate defined goals and new directions for his future.

3. *Vocational and Past Life Readings:* Each soul has its own unique gifts and abilities, which can be latent or developed depending on the circumstances into which the entity is born and the intensity of the desire to self-actualize. If one gives credence to the theory of reincarnation, then a postulate that is an outgrowth of that theory is that on its journey through many existences the soul carries with it a variety of talents, aptitudes, and natural endowments. In one life span handicraft may be a means of earning a living, in another one's natural inclinations may lean toward business enterprises, while in a third incarnation musical endeavors or creativity in writing might fulfill one's needs. The point is that "when a soul enters a new body, in a new environment, a door is opened leading to an opportunity for building the soul's destiny. Everything which has been previously built, both good and bad, is contained in that opportunity."[8] If this is the case, then it behooves each person to make the most of the new opportunity by carefully selecting vocations that provide for optimum use of his particular endowments. Therefore, consultations with psychics who are unusually

endowed with "third-eye vision" for reading past life histories can be of immeasurable value in the vocational choice process.

4. *Futuristic Readings and Predictions:* All of us imagine how exciting it would be to be able to perceive future events. If this were within the realm of possibility, we could then take advantage of each new opportunity that comes our way and avoid the pitfalls and chasms into which we so often stumble or are thrust by the whirlwinds of destiny. The psychic who has this ability has events brought to his awareness that yet may be days, weeks, or months from their appointed date in reality.

   Three questions come to mind when the student of the psychic begins to study prophetic readings:

   (a) *How is prophecy possible?*

   (b) *Is it "evil" for a psychic to prophesy future tendencies?*

   (c) *What are the advantages in knowing future predictions?*

   Mary Ellen Carter's book *Edgar Cayce on Prophecy* seems to contain the answer to the first question. In Chapter 15, "Time and Prophecy," she quotes the Cayce readings as stating "Destiny (the future) is created in Time and Space." . . . "Those activities (of men) make for such an impression on the realm of data, or between Time and Space, as to make for what men have called Destiny—in the material affairs of individuals."[9] We know from our previous discussion of the Akashic Records that each soul writes a unique account of its activities on "the skeins of Time and Space." Therefore, the psychic who possesses the talent to attune her subconscious specifically to read these accounts could envision her client's future with relative ease. The Cayce readings support this contention. "It is from the Akashic Records that knowledge of the future is possible. This is because . . . all time is one: past, present and future."[10]

   The question of "wrongdoing" or "evil" being associated with futuristic psychic readings is often discussed in religious circles. It seems to me this view is very narrow-minded and held by persons who interpret biblical passages to justify their own religious philosophies. There are many passages in the Bible that deal with blessings and benefits bestowed through prophecy. My favorite of all, and the one that clearly condones and even challenges the development of the gift of prophecy, lies in I Corinthians, chapter 12, verses 7 through 11.

To each is given the manifestation of the spirit for common good. To one is given through the spirit the utterance of wisdom, to another the utterance of knowledge according to the same Spirit, to another faith by the same Spirit, to another gifts of healing of the one Spirit, to another the working of miracles, to another prophecy, to another the ability to distinguish between spirits, to another various kinds of tongues, to another the interpretation of tongues. All these are inspired by one and the same Spirit who apportions to each individually as he wills. [*Emphasis by author*][11]

Is evil connected to a gift of God if it is used in his service?

The final question concerns the advantages and benefits gained from being apprised of forthcoming blessings and calamities. The first and foremost advantage, it seems to me, is that if we perceive an event that is possible future reality, such as an accident or illness for ourselves or others, might it not be possible to avoid the tragedy by changing our diets and way of life, or warning another of the impending circumstances? In that way such catastrophes can be avoided or at least minimized. The second benefit to be derived from such prophecies is that even if the foretold event is unavoidable, each of us is better prepared to deal with adversity more effectively if we are able to marshal our forces and plan strategies ahead of time. Then our positions will be strengthened and fortified in the face of such disasters.

Third, knowledge gained from favorable future predictions would enable an individual to revise his current plans in order to derive maximum benefits from the foreseen blessings and perhaps focus more energy upon these occurrences, thus increasing the likelihood of their advent. Blessings anticipated and then experienced tend to make our burdens more bearable.

5. *Universal Truth Readings:* There are some psychics who can be labeled channels of universal truths and laws. These persons exhibit mediumistic abilities. Many could be cited for their philosophical discourses on how the universe functions, the purpose of reincarnation, and the evolution of the soul toward its creator.

   One of the most outstanding mediums known today is the late Jane Roberts. In her *Seth* books she claimed to have received psychically from a spirit personality named Seth entire volumes of materials describing the "nuts-and-bolts" workings of the universe. Several quotes from one of her earliest publications, *Seth Speaks,* provide excellent illustration of universal truth readings.

On illness she writes: "Illness and suffering are not thrust upon you by God, or by All That Is, or by an outside agency. They are a byproduct of the learning process, created by you, in themselves quite neutral."[12]

Concerning God: "God is hidden carefully in his creations, so that He is what they are and they are what He is; and in knowing them, you know Him."[13]

On Love and Joy: "The vitality of the universe is creativity and joy and love and that is spirituality."[14]

On Justice and Rewards: "You reap your own rewards."[15]

On Truth: "You cannot use 'truth.' It cannot be manipulated. Whoever thinks he is manipulating the truth is manipulating himself. You are truth. Then discover yourself."[16]

On Spirituality: "True spirituality is a thing of joy and of the earth, and has nothing to do with false adult dignity. It has nothing to do with long words and sorrowful faces. It has to do with the dance of consciousness that is within you, and with the sense of spiritual adventure that is within your hearts."[17]

Words such as these revitalize our spirits, lighten our hearts, and etherealize our souls.

What conditions are necessary for enhancing the accuracy of psychic information and psychic readings? My own experience and study regarding this question have led me to the conclusion that the essential ingredient that determines the degree of accuracy of the psychic information received is *an intense desire for success*. This desire must not only exist on the part of the psychic giving the reading but coexist in equal intensity in the mind of the receiver. Without this cooperation of minds readings seem to wander rather aimlessly, lacking precise guidance and direction.

It would seem logical to assume, however, that the majority of clients who seek the services of a psychic are sincere and devout seekers of truth and do possess an intense desire to learn about themselves. When this is the case, there would then come to play a hierarchy of five progressive steps each leading closer and closer to the revelation of ultimate truths.

The first step in this progression, and the one least likely to lead to a satisfying outcome, is psychic information obtained from the client's dream material. This is essentially unfocused material, which is largely symbolic and often times a mixture of several problems in one dream. In spite of this, if the client is honest and the psychic an informed student of dream interpretations, some significant insights and life gains can probably be anticipated.

Moving up the hierarchical scale we come to the client who is in a "tug-of-war" situation. At one end of the pole is the desire to learn as much about himself as he can, and in conflict with this, at the other end, lies the intent to cover up any personality characteristics and current life episodes that would be unflattering to him. When such conflicts exist simultaneously in a client, even the best of psychics will receive contradictory signals, which frequently exert a negative effect on the outcome of the reading. This type of client will more often than not request a reading from a distance so he will not be confronted with the prospect of meeting the psychic face to face. Most talented psychics can usually sort through this barrage of conflicting messages and generally complete the reading with satisfactory results. These are not optimum conditions, however.

Arriving at the middle of the hierarchy we come to the client in which no conflict exists, but neither does a strong faith in the process. He will probably request an interview with the psychic and present himself personally in an amiable fashion, but the meeting of minds will be rather loosely knit. This "middle-of-the-roader" will most likely acquire an average reading, but the key to its success lies in whether or not he will profit from its contents by using the information fully, or merely file it away to be reviewed and used at some future date when a calamity befalls him.

On the fourth rung of the hierarchy we encounter the recipient who enters into his psychic reading adventure with an air of confidence and a spirit of cooperation. He is a believer in this venture and presents himself accordingly. In an effort to achieve more satisfactory results he offers a ring, a picture, or some other personal item to enhance the reading psychometrically. At the conclusion of the reading he will carefully review the ideas and suggestions he has received in a effort to improve the clarity of the reading. Positive actions will more than likely be taken in the future, wherever feasible, in accordance with the information given throughout the reading. As a general rule 70 to 80 percent reading accuracy can be anticipated for this type of client.

At the top of this hierarchy resides the peak experience in psychic readings. The superiority of these readings can be traced to a veritable intermingling of consciousness. The mental fabric between psychic and client is so interwoven that the psychic will often respond to a question before the client has posed it. The core of such readings not only focuses precisely on the central issues around which the client's life revolves but defines and discusses methodologies through which these issues may be analyzed and dealt with effectively. Psychic enhancers such as psychometry, guided questions, and the client's physical presence should all be included when enumerating reasons for the excellence of such dissertations. There is one factor, however, that is responsible for their seeming infallibility: *Absolute faith*! Faith in themselves, faith in the psychic, faith in the goodness of others, faith that all things in this existence work together for one's betterment, and above all, faith that the Christ Spirit, which is an integral part of each of us, will provide us with insightful solutions to the most insurmountable of problems.

Many people profess to have faith but when pushed to the wall exclaim, "I have faith but . . . ." The mere utterance of that word implies the seeds of doubt have already taken root.

What is faith? "Faith knows that it has already received and acts accordingly, doubting nothing. It is the builder of the seemingly impossible. It is that which has brought into manifestation all that has ever existed. God is, faith is."[18] "Faith is victory, for where there is faith rightly placed, there is no failure, but true success."[19]

How is faith developed? By maintaining unfaltering belief that events foreseen and desired will come to pass and then translating that belief into positive actions. "Thus shall our faith develop and become to us evidence of things not seen. We must show by our actions in our daily lives that we believe, that we have faith, and that we know as we use what we have, more will be given." (Readings 262-13 to 262-17).[20] When faith is translated into positive actions, the culmination of these rare types of readings is often a complete transformation in attitude or direction in the life of the individual.

A message revealed to me one morning in a dream attests to the supreme importance of faith as related to the psychic: "Faith is that mysterious power which is responsible for proper use of the alpha state."

All of us are psychic in varying degrees, but how does the ordinary person set about developing his psychic skills? Cayce affirmed that meditation practiced daily was the key to the psychic door. Harmon Bro, in his book *Edgar Cayce on Religion and Psychic Experiences*, restates Cayce's views thus: "it was the nature of meditation to free the channels of the person to receive guidance, and if he did not receive it shortly after meditation, he could count on the action of such guidance when next he faced a decision or needed an invention. Through the channels cleared and kept fresh by meditation could come more swiftly the flow of imagery and assurances that made up faith 'the evidence of things unseen' including helpful psychic promptings of all sorts."[21] Cayce, according to Bro, cites three levels of psychic experience:

1. The primary level was a level of natural psychic experiences in daily life and in dreams. These involved warnings of threats to the individual and his loved ones, information on opportunities to be sought, and suggestions for service and guidance to others.
2. The secondary level of psychic experience involves a transcendence beyond one's natural inheritance. With fear set aside and with concentrated practice, a soul could reach beyond its natural endowment and join forces with the universal mind, thus gaining access to the wisdom of the ages. "There were no necessary limits for psychic experience here, when need and opportunity joined with intent."[22]
3. Under duress caused by intense needs or great love a soul might enter an elevated state where "treasures not yet fully earned might be poured into consciousness . . . . In these 'elevated' states not only useful facts but the very bones of the universe, the pulse of creation might come into reach . . . . Psychic ability then became not simply a useful tool for man's day-to-day operations but an

> unforced awareness of 'the way things are' and an invitation to work with the grain of life."[23]

How are these levels measured and how can one be assured he is developing? According to W. E. Butler, in the beginning state of development the would-be psychic perceives an emotional-mental atmosphere that is more vivid than any visual image. As development proceeds, this emotional-mental atmosphere gives way to more graphic visual imagery. The third and ultimate step in development is taken when the visual images recede and a formless intuitional understanding emerges "in which all the details that the visual images and the mental-emotional atmosphere gave are superseded by a clear and exceedingly definite perception."[24] This, then, is the yardstick by which psychic progress is measurable.

The development of psychic potential requires time, effort, patience, and above all prayer and meditation. As with most lessons in life, proficiency comes with experience. The progression of one's psychic abilities is closely aligned with one's religious understandings and practices and one's relationships to his fellow man and the Almighty. "If a person achieves purity of heart and enduring love toward his fellows, he could expect to find as well those times when the psychic stream overflowed its usual channels, and he found himself supplied with whatever was needful for the situation, from the Giver of all good and perfect gifts."[25]

12

Expanding Your Horizons through Psychometry and Psychic Readings

To change the world you must change your thoughts.
Jane Roberts, *Seth Speaks*

Although dreams are the safest method for developing one's psychic abilities, I am certain there are those among my readers who feel relatively confident that they have already mastered the basic tenets of dream interpretation and, being more adventurous, desire to expand their personal consciousness beyond its present scope by venturing forth into the intriguing world of psychometry and psychic readings. This is certainly advisable, for it has been my experience that when one is ready for the next step, the psychic doors open up, flooding the eager student's universe with articles, books, and oral presentations that appear to be specifically designed to meet his current educational needs. For those who fit into this category the methods of techniques discussed in this chapter should prove to be of inestimable value.

The chapter is divided into three sections. The initial portion describes a simple induction method through which the novice can achieve a highly altered state of consciousness. Following these practical exercises involving psychometry, goal realization and precognition are presented. If these are practiced faithfully, excellent progress should be recorded in a relatively short span of time. The final paragraphs of the chapter are devoted to the imminent dangers that exist and begin to become harrowing realities when overzealous students, using unorthodox channels (LSD, Ouija boards) attempt to expand their rapidly developing psychic skills beyond their current capabilities. Alternative methods are cited in lieu of these undesirable pathways. Now that we have charted our course, let us begin.

Exercises for Training Your Inner Eye

I. Focusing Attention through Relaxation

For all beginning students attaining a receptive meditative state is the initial step taken when embarking on a program to develop one's psychic abilities. A successful formula for achieving this altered state of consciousness would be the following:

1. Find a location where you are not likely to be disturbed. Make yourself as comfortable as possible whether it be reclining in your favorite chair or lying down on a couch or bed. Place your hands at your sides and your legs and feet flat on the floor or straight out on the bed.
2. Close your eyes and begin a pattern of rhythmic breathing, taking a series of deep breaths through the nostrils. As the pattern progresses, you will become more and more aware of a sense of increased relaxation flowing through your mind and body. When this occurs, begin to focus your attention on your feet and legs and, working up to the top of your head, instruct each part of your body to relax in turn. Examples of self-suggestive commands would be: "I feel my feet. All tension has vanished, leaving them free and light. I notice all tension is being released in my legs and a sensation of complete freedom now exists." Do not hurry to complete this exercise; the slower pace will enhance the desired results. Continue in this fashion until you reach the top of the head. At this point you should feel energized and buoyant, having reached a peak of mental and physical relaxation.
3. Becoming a highly attuned psychic channel carries with it the requirement of divorcing oneself from preconceived notions and ideas and being absolutely open to the flow of information received. In this manner one truly becomes "a channel of blessings

for others." A prayer of attunement can be initiated through the use of an affirmation such as "*May the protection and knowledge of the Lord so fill me physically, mentally, and spiritually that I become a healing channel in his name.*"

4. Psychic work often involves the need for protection against harmful or negative influences that may intrude upon our subconscious when we open ourselves up psychically. Therefore, it is mandatory to invoke spiritual protection against these unwholesome forces. To do this, imagine that you are surrounded by a coccoon of brilliant white light that acts as a divine shield, neutralizing all negativity that may enter into your auric field. An affirmation such as "I am protected by the love of God" serves a similar purpose.
5. Psychic states can vary from a light trance to a deep hypnotic state of meditative silence. Once having arrived at a state of complete relaxation, the next procedure revolves around a gradual psychic "turning inward." This is accomplished by counting backward slowly from ten to one while simultaneously visualizing yourself walking down a flight of steps. The count should be synchronized with each descending step. At the end of this flight of stairs you will enter into a room and seat yourself in front of a screen. A feeling of reverence should be all-pervasive. You are now ready to view the awe-inspiring presentations of the inner eye.

II. Psychometry

You will remember from Chapter 10 that psychometry is the art of attuning oneself to another human being's vibrational pattern through psychical contact with an object that belongs to that person. All objects carry with them unique vibrational information. The more intensely its owner is emotionally bonded to the object, and the longer the period of proprietorship, the more extensive the amount of psychical data. A relatively simple exercise to attune yourself psychometrically to another soul's vibrational pattern would be:

1. After having attained a heightened sense of awareness through the method described above, enclose the object securely in your hand. (The use of the left hand is optional. Although it appears to work best for me, many psychometrists have found it makes *little difference* whether the right or the left hand is employed. In fact, several

exceptional psychics of my acquaintance claim to receive more precise impressions when the object being read psychometrically is placed against the forehead.)

2. In this state of focused concentration, open up your inner eye to whatever psychic impressions enter in—pictures, words, symbols, and so on. After receiving these initial "intuits," ask yourself what sort of emotions are connected to this person, what are his educational and occupational goals, where is his place of residence, and who are the people most personally associated with him. Lastly, seek to ascertain the central issues around which this person's life revolves and determine if there is any way you can be of service in offering solutions.
3. An important point to remember is: *Be a receptive channel*. Any attempts to interject your personal opinions or interpret the psychic impression according to your own standards or code of values will result in fallacious psychometry.
4. It is a judicious move to register your impressions for future validation. This may be accomplished in one of two ways:
   - (a) By engaging in a partnership whereby your partner may act as a guide as well as recording the information.
   - (b) Through the use of a tape recorder. Continued practice on a regular basis will enhance the chances of psychic accuracy and greatly increase your confidence in your ability to read objects psychometrically.

III. Goal Realization: Fulfillment by Guided Imagery

Is it truly possible to make our dreams come true? Is there a chance that by positively focusing our energies on a desired outcome we can increase the likelihood of goal realization? *Absolutely*! To quote Alan Vaughan in *The Edge of Tomorrow*, "We have a divinity, or a creative consciousness, that partakes of the universe, that is holographic and creates its own universe by means of its powers of mind. Created in the image of God, we are not only endowed with his powers but also his destiny: to create our own universes, to discover our inner destiny and fulfill it by prophesying and creating our own future."[1]

How do we know if we are succeeding in realizing our own

destinies? Again, Vaughan supplies the answer. "There is only one way to know for sure. What feedback from the universe is positive, if your life becomes more satisfying to you and others, if your life works with a new ease and excitement, if barriers fall away, if opportunities open up, if life is a series of 'yes' signs, you know your guiding images are being fulfilled. You are synchronizing yourself with the best opportunities both for your inner self and for the universe. Mostly, of course, this synchronization happens with others who share your dreams."[2]

Because my philosophy of life and views concerning prophecy are so closely aligned with those professed by Alan Vaughan, I have chosen selected points from a short exercise contained in the above mentioned publication to illustrate the method of future goal realization.

1. Choose from your list of desires any goal that seems likely to be reached with a little concerted effort, for example, your daughter's acceptance into the college of her choice.
2. "Now relax and see in your mind's eye an image of the results of your fulfilling that goal. Think of the last time you were successful at a similar task and recreate that feeling of satisfaction. Let the image and feeling of satisfaction stay in your consciousness for about a minute. See yourself being applauded for doing so well. You know it will be easy because you have seen it happen."[3]
3. If you sense any ideas or measures that will improve the chances of attaining the desired outcome, put them into practice immediately.
4. Record your goal image verbally on a 3 x 5 card stating all the positive reasons why the event should come to pass. Carry this with you in your wallet or purse during the day and, when you have a moment of privacy, reread the words and give your subconscious the suggestion that everything of a positive nature is now being done to assure its eventual fulfillment. *Be confident of this.*
5. Review and take action against all negative aspects that could prevent its occurrence.
6. "Keep up your visualization for as long as it takes to accomplish your goal. If the goal is a true guiding image, it will be fulfilled —sooner than you think."[4]

IV. Precognition

In his book *Patterns of Prophecy*, Alan Vaughan refers to an inner "blueprint" of life. According to his theory, "sensitives seem to be able to tap psychically an inner 'blueprint' of life that furnished information about the person's future."[5]

The exercise I am about to present is based on this premise. I use it daily to recharge the psychic flow as well as obtain helpful information concerning my own future and the future of those closest to me. I always focus positive energies on the events previewed that will most favorably affect my future and concentrate on negating events foreseen that will exert a detrimental effect. Through this technique I have often been able to shape my own future.

1. Purchase a notebook that contains pages wide enough for you to divide into two separate columns. The first column should be labeled "Precognition" and the second "Successes."
2. Now, in a relaxed state of mind, reverently request your source to bring to your awareness any and all events that are currently forming just beyond the present. *Be open and receptive*!
3. Program your subconscious to recall observed events. Suggest that you can memorize these easily and recall them in order when you are again in the conscious state.
4. Record all precognitive impressions on the left column of your notebook and then wait. Some of your predictions should begin to materialize within a day or two. Record the exact event and compare it with the initial visualization. On a scale of 0 to 100 percent, award yourself ten points for extreme accuracy, five points for partial accuracy, and zero if the prediction never comes to pass. By this means you can evaluate and measure your precognitive progress.
5. Do not impose time limits on your predictions. It may take weeks or months before some precognitions become actualities.

For the more serious students of psychic readings I recommend as beginning texts Jess Stearn's *The Power of Alpha Thinking* and *Develop Your Psychic Skills* by Enid Hoffman. For those of you who have a precognitive bend I cannot urge you strongly enough to purchase a copy of *The Edge of Tomorrow* by Alan Vaughan. It is a classic in the field and contains exercises far beyond the scope of the basic techniques discussed in this book.

Remember, we all are psychic to some degree, and, as with other talents, some are more highly endowed. However, "There is just no substitute for practice, study and discipline. Mastering the art of prophecy is like learning a foreign language. You have ten thousand mistakes to make. The faster you make them, the faster you learn."[6]

Dangers Encountered on the Psychic Pathway

Up to this point I have emphasized the growth and benefits that are available to one through psychic channels. In truth, devoting one's time to the study and mastery of metaphysical ideas can provide unparalleled rewards. However, on the other side of the coin, psychic investigations by uninformed or unprincipled minds can lead down pathways fraught with incalculable dangers. Promises of unlimited power, mind control of others, and easily acquired wealth lure the unscrupulous into ardent pursuit of unorthodox methods to achieve their goals. In an effort to transform themselves rapidly into another Edgar Cayce or Arthur Ford they select LSD or spirit communication through the Ouija board as a means to achieve their ends. Being unaware of the immutability of universal law (the law of "cause and effect" in the psychic is absolute), they rush headlong down their chosen path, ignoring all danger signals. Inevitably they find themselves sucked into a swirling psychic whirlpool where all efforts to extricate themselves culminate in a continuing downward spiral.

The above is not designed to frighten aspiring students into a state of immobility. I have opted to write this section, however, in a sincere effort to apprise my readers of several occult hazards to which one can unwittingly expose oneself unless adequate spiritual protection or precautions are sought.

What are some of the most prevalent "psychic shortcuts" that might conceivably lead to perilous ends on one's psychic journey? In my opinion, five of the most commonly abused procedures are hypnosis, hallucinogenic drugs, mediumship, the Ouija board, and automatic writing. The most undesirable personality characteristic is lack of psychic balance.

Hypnosis

No one knows exactly what hypnosis is, but under hypnosis, subjects are able to perform extraordinary feats that they find impossible to execute in the conscious state.

There are three stages of hypnosis: *light, medium* and *deep*. In light hypnosis the person's eyes are closed, breathing is relaxed, and there is relatively little talking or movement unless directed by the hypnotist. Under medium hypnosis there may be partial amnesia, lack of response to pain, and acceptance of simple posthypnotic suggestions. In deep hypnosis the person appears entirely conscious, walking about and talking but in a state of complete amnesia and anesthesia. Many gifted psychics are able to receive information in the deep trance state because "the deeper the state of trance, the more activated become the Extra Sensory faculties of the subject. Under these conditions he [the psychic] can be instructed to leave the body and to visit a certain person or place and to report on what he sees and hears."[7]

In electing hypnosis as a means of enhancing your psychic ability the following considerations should be taken into account:

1. Continuous subjection to hypnotic control over a long period of time often can make unstable personalities completely submissive to the will of the hypnotist. The effect of such a symbiotic relationship is the total loss of confidence on the part of the subject to make independent decisions. The relinquishing of self-determination almost always results in physical and mental deterioration.
2. "Actually, whenever one person hypnotizes another, he is assuming a greater responsibility than is customarily realized. Each individual has a distinct mental and emotional make up. He may possess certain inhibitions or complexes or phobias of long-standing, which he has been repressing and which may be brought to the surface, in violent and uncontrollable form, through the

medium of hypnotism. If the hypnotist, under these circumstances, is not equipped with physiological as well as psychological knowledge, he will likely be unable to cope with the situation. Nervous and mental troubles, in addition to physical disturbances, can grow out of the ignorant, however well-intentioned, misuse of hypnotism."[8]

3. It is possible that even the most ethical of hypnotists may experience sexual attraction toward some clients, and, in the course of several hypnotic sessions, these clients become sensitized to the unspoken desires. Such transference of feelings can become an extreme source of embarrassment to both client and teacher, and the sooner such situations are dealt with decisively, the healthier for both parties.
4. "Some subjects may come out of hypnotic sessions with what appear to be either split personalities or possessing entities speaking through them. This may or may not be a good result, depending on the understanding and perception of the individual involved. If one wished to become a medium, hypnosis might be of help in developing such ability. On the other hand, a person having what appears to be some psychic sensitivity, who did not wish to be mediumistic, might find himself dealing with a problem of considerable proportions."[9]

To avoid the above cited pitfalls seek a competent, well-educated hypnotist, who has met the requirement for advanced training in this skill and has several years of experience in hypnotic induction. Engage in one or two sessions in which he can aid you in perfecting the technique of self-hypnosis. Self-hypnosis or self-suggestion carries with it the implication that you are truly the one in command of your life. Others can educate, counsel, and provide all manner of physical and economic assistance, but when entering into a phase of your life that is as important as developing your psychic ability, you are the only one who should really take charge of your thinking and actions.

The Hallucinogenic Drugs

These are a class of drugs that produce marked changes in mood and auditory and visual perception. Among these can be found peyote, lysergic acid diethylamide (LSD), mescaline, and "letter drugs" such as DMT and PCP. Since this class of drugs produces similar reactions, my presentation will center on the effects and adverse reactions of LSD.

LSD was first synthesized by a Swedish chemist named Dr. A. Hoffman. It was initially thought to produce a model of schizophrenic reaction, but later experiments with this drug disproved this theory.

"The LSD experience typically lasts about eight hours. Perhaps the most striking effects of the drug are sensory and perceptual. Chairs, rugs, trees, and other objects become sharper and brighter; details not ordinarily noticed become clear. Ordinary things become endowed with an almost mystical meaning."[10]

To those who choose to experiment with LSD for psychical expansion purposes, the following adverse reactions are cited. These may provide food for thought:

1. Occasionally individuals may undergo "bad trips" that involve dramatic episodes of panic and extreme anxiety. In states such as this, persons have been known to jump from high places or set themselves afire.
2. "The risk of a bad reaction has been estimated to be as high as 10 percent of the times that the drug is taken, a probable estimate that increases with higher dosages, uncertain circumstances (such as taking the drug in unfamiliar environments or among strangers), instability of the user, and the lack of quality control of bootlegged and black market preparations."[11]
3. Sometimes long-lasting or recurring after effects are noted, such as mental confusion, sudden changes of mood, or "flashback" to some previous LSD episode.

In light of the serious side effects of this powerful hallucinogen, avoidance of this particular "gateway in the psychic realm" would seem prudent.

Mediumship

Another gateway to the unconscious is mediumship. This carries with it great benefits for the talented channel, but more often than not ridicule and unforeseen perils for those unschooled in all aspects of this process.

What is the difference between a medium and a psychic? "A Medium is one whose unfolded powers display the fact that there is a conscious existence in another sphere of life. The Medium therefore makes contact with a discarnate entity and produces proof satisfactory to the inquirer. The power of the Psychic is more abstract in nature: it is developed mainly through mental faculties, having no contact with a discarnate entity and not necessarily spiritual in nature."[12]

There are both mental and physical mediums. The former, while entranced, receive the thoughts of the discarnate entity through "voices" speaking to them or through written messages. Among the most famous was Mrs. Lenore Piper, who was the object of a critical investigation by the famous American psychologist William James. (He came away a believer).

Physical mediumship takes place in a trance state also, but the discarnate entity uses the vocal cords of the medium to communicate his messages physically by speaking through that person. Arthur Ford and his control, Fletcher, exemplify this aspect of mediumship.

"The development of mediumship can be greatly beneficial, both mentally and physically, through contact with the Spirit World. A practical understanding of the Philosophies and Laws of Mediumship, and a sincere desire to give out only the highest and best, and a wish to be of service to mankind are the incentives of developing mediumship."[13]

Mediumship demands perseverance, sacrifice, and inspiration, but the essential ingredient is "the spark within." If the ability is there, some students will be successful during the initial sitting. Others, however, may work at developing the skill for a lifetime and never hear a single spirit voice.

"The greatest value of mediumship and communication with the spirits is the assistance it gives us on the road of life."[14]

Now that the rewards of mediumship have been enumerated, let us turn to the dangers associated with mediumistic activities. These should be scrutinized carefully by the novice before any serious thought is given to apprenticeship.

1. In the past there were many fakes and charlatans connected to this vocation. Because of these disreputable persons, the general public

is now hesitant to award credibility to persons professing to be mediumistic. Therefore, even the most gifted practitioners are often subjected to ridicule and scorn.

2. The possibility of being possessed by malevolent spirits when one opens oneself up to channeling information is also a consideration. While it is extremely difficult to prove the existence of such cases, even the possibility of receiving and internalizing negative thought patterns from living persons should provide a strong deterrent for the brash student who would rush headlong down this pathway without giving a second thought to spiritual protection.
3. It is possible for unbalanced persons to experience psychotic episodes when engaging in mediumistic adventures. A part of the unconscious may split off, creating another personality. This is an extremely serious turn of events that may require long-term psychiatric treatment for the "unfortunate seeker of paranormal thrills." However, "A distinction between cases of psychosis and individuals who may be classed as mediums should be made. In severe mental disorders a disassociation with rational thought and action occurs. With mediumistic phenomena the person allows and frequently seeks to be a channel for 'a force' or 'information' which seems to come from outside himself."[15] The medium, therefore, has complete control over his "trance exits and entrances" whereas the psychotic has none.

Arthur Ford, one of the best-known modern-day mediums, always considered helping bereaved persons to a normal recovery after a loved one had passed over one of the most important phases of his ministry. In *Unknown but Known* he writes, "Two things are absolutely essential to the overcoming of the fear of death. The first is to achieve conviction of the survival of human personality after biological death by honest confrontation with the evidence. The second is to sustain this conviction against the eroding forces brought to bear by a materialistic society. These two things accomplished, the truth of survival becomes part of one's core belief—like gravitation, one of the assured certainties of the universe."[16]

The Ouija Board and Automatic Writing

The Ouija board is a board approximately 22 inches long and 15 inches wide. Letters of the alphabet are printed on it in two rows. The word "Yes" is positioned in the upper left-hand corner and the word "No" in the right-hand corner. The numbers 1 through 9 plus 0 are below the alphabet letters. Goodbye is at the bottom of the board. A triangular pointer is operated by participants who place their hands lightly on the pointer, which then is suppose to slide across the board propelled by "spirit forces." In this fashion spirit communications are received.

In automatic writing the spiritual communication takes over the mind or hand of the channel and proceeds to impart wisdom from other dimensions. There have been instances where entire books have been written when entranced or in the sleep state. "It is self-evident that the sensitive individual through whose mind these manuscripts have come, could never, in their normal states of consciousness have created this material . . . . Exhaustive examinations have been made into the past life and experience of some of these automatic writers, proving conclusively that they had had no access to the material they now wrote about."[17]

Problems connected to these two activities are:

1. Here again there is a danger of possession carrying with it all the accompanying traumas described previously in the section discussing mediumship.
2. There are thousands of men and women who dabble in automatic writing. Some of these soon believe themselves in touch with none other than God himself. While these persons may be sincere in their beliefs, such practices are self-deluding. In the aforementioned cases "There is often evidence of the influence of a secondary personality created by this individual as the result of previously repressed desires and frustrations, who now speaks out uninhibitedly in the guise of a 'higher intelligence' or some entity who has 'gone on' and who confers approval upon the thoughts and acts and aspirations of the subject."[18]
3. According to Edgar Cayce, automatic writing does not generally carry with it soul development. Since the kingdom of God is within, to be guided by outside influences could prove detrimental to the majority of individuals. His stand on inspirational writings from within was more liberal, however. "As to the activities of what may be termed the channels through which individuals may receive inspirational or automatic writings, the inspirational is the greater

activities — yet may partake of both earth-earthly things and the heaven-heavenly things, while the automatic writing may partake only of that source or force which is impelling, guiding or directing. The inspirational may but develop the soul of the individual, while the automatic may rarely reach beyond the force that is guiding or directing."[19]

Maintaining Psychic Balance

After being involved in studying and investigation of psychic phenomena for a period of several years and being privileged to meet many psychically gifted individuals from all walks of life, I am finally convinced that the most serious danger encountered along the psychic path is lack of psychic balance. A tipping of the scales in either direction may prove deleterious.

The psychic who lacks confidence in his abilities, even though highly endowed, will often fail at providing adequate guidance for his clientele because of the absence of that magic ingredient called faith. His readings will be disappointing, his predictions inaccurate, and occasionally, directives may be given that, if carried out, might really prove harmful to the reading recipient.

By far the greatest danger for highly successful psychics is the belief in the infallibility of their gift. Having drunk from the "fountain of truth" so often they become intoxicated with their own sense of superpower and come to believe that, rather than being a channel through which the source of information flows, they are themselves the source of all knowledge and universal truth. Any degree of humility that previously existed has long since vanished, and, if they are ever questioned regarding the validity of their prognostications, they become incensed by the mere thought that anyone could be so obtuse as to doubt that their readings could be less than 100 percent accurate. Lord, protect us from these perfected souls. In a state of such perfection, however, it is likely that their souls might leave their bodies and the existing problem would be solved for both parties.

Considering that neither of these skewed states is conducive to acquiring a sense of balance, how might an aspiring psychic achieve and maintain psychic equanimity?

Guidelines to Promote Spiritual Attunement for Accurate Psychic Readings

Goal Setting

The first step in psychic development is to know the proper course to set and then determine the most efficacious methods of realizing your goals. Listed below are seven rules that will provide you with guidelines when initially organizing your psychic curriculum.

1. *Formulate realistic goals:* How do you want to put your futuristic psychic skills to use? Do you desire to become a healer? Do physical readings appeal to you? Are you interested in focusing your talents on the financial and business aspects of this field? Do past lives intrigue you? Are you a spiritual philosopher at heart? In short, determine realistically where your interests and *abilities* lie and then *allow adequate time* for your goal realizations.
2. Once you have decided on your course of psychic development, make the metaphysical section of the library your home away from home for a period of time. Browse through all publications that contain information and practical guidance in your chosen field of endeavor. Take voluminous notes from such publications.
3. After you have acquired sufficient knowledge concerning your subject or subjects and are confident of the course you wish to pursue, outline *specific* step-by-step procedures that will allow you to approach your goal in an orderly fashion.
4. It is not only rewarding but almost mandatory to choose a partner to accompany you on the psychic path. This companion will prove to be a source of insight and encouragement during times of despair (and these will come) and can also analyze your mistakes and offer corrective suggestions. Psychic partnerships are both energy-producing and inspirational, and these qualities are essential for periodic psychic renewal.
5. Psychic skills cannot develop adequately without daily practice. Therefore, select a time when you feel you are at your psychic best (mine is 9:00 A.M. or 9:00 P.M.) and engage in your outlined program of mental exercises. Whether this is 20 minutes or one hour, the important point is consistency. To quote Alan Vaughan again, "There is just no substitute for practice, study and discipline."[20]

6. Keep records of your psychic successes and progress. Did you correctly predict an event that happened within several days of your previewing it? Was your intuitive impression concerning your brother's health correct? Applaud yourself and award yourself points for accurate insights. Detailed records over a period of several months provide invaluable feedback and clues regarding your strengths and weaknesses.
7. You must believe that what you desire will eventually become reality. "Your higher sensory faculties are the channels through which the God Consciousness is reached. They exist ready to function, just beyond the outermost limits of the five physical senses and the *key that* unlocks the invisible door to these powers is your faith."[21]

Self-appraisal

Once you have begun to perceive some degree of psychic progress, you will want to engage in some self-appraisal. The ideas discussed below are designed to assist you in this process:

1. Enumerate the personality characteristics you have observed in both outstanding and deplorable sensitives. Among those exhibited by the latter would be arrogance, intolerance, self-righteousness, inflexibility, and greed. Qualities almost always noted in the most highly attuned spiritual souls are humility, generosity, reverence, patience, and an overpowering sense of love and service to all with whom he comes in contact. Choose wisely the attitudes you wish to develop within yourself.
2. The passage of time will act as an excellent barometer to gauge your psychic progress. Some of you will develop so rapidly that after a short period of time you will begin to uncover exciting new psychic talents in the course of your progression. Others may find that what they perceived to be psychic abilities were, in actuality, only intense interest in that subject, and, therefore, a change of goals will be necessitated. Still others may become completely disenchanted with the amount of study and self-discipline required for psychic refinement and turn their attention elsewhere. Whatever your experience, be true to yourself in your appraisal of your abilities.
3. Refine your techniques and basic methods of operation as you proceed. If you find that you can switch to a trance state via a

shorter method of induction, discard the old way. If long-distance readings are not for you, but you can read your client face to face, use this mode of operation. If the Tarot cards or astrology charts suit your particular talents, employ them as a method of focus. Weed out and continuously reseed your "psychic garden" as you grow.

4. Finally, set ideals for yourself and then practice them daily. Whether your ideal be dedication to live a healthy life, intellectual open-mindedness, or a healing attitude toward others, live by it. To quote Edgar Cayce on ideals, "These are what we mean by constructive thinking, and as they are applied within the experience, we will come to see what a spiritual life means. Not eliminating of pleasures, for the purpose of life is pleasure, but that which is constructive and not destructive" (1995-1).[22]

Use of Meditation and Prayer

In the final analysis none of what has been discussed up to this point can become actuality without meditation and prayer.

1. Why does one need meditation? "Through meditation the body becomes not a prison from which to escape but rather an instrument through which the highest spiritual aspirations of the 'real self' can be expressed."[23]
2. What gains and benefits are realized through the practice of daily meditation? This varies from person to person, but in general, memory and concentration improve, creativity expands, psychic sensitivity increases, dreams become more graphic, intuitive insights and hunches multiply, and there is a sense of serenity and inner peace that flow freely from a personal attunement with one's Creator.
3. How are prayer and meditation connected and how is prayer most effective? "You must believe what you desire, as expressed in prayer, you not only desire but have the power to receive. This faith must be positive, expectant and unwavering or it will not energize your God-given Creative Power which must be activated before the prayer, itself, can be answered. Utter sincerity, unselfishness, simplicity and directness should be the attitude in which you approach prayer. You should carry into each meditation the conviction that what you are about to pray for has already been realized by you in mind and requires only to be vitalized by

attunement with the God Power within to become, eventually, a reality in your outer life."[24]

4. What types of prayer are most meaningful? In Harold Sherman's *Know Your Own Mind* I ran across five types of prayers, each of which accomplishes a great fundamental purpose in your life. These made such an impression upon me that I have never forgotten them. I would like to share them with you.

   (a) *The Prayer of Inspiration* opens the channels of one's mind so that creativity, guidance, and intuition may flow freely. Such a prayer might be expressed as "Father, I am aware that I am never forced but always have the privilege of following Your Instructions. I pray in Faith knowing that you answer prayer. I now open the channels of my mind to receive Inspiration and Guidance from Your Creative Power."

   (b) *The Prayer of Adjustment* assists in overcoming any prejudices and ill will toward others. An example might be "Father, grant me tolerance of others' imperfections just as I would wish them to offer me understanding with my shortcomings. Help me to apply this tolerance to family and friends and provide daily support so that through service to others I may build a happier life and better world for all."

   (c) *The Prayer of Re-creation* "is designed to give you a conscious awareness of the functioning of the Creative Power within as it applies to the re-creation of any and all body imperfections which have developed through wrong emotional and mental reactions to life experiences."[25] These words illustrate re-creational prayer. "Lord God, cause me to realize that thoughts are things and imperfect thinking creates bodily disharmony. Help me to turn my thoughts towards Divine Goodness so that every cell of my being is directed toward harmony and bodily perfection."

   (d) *The Prayer of Abundance* replenishes your resources through a change of attitude. "Heavenly Father, let me be constantly aware that by envisioning gain instead of loss, and focusing my mind on total success, all my needs will be amply met."

   (e) Finally, *The Prayer of Attunement* "is designed to help you come into full conscious awareness of your personal relationship to God, the Father, in consciousness."[26] One might pray thus: "Our Father, release all feelings of hate, fear and animosity in me. I would request Your Forgiveness as I would forgive others. I will forever trust in Your Wisdom and Guidance and,

> remaining steadfast in Your abiding Love, I know I need never walk alone."

A message given one morning in dawn's early light expresses succinctly the thoughts I have tried to convey. The words came, "In preparation for all things, begin by praying."

Development of your psychic potential can be one of the most spiritually exhilarating adventures of your entire life. Apropos to this point is Luke 11:34. "The light of the body is the eye: therefore, when thine eye is single, thy whole body is also full of light."[27]

13

Ideals for Successful Living

> Love. There is no difficulty that enough love will not conquer; no disease that enough love will not heal; no door that enough love will not open; no gulf that enough love will not bridge; no wall that enough love will not throw down; no sin that enough love will not redeem. It makes no difference how deeply seated may be the trouble, how hopeless the outlook, how muddled the tangle, how great the mistake; a sufficient realization of love will dissolve it all. If only you could love enough you would be the happiest and most powerful being in the world.
>
> Emmet Fox

One of the most edifying aspects of my investigation into the psychic has been the impartation of ideals for successful living. Over a two-year period I received a broad range of philosophical and religious oratory that varied in scope from messages containing short maxims to sermonettes proposing recipes for the acquisition and maintenance of proper physical, mental, and spiritual attitudes to be assumed in daily living, and,ultimately, to lengthy discourses on the immutability of spirituality, which serves as a basis for the operation of all universal laws.

I cannot lay claim to any of these ideas as originating from either Jim or myself. Although my husband has a degree from Colgate Rochester Divinity School, his role was primarily that of recorder rather than disperser of the treatises as they were channeled through me. I myself have taken only one philosophy course during my years of graduate studies, and its focus was on the philosophy of education. Therefore, it would seem to be a judicious assumption that the authorship of the philosophical doctrines summarized in this chapter had their origins from a higher level of consciousness.

A second assumption originating from a thorough study of the types of communications we have been privileged to receive suggests there may be several spiritual orators rather than just one. The types of expressions, styles of presentations, factual data, and even the humor often vary from one trance session to another. Examples of literary puns are sprinkled throughout the works, affording comic relief from the exacting self-knowledge and self-alterations that the ideals require of one, if through the application of the lessons, he is to develop and grow.

A third phenomenon I have observed in connection with these discourses is the variation of interpretations among consumers, yet each inferential interpretation is uniquely and personally fitting, based on that individual's own philosophical stance toward life. It would seem that each profits in accordance with his own particular needs.

I have done extensive soul searching in a concerted effort to determine if any or all of these ideas could originate from my husband or myself. Even in deepest meditation the response has always been a resounding "No!" Thus, I am satisfied that what I am about to present does truly represent the spiritualistic ideations of a higher dimension and that I am but the instrument for its dissemination.

With these thoughts in mind the remainder of this chapter will be devoted to the impartation of these ideals.

Messages

These were received either in the hypnogogic state between sleeping and waking or in deep meditation.

ACCESS TO THE RECORDS

When I first began to record dream messages, a voice said, "We have the records."

TWO TURRETS

"There are two turrets that exist in a person: immediacy and generosity."

MA PAROLE (MY WORD)

I heard a voice say in French, "Ma parole." I did not respond. I heard the voice say in a loud commanding tone, "Ma parole." I arose and wrote the message given to me.

ONENESS OF ALL MINDS

Reality consists of the oneness of all minds. It is body, mind and soul and the Oneness of Force.

DREAMS FOR DAILY LIVING

Dreams are entertaining, but they give you valuable messages that you can use in daily living.

ONE'S TREASURE (IN FRENCH)

Your treasure of gold lies where you spread your heart around.

SUFFERING FOR GROWTH

When there is winter all around, the light snow in high places makes it excellent for growth. [In this case light snow means solitude, introversion, or mild suffering.]

PSYCHIC BUILDING BLOCKS

There are psychic building blocks, large and small. Which building blocks are used depends on the appropriateness of the situation.

DR. WAINWRIGHT ARRIVES

Dr. Wainwright lives on Apollo *Road. [In looking up Apollo I learned in Greek religion he was the god of poetry, music, and oracles, as well as the god of healing and sender and stayer of the plague. Jim and I wonder if this is the name of one of the medical guides.]*

SUGGESTIONS FOR IMPROVING READINGS

Meditate twice per day at the same hour.

Daydream several times per day. This will put you in touch with a higher dimension.

BALANCE AND HARMONY

Be willing to be supportive of one another while developing one's own abilities.

SYMBOLISM

Symbolism is contained in all actions.

PSYCHIC DEVELOPMENT

All psychic development is self-creation.

THE THIRD AND FOURTH DIMENSIONS

The third and fourth dimensions are surrounded by pink clouds. (Pink clouds implies enveloped in love.)

THINK WITH YOUR HEART

Wear your heart on your head.

MARRIAGE

Marriage is an agreement in which two people work side by side.

Those who sail on the sea of matrimony have to learn to rig boats.

A SINGING ENTITY

The entity would like to sing and entertain you concerning law and order.

WISDOM

With understanding comes wisdom.

HELP FOR HIGHER LEVELS

I am a help in present times of trouble.

FAITH

Faith is the mysterious power that is responsible for the proper use of the alpha state. (The alpha state is the trance state.)

THE SCHOOLHOUSE EARTH

The Schoolhouse Earth transforms a rough-hewn stone into a polished gem.

EXPLORATION WITHOUT RESERVATION

In the second phase of development one should be willing to explore the knowledge and mysteries of the universe without reservations.

GOOD HEALTH AND UNIVERSAL LAWS

Good health is clearly related to universal laws.

A UNITED UNIVERSE

As above, so below.

SHARE BLESSINGS WITH OTHERS

You have been given love and properties in abundance. Share these commodities with others.

THE IMPORTANCE OF EXERCISE

Tumors are not published on the sports page. (This advice was imparted to emphasize the urgency of an ongoing program of exercise as a preventative measure against developing new cysts.)

DEVELOPING THE SOUL'S FULL POTENTIAL

Spiritual love enhances soul development in such a way that, through the evolutionary process, the attainment of the soul's fullest potential is a distinct possibility.

SPIRITUAL QUIPS

While working on the section "On Heaven and Hell" my secretary, Betty, typed the word simmer *rather than* sinner. *We both laughed heartily at this error. The scene that we visualized was a group of "sinners" attending a "cookout" in an "extremely torrid zone" and eventually realizing that participation in the event required that they serve as the entree.*

As if to chastise me for not always living the philosophy channeled through me, I received the following message one day:

"Be not professors *but also* doers *of the Word."*

In response to an inquiry by Elizabeth as to how often Jim and I were scheduling readings, the words issued forth from my lips:

"When the spirit moves me."

On one occasion Jim requested personal guidance for being a successful husband. The response was:

"For you, find a happy medium and keep her that way."

IDEALS FOR DAILY LIVING

"Review, consider, formulate goals — then Act! Thoughts such as these translated into action are the stuff of which most effective lives are composed."

"All marriages are made in heaven, but each soul is responsible for his own happiness on earth. If your marriage is to be one of mutual trust, understanding, loyalty, and devotion, then you must look inward to yourself to see that these qualities are applied to your marriage and hope that the same qualities will be reciprocated."

"A husband and wife fit each half of the heart together to make a whole-hearted *effort toward a successful marriage."*

"Children can be compared to young plants that grow. The youngest needs the firmest roots. Keep in mind when raising children that it is not wise to force a flower to bloom before its time."

"One can give birth to children, but one should not rule their lives or take on their problems. Each soul must choose his own gifts, problems, skills, and situations that must be overcome or experienced through success or failure. A parent may not assume the child's burdens. Each soul must learn through his own growth pattern. This is wise to give the rules of life so that one might learn and succeed in the Schoolhouse Earth. Thus, each might progress in his own lifetime.

DISCOURSES ON UNIVERSAL LAWS

Disseminating Psychic Information

What comes through is needed. There is nothing that comes through that is not needed. It is essential that the information that comes through be passed on. Each of the pieces of information is meant for some purpose,and that is why you get specifics. These are to be used for each soul's growth and development. Therefore, use as much as possible. To store the information is ridiculous.

On Heaven and Hell

Heaven and Hell are creations of your own mind. This is the way things evolve. It is the way the soul's development evolves up and down. You create your own reality. What you perceive will be. If you conceive of hell in the literal sense, your perception will become reality at death. This relates to all laws and perceptions of reality and it carries over to the perceptions of heaven and hell. If your concept of heaven is resting in the bosom of God until Judgment Day, this may be what occurs to you because of your concept. When your perception alters, you will then have a new view of heaven and hell. At times what you do is create your hell here on earth with the negative vibrations, disharmonies, and chaos you attract in your own lives. Thus, hell may be begun on earth but there is a continuation of the life pattern after the soul has left the body. You do not escape this until you accept God and begin to evolve toward higher levels of consciousness.

There is no eternal damnation — be sure of that*!* There is no eternal damnation*! Have this written in capital letters and stamped on the hearts of all. You may lower your vibrations into the world of chaos through dastardly deeds and thoughts of your own making, but if you but change your own reality and set your feet on a higher path, the law of grace works and there is always forgiveness. You can be sure that God accepts a sinner who sees the error of his ways.*

Hell is a place of your own creation. *Therefore, make love, not war. This is trite, but it is one of the eternal truths. The source of love is in all human beings the origin of which is the Godhead.*

On Soul Growth and the Soul's Purpose

You should be aware that universal truths exist and they do apply to all persons. No one escapes the universal realities or the laws. If one abides by these and is lawful, he will progress and learn and thus become a more highly elevated soul. If he does not believe these exist, and he struggles against or breaks these laws, then he diminishes in stature and becomes a less elevated and more troubled soul. He continues down paths that are of no consequence in his ultimate growth. These are byways that ultimately lead to dead ends *and in this case,* dead ends *are to be taken in the literal sense.* Dead ends *mean you begin over again in another existence. This truly does apply because when you have come to the end of your life and have made no progress, it is truly a* dead end, *is it not?*

This one law that you must know is God is love. Love is law. *Laws are to be obeyed. Therefore, God is to be obeyed.* Question: *"If there are laws to be obeyed, how do we know what God's laws are?"*

Search your own hearts. He is in our hearts. He is in each person's heart. If we search within through meditation, prayer, and inward vision, we perceive and begin to understand what he desires of each of us. For each of us has a different purpose. None comes with the same lesson to learn but it is his will that we learn those tasks of our own choosing. By looking within ourselves and learning what he desires of us, we then can choose the paths that would most likely lead to the culmination of the projects we have chosen.

The general purpose of each soul is to glorify his Creator through his chosen endeavors on each plane of consciousness.

There is in the universe a final point or goal to be reached. This is to dwell in peace and harmony with all others and to be molded into one ultimate and final existence with our Creator.

Comments on the Book

The ideas, philosophy, and experiences contained in this book are provided for persons who are seeking a new way or a new philosophy to be integrated into their lives. There are many seekers at this point who will benefit from its publication. The ideas contained are elemental enough so the common man will be able to understand and internalize the spiritual truths, and yet for the most highly developed souls there will be found meanings that will be entirely different from those not as highly evolved.

The purpose of the book is to have the reader enter into adventures of the mind himself. This is an experience that should not be unique to you both, for it will provide others with an avenue of exploration that they may explore their own soul's purpose and lend service to others. It is not to make a grandiose drama of your experiences. It is primarily a handbook for others who seek the same sort of viable experiences. This resource will provide them with that.

The universal truths in this book were given so that others may understand the existence of not only Our Creator but of other little creators in that all of us are part of the whole. Each Creator and Creation is absolutely mandatory for the full energies of the whole to be used effectively.

The universal truths contained in this volume received through messages, altered states of consciousness, and dreams are of little and great magnitude in the sense that the understandings will reach all levels of minds in development. The term minds *is used in the universal sense in that all minds are one and the understandings gained through this book will bring others to seek the truths, and the minds of each will be connected to other minds of similar propensity and origin so that the united philosophies will become the sum of the whole.*

On Eternal Love

Eternal love is found in all of our actions, all of our deeds and thoughts, in spite of the fact that sometimes we cut off its source. It is the basis of each soul's existence, and if we merely turn inward to its source, we find refreshment, new energies, and the eventual emergence of the true meaning of life itself. Therefore, the maxim "Turn inward, little one, unto yourself to find the meaning of your own unique existence and ideas."

Love is all-encompassing, never-ending, absolute, consciousness-raising, and, as the mystic rose, flowers continuously in eternity.

I have come to the end of my journey in writing this book. My family and friends have questioned the wisdom of making our psychical research public. I requested guidance in meditation and received the following:

"It is necessary to give away a portion of oneself to become a part of humanity, for the gain far surpasses the loss, and in doing so one becomes part of the whole."

Many fears beset individuals. Among the most horrifying are fear of poverty, old age, failure to achieve success in one's chosen career, physical illness or deformity, mental aberrations, and finally personal death. In my own hierarchy of demons death ranked rather low on the list. I seemed to have dealt with that question many years before. Death is not to be courted but rather to be accepted as a friend when the appointed time comes. For me the most terrifying thought that entered my consciousness was the loss of love. The idea of absenting myself from the love of my husband, children, family, and friends was almost unbearable to me. In searching for understanding and an ultimate resolution to my dilemma, I prayerfully turned to my guides for advice. Their response was loud and clear:

"You are love, *and in experiencing a loss of love, you are truly feeling the loss of a portion of yourself. But understand that love is never lost. There is merely a transformation of energy that returns again to its origin. Be still and know, ma cherie, that* Love is the core of the universe and its source is rooted in eternity."

APPENDIXES

Appendix A
How to Set Up a Dream Journal

The most effective way to work with your dreams is to record them in a dream journal daily. The suggestions below are presented so that you may begin keeping an organized and efficient ledger of this journey through the dream landscape.

1. Purchase a large notebook with several hundred pages of lined paper. You will probably want one that has widely spaced lines to facilitate readability when reviewing past dreams.
2. It is generally better to record dreams on the left side of the notebook, numbering each dream as you recall it. (Dream I, *title*; Dream II, *title*; etc.) The right-hand side of the notebook can be reserved for the interpretation of each dream episode as well as additional notations and new insights as they occur with the passage of time.
3. Each dream should have a separate title that conveys specific elements contained in the dream that will bring the theme to mind when the title is reread in the future. The date of the dreams should be written on the top of the left-hand page.
4. The first few pages of your dream journal should be reserved for the index. The format suggested is:

April 30, 1984

(1) Dream I, *title*

(2) Dream II, *title*

(3) Dream III, *title*

(4) Dream IV, *title*

(5) Dream V, *title*

May 1, 1984

(1) Dream 1, *title*

(2) Dream II, *title*

(3) Dream III, *title*

(4) Dream IV, *title*

(5) Dream V, *title*

5. It is wise to keep a file box for your own personal dream symbol associations. These can be alphabetized and categorized for easy retrieval. A sample card might read:

   Dog: (My own collie) - Faithful friend
   (My neighbor's dog) - Aggressiveness
   (A cocker spaniel) - A playful companion

   Remember, the more personal associations you can identify, the faster you can interpret the meaning of your dreams.

6. Be sure to describe all aspects of the dream. Note the colors and types of people's clothes, what position they assume, where they are in the scene, how they relate to the dreamer, the weather in the dream, the surrounding landscape, whether the characters are living or dead, and so on. Each part of the dream is important and the omission of one symbol might by chance be the key symbol for the entire dream.

7. Don't worry if you cannot recall your dreams completely. What is forgotten will almost invariably show up in a future dream.

   GOOD LUCK!

Appendix B
Common Dream Symbols

The key to all successful dream interpretations lies within the dreamer. The dreamer is the main pivot around whom revolve innumerable constellations of past, present, and future thoughts and events. Psychologists, dream interpretation gurus, and books designed to interpret dream symbology will offer all manner of "correct" translations. Unless, however, the still small voice within offers final approval for the interpretation, be wary of accepting such pronouncements.

With this in mind, the following list of common dream symbols is presented only as a guide from which to begin formulating your own dream associations. Your personal symbology is by far the most important component for accurate dream interpretations.

The dream symbols listed below are a composite of explanations selected from *Dreams: Your Magic Mirror* by Elsie Sechrist, *How to Interpret Your Own Dreams* by Tom Chetwynd, and *Dreams and Dreaming*, Paris I and II of the Edgar Cayce readings compiled by Marilyn Lindgren Peterson.

ACCIDENT: Conditions brought about by indulgence. Self-punishment.

AGE: Someone being a certain age. Perhaps the dreamer at that age. Look at the dream to see what was relevant in the dreamer's life at that time.

AIRPLANE: (Sun, moon, stars, comets, planets) represent spiritual ideals.

AMBULANCE: Physical help being given.

ANGEL: Freedom. Pure being. Source of help. *Angel of warning*: Not the way to go.

ARROW SHOT: Message coming.

ATTIC: Conscious mind.

BABY: A new birth. Rebirth of self to higher and nobler ideals if the baby is beautiful and often able to speak. It can also represent a real individual.

BATH: A cleansing.

BATHROOM: Cleansing needed.

BATHTUB: Physical cleansing required.

BATHTUB OVERFLOWING: Uncontrolled emotions.

BED: Rest or sex.

BEDROOM: Desire for pleasure.

BIBLE: God's laws.

BIRD: At the highest level, related to beauty, joy, and love. These are frequently in dreams at a critical period in one's life. Note the type of bird.

BLACK FIGURE: Repressed desires. The dark side of oneself. Death. The devil. Whatever is taboo.

BLACKBOARD IN A CLASSROOM: Conditions from which one can draw conclusions.

BLANKET: Comfort, rest

BOAT: The voyage of life. "Smooth sailing"; "stormy crossings"; "shipwrecked individuals."

BOOKS: Study.

BREAD: Essence of life itself. "The bread of life"; satisfaction and peace.

BRIDGE: State of transition.

BUSES: A short phase or stretch of the dreamer's life.

CAR: The physical body. The driving mechanism of the car can represent the various anatomical parts of the dreamer. *Use of brakes*: use of will. Driving the wrong way is a warning concerning health as is a car out of control. A *truck* is a work vehicle.

CASKET (coffin): Death.

CAT: Independence but often uncooperativeness and isolation. Petting a cat often suggests pleasure in a negative emotion. Note cat's color and disposition. Also "cattiness."

CELLAR: Subconscious.

CHICKEN: Timidity or lack of courage. A chicken with no head means hysterical futility.

CHILDHOOD HOUSE: Family ties.

CHURCH: A place of peace and refuge. Sometimes, the self. A place of baptism and therefore rebirth. Background for moral and religious ideas.

CIGARETTES (*smoking*): Not seeing clearly. Negative aspects of personality.

CIRCUS: The circus of life.

CLIMBING: Movement upward. Note how difficult the ascent is.

CLOCK: Time. *Clock with hands still*: Death. *Clock with hands racing*: time running out.

CLOSET: Inner self closed off, separated.

CLOTHES: Representation of activity or attitude of the dreamer. *Work clothes*: work; *Swim clothes*: relaxation; *Formal attire*: formality; *Quality material and beautiful color*: positive qualities; *Disheveled clothes:* disorderliness; *Tight clothes:* ill-fitting characteristics.

CORN: Food for physical and mental development.

CORPSES: Life and death.

CROSSROADS: Alternate courses of action.

CRYING: Warning of trouble.

DARKNESS: Subconscious, unknown, lack of awareness. "In the dark."

DAWN: A second choice, new understanding, an enlightenment.

DEPARTMENT STORE: Things stored. A selection from various items.

DESK: Your work.

DINING: Watch what you are eating. The dream may give a clue.

DINING ROOM: Consumption of food, mental or physical.

DIVING: "Diving down" into the mind, possibly in search of childhood memories. Delving into the unconscious.

DOCTORS: Authorities. *The Great Physician*: Christ. *Going to a doctor*: Be aware of physical health problems.

DOG: Faithful companion. The dog can represent both faithful and unfaithful aspects of self in a relationship of trust given to you. Note the manner and type of dog.

DOOR: Entrance into self. *Locking a door*: Locking out unpleasant conditions. *Opening the front door*: Receiving spiritual help. *Closed door*: Negative attitudes that close out people and help.

DRESS: Attitude. *New Dress*: New thoughts or ideals.

DRINKING: Note what you drink and how much. It may be a physical warning.

ELEVATOR: Changes, desire. Way of escape. On the right side the correct way. On the left side the wrong way.

ENEMY: A true rival. It may also be the dreamer himself and those aspects of his character that are robbing him of a more perfect nature.

ESCAPE FROM PRISON: The dreamer has managed to evade the current "threat." This could come at the end of a series of dreams in which a particular conflict has been concluded. Note theme of the dream.

EXPLOSION: Burst of temper. It may also represent a demand for a change of attitude. A change of consciousness to a more peaceful situation.

EYES: The windows of the soul. It shows the intelligence of the individual as well as often revealing his spiritual state. Spiritually minded people may even dream of having three eyes. *Blindness*: A refusal to face certain realities. *Glasses*: Enable one to see more clearly. *Dark glasses*: Seeing less clearly.

FACE: Reflection of the dreamer's character. *Unusually shaped head*: "Egghead," "square head," "shrunken head." It is more advisable to note which part of the face is emphasized and how it is depicted.

FATHER: Embodiment of authority, law, order, social conventions, patterns of behavior, as well as masculine protectiveness. He can be seen as an oppressive person who commands the dreamer to mold to conformity. He can also represent the father archetype in himself or an actual relationship with the dreamer's own father.

FENCE: Obstacles or dividers.

FIGHT: A moral struggle or mental conflict.

FIRE: It represents the heart of man. All great forces in nature have a duality. Fire may either purify or destroy. It can signify uncontrolled temper, jealousy, vengeance, hatred and unbridled zeal, patriotic fervor, patience and enthusiasm. Dreams of fire that suggest carelessness should be taken literally.

FISH: This is often related to the spiritual side of life because a fish was the early symbol for Christ. A beautiful fish represents growth of the self. An ugly fish signifies spiritual weakness. Fish eyes represent perpetual attention because they never close. Eating fish suggests renewal.

FLAG: The standard set.

FLOOR: Foundations of self. Principles.

FLYING: Wishful thinking. Astral projection. Suggestions to rise above the problem. Sex.

FOOD: Appetites. Food for the spirit. Specific foods may be those one has a need for or should avoid. *Ice cream*: Special items "frozen" for future use and delight. This may also carry the suggestion to use immediately.

FOREIGN COUNTRIES: Traveling to another "state." Actual dream of travel.

FORK: To pick carefully.

FURNACE: Digestion, stomach.

GAME: The game of life. A reluctance to become involved in life. A conflict in life. The two opposing sides may represent parts of the conflict. Note how the game is played and what it takes to win.

GARBAGE DISPOSAL: Something needs to be eliminated.

GHOSTS: The spiritual nature of the dreamer. A ghost may be an archetype or a dead person from the dreamer's past who may have an important message for him.

GLASS: Reflection of oneself as seen by others. The barrier from the material to the spiritual world. Passing through this means astral projection into the spiritual realm.

GLOVE: Blue on gloves means beautiful service. Dirty gloves mean improvement in performance can be achieved. Gloves may also mean covering up of abilities to be used.

GOD: When the image of God appears in dreams, it may point to the dreamer's need to realize his fullest inner potential. A person may feel his ego is destroyed by "an experience resembling death," but the result is he will be at one with the enduring spirit of which he is a part.

GOOSE: A "silly goose."

GRAVE: Death. Thoughts about someone who is dead. The past, what is dead and buried.

GUN: An emotional explosion.

HAIR: Thoughts. *Kinky hair:* Straighten out thinking. *Bald head:* Do more thinking. *White hair*: Wisdom or maturity. *Golden hair*: Golden or spiritual thoughts. *Bright shiny black hair*: Ever-intriguing mysteries of the mind. *Black dull hair*: Mental depression. *Red hair*: Temper. *Golden red hair*: Constantly active mind. *Stiff hair*: Rigidity. *Disheveled hair*: Mental imbalance. *Dirty hair*: Cleanse one's thoughts. *Combing of the hair*: reasoning.

HANDS: Beautiful hands mean beautiful service. *Hands applauding*: Approval unless accompanied by negative symbols which then mean self-applause. *A wagging of the index finger*: A warning or reproach. *Shaking hands*: Lack of gentleness in one's approach. *Clawlike hands*: A grasping or holding on.

HATS: Mental conditions. *High silk hat*: Thinking. *Straw hat*: Mental telepathy.

HALLWAYS: Transition. Changes.

HEAD ON BACKWARDS: Approaching things in a backward or incorrect manner.

HELL (*Devil*): A situation or person is confronted with when he is thinking of abandoning his inherited standards in favor of something chosen for himself. This challenges him to reassess his principles.

HORSE: Tempestuous emotions. Message. *White horse*: Master creative energies, which can lead to genius, ESP, creativity that enables one to serve well. *Red horse*: Persistence, patience, drive. May also mean "Stop!" *Black horse*: Necessity to balance male and female qualities of the soul.

HORSE AND RIDER: Messenger.

HOSPITAL: A hospital may relate to a physical imperfection or the necessity of correcting a mental or physical ailment.

HOTEL: A temporary or transitory state.

HOUSE: The activities of *self*. The condition of the house, building, or room represents the dreamer's own state and his recent relationships or activities to people in the dream or those in the background.

ILLNESS: Dreams of illness often contain treatments or suggestions to heal that condition.

JEWELRY (Gold, money, valuables): Symbols of spiritual graces at their highest level. A beloved person. *Diamond*: Center of consciousness is shifted from the ego to the original source. *Pearl*: The mind. *Ruby*: Rose color or mystic rose; highest form of true love.

JOURNEY: The journey through life.

KEYS: The solution to a problem. The key to happiness. *Keys*: Safety.

KING: A sleeping spiritual state. A father figure. A ruling principle.

KITCHEN: Preparation of food.

KNIFE: To cut out. Sex.

LADDER: A climbing upward or descending backward. Note the direction. *Jacob's ladder*: A spiritual ascent.

LAUNDRY: Improving one's attitude or activities. Dirty laundry: Need for improvement.

LEGS: Spiritual foundation or support.

LETTER: Communication. Note contents.

LIBRARY: Research.

LIGHT: Directing force. Spiritual light.

LIGHTNING: Flashes of intuition or revelation. Sudden unexpected and overpowering change within.

LOCK: Locking out unpleasant conditions.

LIVING ROOM: Daily activities.

LUGGAGE: Baggage of life. Marriage.

MARRIAGE: Literal marriage. Union with higher self. Integration.

MEDALS: Awards for accomplishments. That which may be presented in life.

MEDICINE: Actual treatment. Treatment to cure a problem.

MILK: Immaturity. "Milk of human kindness." Calling attention to one's diet.

MIRROR: Reflection of oneself. Look at yourself.

MONEY: Anything of value. Exchange. This can be at the highest spiritual level, at the practical everyday level as a necessity to have or its lowest level as in "money is the root of all evil."

MOTHER: The archetype representing wholeness or potential wholeness in a woman. One's own mother. Basic family relationships as they affect one's current life.

MOUNTAIN: Obstacle. Highest mental development.

MOVIE: Mind laid bare. One's own life story or that of another individual.

MUD: Departure or neglect of the moral way.

MUSIC: Divine influences in life; harmony. *Singing or hearing beautiful music*: Activities of divine forces in the self.

NEWSPAPER: Daily activities.

NUDITY: Undressed and exposed.

NUNS: Highest spiritual forces in our lives.

OCEAN: The moods and mystical powers of the psychic. The cosmic unconscious. *Deep versus shallow water*: Profound versus superficial. *Waves*: Waves of emotion. The ocean itself.

OFFICE: The meaning depends on the activity carried on there. One's own office means one's work.

OIL: Removing friction. Smooth out.

OPERATION: Interference with one's way of life, his thoughts, his values. Healing wounds. Sacrifice. Note the area of the operation and the outcome. *Doctor*: Higher authority.

ORCHESTRA: The music of life with its harmonies and discords. The dreamer's mind and especially emotions.

OUTSIDE/INSIDE: Outer versus inner life.

OVERSHOES: Protection on life's way. When these are missing in bad weather, it is a warning toward exposure to trouble, physical or spiritual.

PARALYSIS: Unable to move, frozen. Conflicting emotions or impulses. The dreamer longs to do something but is immoblized by its consequences.

PEACOCK: Self-love symbolizing a warning. "Proud as a peacock."

PEARLS: "Pearls of wisdom." The whole self.

PEN AND PENCIL: Communication. Writing.

PERFUMES: Intermingling in the atmosphere that brings thoughts and actions to the dreamer.

PHOTOGRAPH: Reflection of the person. *One's own photograph*: Self-examination required.

PIANO: Harmony in self or others.

POCKET: Within.

POLICE: Highest spiritual authority. Control. Law and order.

PORCH: Outside of self. Insecurity.

PREGNANCY: Potential new life. Anything full of possibilities and hopes.

PRISONER: Controlled by conditions.

PROFESSOR: Higher teacher. The conscience within.

RADIO: Message from the unconscious.

RAILROAD: A trip or change. *Single track*: One-track mind. *Getting derailed*: Going off the track. *On the right track*: Literal interpretation. *Arriving at a station*: Death.

RAIN: A cleansing process within. Rain provides for richer growth.

RIVER: Life and the twists and turns of fortune especially in the dreamer's destiny. *Crossing a river*: person has died.

ROAD: The individual way or destiny that leads to the culmination of one's aims or objectives. *A stretch of road*: A period of time. *A choice of roads*: Alternate courses. *Turn in the road*: New events lie ahead. *Dead end*: Road leads to no where. *Going downhill*: Literal interpretation. *Going uphill*: State of tension.

ROBBERY: Stealing one's valuables.

ROCK: Cornerstone. Christ. "Rock of our salvation." Impressionable spirit. *On the rocks*: Trouble.

ROOF: Highest point or ideals.

SAND: Poor foundation or poor building materials.

SCALES: Justice.

SCAR: Lasting mental effects.

SCHOOL: Issues of life.

SCHOOL CLASSROOM: Lessons to be learned. Note the level of education.

SCISSORS: To separate. Death.

SEA SHELLS: Various phases of life represented by Mother Sea.

SEED: Potential for growth.

SERVANT: The flesh must be the servant for greater truths to be gained. The master must be the servant to all.

SHOES: Foundations.

SHOWER AND TUB: Cleansing and baptism.

SILVER: Light. Self-knowledge. Wisdom, purity, valuable commodity.

SNAKE: Temptation or evil. Wisdom. Sneakiness. Note the manner and type of snake.

SNOW: Cold. Frigid emotion. Trouble or warning.

SOAP: Purity indicated or a need for cleansing.

SPIDER: A web or trap into which the dreamer is falling. A bad habit, a coming temptation, a recent indiscretion, or warning of bad business ventures. Note the dream content for the situation.

SPOON: Small dose.

STAIRS: A moving upward or downward.

STARS: Destiny. Whatever gives life its direction and guides to an inner goal. *Bright star*: Mystical achievement. *Falling star*: Failing hopes.

STORM: Outburst of emotion, desire, or instinct. Extreme mental agitation. Difficulties encountered in life.

SUICIDE: Look into self for problems. Occasionally, seeing another person's intentions.

SUN: Light of consciousness. Intellect. *Sunrise*: Dawn of consciousness. *Noon*: Maturity. *Sunset*: Decline of creative energy. Old age. *Black sun*: Death or profound depression.

SWIMMING: Spiritual activity.

SWORD: Erection. Power or justice.

TEETH: Speech.

TELEPHONE: Message or communication coming.

TEMPLE: The temple of the soul. The self.

TEST: Some new "test" in life.

TOOLS: Abilities. Knowledge.

TRAIN: Journey. "Trains of thought." Death.

TRIP: Changes.

TURKEY: Food. Unintelligent person or decision. "A turkey."

TURTLE: Strength. New life. Long life. Resistance to disease.

UNIFORMS: Trains of thought.

VEIL: Something only partially recognized by himself. Veil to the unknown or future.

WALL: Obstacle or divider.

WATER: Mother of creation. Spiritual symbol. Symbol of unconsciousness. "Water of life." Note beauty of water. *Clearness*: Purity, spirituality. *Muddy water*: Uncleanliness. Death.

WINDOW: Light, perception, eyes, awareness.

WOODS: Maze.

Colors

If colors are bright, elated states or great vitality exists. Muddy colors are negative associations. This chart shows the general meaning of colors. Personal associations may differ.

GRAY: Gray matter (brain). Ill health.

WHITE: Purity, light, innocence, divine mind.

BLACK AND WHITE: Right and wrong.

BLACK: Mystery, death, evil, darkness.

RED: Life force, new life, anger, sex, stop sign, fire.

ROSE PINK: Love, joy, happiness.

CERISE: Passion.

PALE PINK: Weakness.

GREEN: Healing, growth, hope, jealousy.

YELLOW: Sunshine, mind, cowardice, or "yellow streak," intuition.

ORANGE: Health, energy, occult power.

BROWN: Earthy, practical, depression. Gold or money.

MAROON: Poor health.

BLUE: Celestial, spiritual energy, "true blue" fidelity.

GOLD: The sun, intuition, something of value.

LILAC: Death.

Numbers

ONE: Universal Force, Creative Energy, God.

TWO: Weaker number than one. Two is a combination of 1 and 1 but is a division of the whole.

THREE: Combination of one and two. The Trinity. Great strength.

FOUR: Elements of earth, air, wind, and fire. The body. *Forty*: cleansing, preparation, or testing.

FIVE: Activity. An immediate change in activity from whatever it is associated.

SIX: Beauty and symmetrical forces of all numbers. It may also represent Satan.

SEVEN: A healing number. The spiritual forces in all ritualistic orders. A mystical relationship.

EIGHT: Double weakness of form. Vacillation.

NINE: A completion or finish. A termination of the order of things.

TEN: A completion of all numbers in a strength seldom found. From ten all numbers return to one.

Time and Position

FUTURE: Approaching objects or the right side of the scene.

PAST: Receding objects, left side of the scene. The past is also seen through pictures of ancient dwellings, ancient clothing, old things, old people, a date in history, or a scene from childhood.

RIGHT SIDE: Right way.

LEFT SIDE: Wrong way.

Appendix C

Sample Dream Interpretations

Now that we have progressed sufficiently to have mastered some of the basic techniques of dream interpretation, let us test our newly acquired knowledge. The dreams listed below have been selected for their ease of interpretation as well as for their employment of a multiplicity of varying themes in order to cover the widest possible range. Any actual precognitive events will be noted after the dream if the events occurred to improve the accuracy of the interpretation. The key to the suggested interpretations is listed at the end of this chapter. Try your luck and see how precise you are in your perception of the underlying meaning contained in each fantasy:

HOUSE ON FIRE

We appear to have two fires in the living room of the house. They were contained in the fireplace for a while. I tell my husband to watch them so they do not get out of control. I walk upstairs and from my bedroom I can look down between the wall and the outside. I see flames slowly creeping up and burning the insulation. Suddenly, the flames leap into a raging inferno that damages the room and walls. I race downstairs, but, by that time, the fire has been brought under control. There has been extensive damage to the lower floor. (Trend suggestion)

PICK UP PEARLS

I see an envelope that says, 'Put your hand in here and you may pick out a valuable pearl.' I place my hand in it and feel junk, paper, and candy around the pearls. The pearls are hidden in the envelope thus making it necessary to search for them.

NEW JOB AND NEW HOUSE

Arlene and I have gone to a beauty parlor to get our hair styled. It is owned by three brothers. One has his hair cut very short, although he has worn it longer in the past. He is dressed in a business suit such as executives would wear. He begins to set my hair and the color seems darker. As I arise from the chair after the set is completed, I ask if he is thinking about buying a new house. He says, "Yes. How did you know?" I say the words just came out of my mouth. I write them down because I don't want to forget them. (Actual happening at a later date)

AN OLD PICTURE ALBUM

I am looking through an old picture album. All pictures I look at I have seen before. In one picture a man is looking at a dead pope lying in state. In a second the man is dressed in a colonial outfit and carries a gun. I tell the man to take the gun off for the picture and he does. In the final picture he wears a business suit and is attending a board meeting. All pictures except the last are on black backgrounds.

OLD RECORDS ARE WORTH MONEY

Someone says that old records, especially those recording Bing Crosby's voice, are worth a lot of money.

OLD LADIES OF WILLIAMSBURG

I am looking through a newspaper clipping of five ladies dressed in colonial garb. They are attending a social gathering and drinking tea. Among them are Mrs. Hugh Miller and Mrs. Bolling.

A LOSS OF VOICE

I call my husband at work as I have a message for him. His secretary wants to know who is calling. I give my name. I finally get him on the telephone and hear raspy sounds. No intelligible words can be understood. (Actual happening at a later date)

RECEIVING A NEWSY LETTER

A letter written to me by Elizabeth. It contains news of current books she is reading, talks of a promotion for her husband, and discusses plans for a vacation together. She has just written it. (Actual happening simultaneously)

A TRIP TO MANDEVILLE

I am visiting a friend in Mandeville. I travel across Lake Pontchartrain and then across a smaller bridge. As we travel up the hill, I notice a large water tower. Then my friend and I are seated in a restaurant built near water. It has a nautical decor and many captain's chairs. I can see the water from a terrace. My friend introduces me to her husband's relatives, who are eating there. They frequent this establishment often. (A feeling of having actually been there accompanied this dream)

THE BLUE VEIL

There is a table with a blue veil on it. A celestial being stands behind it but does not speak. I feel that if one has an inquiring mind and a strong desire, one can see through the blue veil. The angel is the guardian of the veil.

A PLANE CRASH

I am at an airport. A small plane taxis down the runway, flies a short distance, and then noses over and crashes. Flames shoot out as the two aviators jump out of the wreckage. One pilot tries to put out the flames surrounding his companion, who is on fire. The equipment arrives, but they are too late; the flames have engulfed him. (The event occurred and was written up in a newspaper)

AN AFTERLIFE LESSON

My mother is ill, and no one seems to be able to cure her. I am sweeping out auto repair garages so when the cars are repaired, the places are clean. Finally, my mother dies. After a period of time, my husband dies. I walk along further and I die. There are people waiting for all of us who say, 'Don't be afraid. We will teach you more here. There are many more lifetimes for you to live.'

JOHNNY'S ALLERGIES

I see the Hunt children playing on a beach. I see Johnny Marsh swimming very fast in the water. I swim quickly, catching up to him, and inquire why he is swimming at such a pace. He says, "I have eaten dextrose, fructose, saccarin, and chocolate." Then we are traveling on a bus, and Johnny is there looking very unhappy. I see the front of his pants is wet. He has little control over his bladder. I take him off the bus. He is very upset! (I had a client whom I shall call Johnny Marsh although that was not his real name.)

JIMMY'S CAR ACCIDENT

Jimmy's car appears to be in an accident. He is hit from the side and the door dented in. Jimmy appears to be unhurt, but the car is damaged extensively. (This occurred three weeks later.)

JIMMY'S ANKLE INJURY

I feel my foot has been amputated. I am trying to hop around on the other. I rest at my home. I feel bad that I have lost my foot. (Actual happening one day later.)

THE VIRGINIA BEACH MEETING

My husband and I are in a large meeting room. There appears to be a lawyer present. It is a Mental Health Meeting. People in the audience are listening attentively. (This was dreamed August 15, 1981, and occurred September 19, 1981.)

THE COFFIN

I walk across the street from my father's house to the dwelling of a neighbor who is a good friend of ours. I see in their picture window a coffin. There is a figure in white cloth in the coffin. I see the figure raise his right hand. (The neighbor died six months later.)

THE LAWSUIT

There was a lawsuit between someone else and me. The suit was over some misrepresentations or breach of contract, and just as I was assured of victory in the lawsuit, the other party won by devious means. (Trend suggestion)

REFLEXOLOGY HEALS

I see a chart with lines on the foot. It shows various parts of the body connected to these lines. I am in a reflexology class.

LAW SCHOOL PARTNERS

A friend and I are attending law school together although she is more advanced than I am. Our husbands are law partners with us. We place our hands together in a square. (Not an actual event.)

A PSYCHOLOGICAL STUDY OF A COLONIAL LADY

Several psychologists are doing a study concerning a colonial lady. I look at a blue book, which contains each day of her life. She died in 1781.

A DILIGENT WORKER EARNS REWARDS

You must work diligently to be worthy of your rewards.

NEW BEGINNINGS

An ending is in truth a 'knew' beginning if one will but accept and acknowledge its commencement.

FOUR BUILDING TOOLS

I am on a beach near an ocean. I see a carpenter's apron with four building tools. On the first is engraved Love, *on the second* Faith, *and on the third* The Psychic. *The fourth word is unclear as yet.*

Key to Dream Interpretations

Listed below the reader will find suggested interpretations for the sample dream exercises. More than one category has been selected for several dreams, so give yourself credit if your response matches any one of the several classifications cited. The dream samples and commentaries were drawn from personal experiences. Each accurate selection for the dream type is worth four points. Your total score for all dreams may be rated according to the following scale:

0 — 32: More intensive dream study is indicated.
33 — 60: Above average mastery of dream concepts.
61+ : superior dream interpretation.

Share your knowledge with others.

HOUSE ON FIRE (GUIDANCE FOR SELF AND OTHERS):

This dream appeared to warn me of an impending danger regarding a fire in my fireplace. I was concerned by the implications of the dream and immediately contacted a chimney sweep. Upon inspecting he advised that there was a strong possibility of a fire breaking out due to the amount of residue that had accumulated in our chimney over the years.

PICK UP PEARLS (VISIONARY):

This dream carries with it strong symbolic overtones. The pearls depict pearls of wisdom or concepts of value. The envelope suggests a form of communication. The message I felt to be implicit in the dream was if I searched discriminately among the many communications I received, I could locate "pearls of wisdom."

A NEW JOB AND A NEW HOUSE (CLAIRVOYANT, PRECOGNITIVE):

At the time of this dream, Betty's son was thinking of changing his business position and also contemplating the purchase of a new home. Confirmation of these events occurred within three weeks.

AN OLD PICTURE ALBUM (PAST LIFE):

The old picture album provides the primary clue that this particular dream may involve past life information. The initial incarnation seemed to be as a priest, and the second apparently centered around colonial times. In the current existence the subject leads the life of a business executive. The black background, except for the final picture, represents death.

OLD RECORDS ARE WORTH MONEY (GUIDANCE FOR SELF AND OTHERS, BUSINESS):

This sentence was recorded by me two months before my father's passing. In one section of the attic my sister and I found several piles of outdated records that belonged to my grandmother, who had died years before. This dream alerted me to the fact that those could prove to be a valuable financial asset.

OLD LADIES OF WILLIAMSBURG (PAST LIFE):

The colonial clothes hint of a past life theme. On checking in Swem Library I located the names of the two ladies mentioned.

A LOSS OF VOICE (CLAIRVOYANT):

The situation I beheld just before awaking on Friday morning as I slept late was actually taking place in my husband's office. When he arrived home early that afternoon voiceless, I realized the significance of the previewed scene.

RECEIVING A NEWSY LETTER (TELEPATHY):

The contents of this particular letter from Elizabeth seemed vaguely familiar to me as I read it. Upon checking my dream diary I was surprised to find that both the date of her letter and the events she described coincide precisely with the account recorded in my journal.

A TRIP TO MANDEVILLE (OUT OF BODY):

The vividness and sense of reality I experienced during this dream episode prompted me to phone a dear friend. Although I have never seen Mandeville up to that point in time, my friend confirmed the accuracy of my descriptions of the countryside surrounding Mandeville as well as the decor of her husband's favorite restaurant, which she and his family often frequented.

THE BLUE VEIL (VISIONARY):

The celestial being personifies guidance from a higher realm. For me the blue veil represented the revelation of truths. The advice imparted is self-explanatory.

A PLANE CRASH (CLAIRVOYANT, LOCAL EVENT):

I feel I read this local event clairvoyantly either through the newspaper article or by viewing the event as it unfolded.

AN AFTERLIFE LESSON (DEATH — RECORDED DECEMBER 31, 1982):

This dream was perhaps in preparation for my father's impending death, but, in a broader sense, it was apprising me of the future opportunities afforded each soul in the after-death state.

JOHNNY'S ALLERGIES (HEALTH, GUIDANCE FOR SELF AND OTHERS, TELEPATHY):

This dream was received in response to a before-sleep inquiry I formulated about a 10-year-old male client afflicted with enuresis. The reply supplied the cause of the problem and the direction to proceed in for its elimination. The answer appeared to be furnished telepathically by the boy himself.

JIMMY'S CAR ACCIDENT (PRECOGNITIVE):

An accident involving our car occurred exactly three weeks after the date of this dream, but the discrepancy noted was that it was my husband, not my son, who was involved. His mother often called him Jimmy in his youth, however.

JIMMY'S ANKLE INJURY (HEALTH, PRECOGNITIVE):

I recorded this April 7, 1982. Jimmy sprained his ankle April 8 and had to have it in a cast for six weeks, thus losing the use of his foot. Here again it was not I but my son who had the disaster, yet in the dream I vicariously sensed his feeling of helplessness and loss.

THE VIRGINIA BEACH MEETING (PRECOGNITIVE):

The dream seemed to have no real significance other than proving to my unbelieving mind the reality of precognition at a point in time when my consciousness was undergoing considerable expansion.

THE COFFIN (DEATH, PRECOGNITION):

Here again I was being warned in advance of the forthcoming death of my father's best friend. The right hand's being raised indicates this will happen in the future. The dream was therefore one of preparation.

THE LAWSUIT (BUSINESS):

The trend of the dream suggests if the dreamer continues to pursue the same course in the future, he will suffer a considerable financial setback.

REFLEXOLOGY HEALS (GUIDANCE FOR SELF AND OTHERS, HEALTH):

The dream recommends an alternative method of healing for myself and others.

LAW SCHOOL PARTNERS (GUIDANCE FOR SELF AND OTHERS, TELEPATHY):

Since my husband and I have entered into an intensive study of the psychic, we have been blessed with many new friendships. We feel so comfortable with these new acquaintances, however, that we suspect the bounds of friendship may extend far beyond this life. This belief is well illustrated by the "Law School Partners" symbology.

A PSYCHOLOGICAL STUDY OF A COLONIAL LADY (PAST LIFE):

The records of an eighteenth-century life with the date of death being 1781 indicate a review of the past life, perhaps from the Akashic Records.

A DILIGENT WORKER EARNS REWARDS (MESSAGE):

The dream is self-explanatory.

NEW BEGINNINGS (MESSAGE):

The events of the past two years have so renewed my faith in God and spirituality that my entire existence is living proof of the truthfulness of this axiom.

FOUR BUILDING TOOLS (VISIONARY):

The three tools represent the means with which to build one's future and are already available to the dreamer. The fourth is yet to be revealed.

Appendix D
Preparation of a Castor Oil Pack

One of the treatments most frequently recommended by Edgar Cayce was the application of a castor oil pack. Although it is primarily used over the abdomen or intestinal area, in the case of cystic fibroid disease, the pack is situated directly over the cyst. Directions for preparation of such a pack are as follows:

1. Secure a soft cotton or wool flannel cloth and fold until it measures eight inches in width and ten to twelve inches in length.
2. Pour enough castor oil in a pan so that the flannel is soaked in the liquid but not saturated.
3. Protect the bed clothing with a plastic sheet placed under the body.
4. Apply the castor oil - soaked flannel to the area that is to be treated. A plastic covering is placed over the cloth followed by the heating pad on top of the plastic. The initial setting should be "medium" but switched to "high" if the patient can tolerate this elevated temperature.
5. The entire pack is then wrapped in a towel and must remain in place for a period of one and one-half hours.
6. At the end of this time period the skin over which the pack has been placed should be cleansed with a solution of a quart of water to which 2 teaspoons of baking soda have been added.
7. For optimum results use the pack for three days in succession and then discontinue for a day or two. Repeat the process. Swallow a teaspoon of olive oil by mouth after every third treatment.
8. The flannel pack can be stored and used again and again for other illnesses of varying types.
9. Each person should have his or her own individual castor oil pack.

(Portions of the above material were summarized from *The Physician's Reference Notebook* compiled and written by William A. McGarey, M.D. and Associated Physicians of the ARE Clinic in Phoenix, Arizona.)

In conjunction with the castor oil pack treatment healing is enhanced through the ingestion of 1000 milligrams of vitamin E (as found in d-alpha tocopheryl acetate) daily for 10 days or for the period required to eliminate the cyst. Vitamin E appears to possess softening properties for internal cysts.

For women with persistent cystic fibroid disease I recommend massaging each breast daily with Mastitis Formula 1. This preparation is available from Cayce's Corner, The ARE Clinic, 4018 North 40th Street, Phoenix, Arizona 85018 (Telephone number 1-602-955-0551).

Notes

Chapter 1

1. Elsie Sechrist, *Dreams: Your Magic Mirror* (New York: Warner Books, 1968), p. 13.

2. Harmon Bro, *Edgar Cayce on Dreams* (New York: Paperback Library, 1968), p. 59.

3. Ibid., p. 149.

Chapter 2

1. Roy Udolf, *Handbook of Hypnosis for Professionals* (New York: Van Nostrans Reinhold Company, 1981), p. 264.

2. Harmon Bro, *Edgar Cayce on Dreams* (New York: Paperback Library, 1968), p. 151.

3. Edgar Cayce, "Address," February 6, 1933, quoted in Doris Agee, *Edgar Cayce on ESP* (New York: Warner Books, 1969), p. 25.

4. Ibid., p. 224.

Chapter 3

1. Roger Pile, correspondence, Chester, Ct., June 1982.

2. Roger Pile, "On Body Communication, Illness and Spiritual Healing," Chester, Ct., August 1982.

3. Roger Pile, "Healing with the Word," Chester, Ct., August 1982.

4. Roger Pile, "Sources of Psychic Energy," Chester, Ct., August 1982.

5. Roger Pile, "On Psychic Readings," Chester, Ct., August 1982.

6. Roger Pile, "Why We Should Develop Our Psychic Talents," Chester, Ct., August 1982.

7. Nancy Pile, unpublished psychic reading, Chester, Ct., August 1982.

Chapter 4

1. Albert Bowes, "My Experience as a Professional Psychic," Virginia Beach, Va., Association for Research and Enlightenment, conference tape, June 1982.

2. Charles Thomas Cayce, "Problems on the Path of Psychic Development," Virginia Beach, Va., Association for Research and Enlightenment, conference tape, June 1982.

3. Charles Thomas Cayce, "Synchronicity and Divination," Virginia Beach, Va., Association for Research and Enlightenment, conference tape, June 1982.

4. Norman Shealy, *Association for Research and Enlightenment Conference Bulletin,* Virginia Beach, Va., Association for Research and Enlightenment Press, September 1982.

5. Norman Shelby, "Self-regulation: Avoiding Burnout," Virginia Beach, Va., Association for Research and Enlightenment conference tape, September 1982.

6. Elizabeth Hollis, "Astrological Reading for Joan Windsor," Charlotte, N.C., October 1982.

7. Elizabeth Hollis, "Astrological Reading for James Windsor," Charlotte, N.C., October 1982.

8. Elizabeth Hollis, "Astrological Reading for James L. Windsor," Charlotte, N.C., October 1982.

9. Elizabeth Hollis, "Astrological Reading for Robin Windsor," Charlotte, N.C., October 1982.

10. Elizabeth Hollis, correspondence, Charlotte, N.C., November 1982.

11. Cynthia Leonard Miller, ed., *The General Assembly of Virginia: June 13, 1619 to January 11, 1978: A Bicentennial Register of Members* (Richmond: Virginia State Library, 1978), p. 130.

Chapter 6

1. Carl G. Jung, with M. L. von Frantz, Joseph Henderson, Jolande Jacobi, and Aniela Jaffe, *Man and His Symbols* (Chicago: J. G. Ferguson Publishing Company, 1964), p. 36. Copyright 1964, J. G. Ferguson Publishing.

2. Carmen Blacker, "Japan," in Michael Loewe, and Carmen Blacker, eds., *Oracles and Divination* (Hemel Hempstead, England: George Allen and Unwin, 1981), p. 75.

3. R. B. Serjeant, "Islam," in Michael Loewe, and Carmen Blacker, eds., *Oracles and Divination* (Hemel Hempstead, England: George Allen and Unwin, 1981), p. 224.

4. Ibid., p. 225.

5. Carl G. Jung, *Man and His Symbols,* p. 162.

6. *The Holy Bible,* Revised Standard Version, copyrighted 1946, 1952, 1971, 1973 (New York: National Council of the Churches of Christ, 1946), I Kings 3:5–14, p. 355.

7. *The Holy Bible,* Revised Standard Version, copyrighted 1946, 1952, 1971, 1973 (New York: National Council of the Churches of Christ, 1946), I Samuel 3:6–9, p. 287.

8. *The Holy Bible,* Revised Standard Version, copyrighted 1946, 1052, 1971, 1973 (New York: National Council of the Churches of Christ, 1946), I Samuel 3:10–14, p. 287.

9. *The Holy Bible,* Revised Standard Version, copyrighted 1946, 1952, 1971, 1973 (New York: National Council of the Churches of Christ, 1946), Daniel, 4:10–17, pp. 922 and 923.

10. Kevin Riley, Unpublished Term Paper: "What I Tell You In Darkness, That Speak Ye In Light," Williamsburgh, Virginia. May, 1984, p. 7.

11. *The Holy Bible,* Revised Standard Version, copyrighted

1946, 1952, 1971, 1973 (New York: National Council of the Churches of Christ, 1946), Joel 2:28, pp. 949 and 950.

12. *The Holy Bible,* Revised Standard Version, copyrighted 1946, 1952, 1971, 1973 (New York: National Council of the Churches of Christ, 1946), Job 33:14–16, p. 553.

13. Carl G. Jung, with M. L. von Frantz, Joseph Henderson, Jolande Jacobi, and Aniela Jaffe, *Man and His Symbols,* pp. 9 and 10.

14. Carl G. Jung, "The Individuated Man" quoted in D. Caprio and S. Nicholas, *Personality Theories: Guides to Living* (New York: Holt, Rinehart and Winston, 1974), p. 471.

Chapter 7

1. Doris Agee, *Edgar Cayce on ESP* (New York: Warner Books, Inc., 1969), p. 216.

2. Harmon Bro, *Edgar Cayce On Dreams* (New York: Paperback Library, 1968), p. 160.

Chapter 8

1. Elsie Sechrist, *Dreams: Your Magic Mirror* (New York: Warner Books, 1968), p. 34.

2. Harmon Bro, *Edgar Cayce On Dreams* (New York: Paperback Library, 1968), p. 47.

3. Mark Thurston, *How To Interpret Your Dreams* (Virginia Beach, Virginia Association of Research and Enlightenment Press, 1978), p. 87.

4. Harmon Bro, *Edgar Cayce on Dreams,* p. 144.

5. Harmon Bro, Ibid., p. 145.

6. Harmon Bro, Ibid., p. 146.

Chapter 10

1. Harmon Bro, *Edgar Cayce On Dreams* (New York: Paperback Library, 1968), p. 195.

2. Mark Thurston, *How To Interpret Your Dreams* (Virginia Beach, Virginia, Association for Research and Enlightenment Press, 1978), p. 86.

3. Harmon Bro, *Edgar Cayce on Dreams*, p. 203.

4. Harmon Bro, Ibid., p. 159.

5. Mark Thurston, *How To Interpret Your Dreams*, p. 118.

6. Ibid., p. 120.

7. Ibid., p. 120.

8. Ibid., p. 121.

9. Harmon Bro, *Edgar Cayce on Dreams*, p. 168.

10. Ibid., p. 168.

11. Ibid., p. 175.

12. Ibid., p. 189.

13. Ibid., p. 190.

14. Ibid., p. 191.

15. Mark Thurston, *How To Interpret Your Dreams*, p. 179.

16. Ibid., pp. 181, 182.

17. Cbid., p. 182.

18. Ibid., p. 108.

Chapter 11

1. W. E. Butler, *How to Read the Aura, Practice Psychometry, Telepathy and Clairvoyance* (New York: Warner Books, Inc., 1978), p. 17.

2. Ibid., p. 27.

3. Doris Agee, *Edgar Cayce on ESP* (New York: Warner Books, 1969), p. 36.

4. Ibid., p. 37.

5. Ibid., p. 38.

6. Ibid., p. 41.

7. Ibid., p. 122.

8. Ibid., p. 130.

9. Mary Ellen Carter, *Edgar Cayce on Prophecy* (Virginia Beach,

Va.: Association for Research and Englightenment Press, 1968), p. 182.

10. Ibid., p. 190.

11. *The Holy Bible,* Revised Standard Version (New York: National Council of the Churches of Christ, 1946), pp. 195 and 196.

12. Jane Roberts, *Eth Speaks* (New York: Bantam Books, 1972), p. 358.

13. Ibid., p. 480.

14. Ibid., p. 481.

15. Ibid., p. 208.

16. Ibid., p. 476.

17. Ibid., p. 481.

18. Study Groups of the Association for Research and Enlightenment, *A Search for God,* Book I (Virginia Beach, Va.: Association for Research and Enlightenment Press, 1945), p. 47.

19. Ibid., p. 48.

20. Ibid., p. 49.

21. Harmon Bro, *Edgar Cayce on Religion and Psychic Experience* (New York: Warner Books, 1970), p. 199.

22. Ibid., p. 36.

23. Ibid., p. 37.

24. Butler, *How to Read the Aura,* p. 24.

25. Harmon Bro, *Edgar Cayce on Religion and Psychic Experience,* p. 42.

Chapter 12

1. Alan Vaughan, *The Edge of Tomorrow* (New York: Coward, McCann and Geoghegan, 1982), p. 182.

2. Ibid., pp. 183, 184.

3. Ibid., p. 190.

4. Ibid., p. 191.

5. Alan Vaughan, *Patterns of Prophecy* (New York: Hawthorn Books, 1973), p. 72.

6. Alan Vaughan, *The Edge of Tomorrow* (New York: Coward, McCann and Geoghegan, 1982), p. 141.

7. Harold Sherman, *How to Make ESP Work for You* (New York: Fawcett Crest Books, 1964), p. 164.

8. Ibid., p. 159.

9. Hugh Lynn Cayce, *Venture Inward* (New York: Harper and Row, 1964), p. 95.

10. Barclay Martin, *Abnormal Psychology: Clinical and Scientific Perspectives* (New York: Holt, Rinehart and Winston, 1977, 1981), p. 479.

11. Ibid., p. 480.

12. Janet Karcher and John Hutchinson, *This Way to Cassadaga* (Deltona, Fla.: JH Productions, 1980), p. 79.

13. Ibid., p. 81.

14. Ibid., p. 85.

15. Cayce, *Venture Inward,* p. 100.

16. Arthur Ford, *Unknown but Known* (New York: Harper and Row, 1968), p. 73.

7. Harold Sherman, *How to Make ESP Work for You,* p. 166.

18. Ibid., p. 167

19. Cayce, *Venture Inward,* pp. 142, 143.

20. Alan Vaughan, *The Edge of Tormorrow,* .p. 141.

21. Harold Sherman, *Know Your Own Mind* (New York City and Canada: Random House, 1953), p. 57.

22. Hugh Lynn Cayce, *Faces of Fear: A Practical Guide to Overcoming Life's Anxieties* (New York: Harper and Row, 1980), p. 134.

23. Hugh Lynn Cayce, *Venture Inward* (New York: Harper and Row, 1964), p. 198.

24. Harold Sherman, *Know Your Own Mind* (New York City and Canada: Random House, 1953), p. 57.

25. Ibid., p. 64.

26. Ibid., p. 67.

27. *The Holy Bible,* Revised Standard Version (New York: National Council of the Churches of Christ, 1946), Luke 11:34, p. 81.

Bibliography

Agee, Doris. *Edgar Cayce on ESP*. New York: Warner Books, 1969.

Bowes, Albert. "My Experience as a Professional Psychic." Virginia Beach, Va.: Association for Research and Enlightenment conference tape, 1982.

Bro, Harmon. *Edgar Cayce on Dreams*. New York: Paperback Library, 1968.

Bro, Harmon. *Edgar Cayce on Religion and Psychic Experience*. New York: Warner Books, 1970.

Butler, W. E. *How to Read the Aura, Practice Psychometry, Telepathy and Clairvoyance*. New York: Warner Books, 1978.

Carter, Mary Ellen. *Edgar Cayce on Prophecy*. New York: Paperback Library, 1968.

Cayce, Charles Thomas. "Problems on the Path of Psychic Development." Virginia Beach, Va.: Association for Research and Enlightenment conference tape, 1982.

Cayce, Charles Thomas. "Synchronicity and Divination." Virginia Beach, Va.: Association for Research and Enlightenment conference tape, 1982.

Cayce, Hugh Lynn. *Facts of Fear: A Practical Guide to Overcoming Life's Anxieties*. New York: Harper and Row, 1980.

Cayce, Hugh Lynn. *Venture Inward.* New York: Harper and Row, 1964.

Chetwynd, Tom. *How to Interpret Your Own Dreams.* New York: Bell Publishing Company, 1980.

DiCaprio, Nicholas S. *Personality Theories: Guides to Living.* New York: Hold, Rinehart and Winston, 1974.

Ford, Arthur. *Unknown But Known.* New York: Harper and Row, 1968.

Fox, Emmet. Card #25, Marina del Rey, California, Devorss and Company, Publishers.

Hollis, Elizabeth. Correspondence, Charlotte, N.C. November 1982.

Hollis, Elizabeth. Astrological Charts, Charlotte, N.C. October, 1982.

Jung, Carl G. with von Frantz, M. L., Henderson, Joseph L., Jacobi, Jolande and Jaffe, Aniela, *Man and His Symbols.* Chicago, Illinois: J. G. Ferguson Publishing Company, 1964.

Karchner, Janet and Hutchinson, John. *This Way To Cassadago.* Deltona, Florida: Creative Communications, 1980.

Lowe, Michael and Blacker, Carmen. *Oracles and Divination.* Hemel Hepstead, England: George Allen and Unwin, 1981.

Martin, Barclay. *Abnormal Psychology: Clinical and Scientific Perspectives.* New York: Hold, Rinehart and Winston, 1977, 1981.

Miller, Cynthia. *The General Assembly of Virginia, June 13, 1619 to January 11, 1978: A Bicentennial Register of Members.* Richmond, Va.: Virginia State Library, 1978.

Peterson, Marilyn. *Dreams and and Dreaming* — Part I, Part II. Virginia Beach, Va.: Association for Research and Enlightenment Press, 1976.

Pile, Nancy. *Unpublished Psychic Reading.* Chester, Ct. August, 1982.

Pile, Roger. Correspondence, Chester, Ct. August 1982.

Pile, Roger, "Healing with the Word." Chester, Ct. August 1962.

Pile, Roger. "On Body Communication, Illness and Spiritual Healing." Chester, Ct. August 1982.

Pile, Roger. "On Psychic Readings." Chester, Ct. August 1982.

Pile, Roger. "Sources of Psychic Energy." Chester, Ct. August 1982.

Pile, Roger. "Why We Should Develop Our Psychic Talents." Chester, Ct. August 1982.

Riley, Kevin. Unpublished term paper, "What I Tell You in Darkness, That Speak Ye in Light." Williamsburg, Va.: May 1984.

Roberts, Jane. *Seth Speaks.* New York: Bantam Books, 1972.

Sechrist, Elsie. *Dreams: Your Magic Mirror.* New York: Warner Bookes, 1968.

Sergeant, R.B. "Islam." In Loew, Michael, and Blacker, Carmen, eds., *Oracles and Divination.* Hemel Hempstead, England. George Allen and Unwin, 1981.

Shealy, Norman. *Association for Research and Enlightenment Conference Bulletin.* Virginia Beach, Va.: Association for Research and Enlightenment Press, September 1982.

Shealy, Norman. "Self-regulation: Avoiding Burnout." Virginia Beach, Va.: Association for Research and Enlightenment conference tape, 1982.

Sherman, Harold. *Know Your Own Mind.* New York City and Canada: Random House, 1953.

Sherman, Harold. *How to Make ESP Work for You.* New York: Fawcett Crest Books, 1964.

Study Groups of the Association for Research and Enlightenment. *A Search for God,* Book I. Virginia Beach, Va.: Association for Research and Enlightenment Press, 1945.

Thurston, Mark. *How to Interpret Your Dreams.* Virginia Beach, Va.: Association for Research and Enlightenment Press, 1978.

Udolf, Roy. *Handbook of Hypnosis for Professionals.* New York: Van Nostrand Reinhold Company, 1981.

Vaughan, Alan. *The Edge of Tomorrow.* New York: Coward, McCann and Geoghegan, 1982.

Vaughan, Alan. *Patterns of Prophecy.* New York: Hawthorn Books, 1973.

Index

A

B

C

Q

R